FOUNDATIONS OF THE CHRISTIAN FAITH

FOUNDATIONS OF THE

CHRISTIAN FAITH

by

Roger Weil

GRACE PUBLICATIONS TRUST
7 Arlington Way
London EC1R 1XA
England
e-mail: editors@gracepublications.co.uk
www.gracepublications.co.uk

First published 2011
This edition with minor corrections 2017

ISBN 978-1-912154-03-6

Printed and bound in UK by Ashford Colour Press Ltd.

Contents

Introduction

1 What is the purpose of this book?

To help individual Christians to gain a clearer understanding of the fundamental teachings of their faith.

To provide preachers and Bible-class leaders with outlines of the central themes of the Bible in order to help them in their preaching and teaching.

2 Why is it needed?

a) For the past fifty years in many parts of the world Bibles, hymn-books and Christian literature have been very scarce or non-existent. Believers were deliberately deprived of Christian literature.

b) For many years pastors were compelled to work in secular employment, had no opportunity for Bible training, and had little time to devote to study of the Word of God.

c) Much of the spiritual literature which is now available does not present the truth within the context of the Bible as a whole and is therefore often 'one-sided'. For example, books on healings, miracles and tongues.

3 What is the remedy for this situation?

a) The Church must provide a teaching ministry

For teaching to be successful it must be continuous and systematic. This is the way children learn in school. Their teachers prepare a syllabus of lessons which take the children step by step through the different subjects they must study. The teachers have to spend a lot of time preparing the lessons they will teach. They plan ahead so that the children are taught in a continuous and systematic way. In this respect the School is more successful than the Church. Although there are obvious differences between the Church and the School, there are points of similarity too. Both institutions exist to impart knowledge to their members, and both want them to understand and benefit from what they hear and the information they are taught. Both Jesus and Paul gave a high priority to teaching.

Someone once showed Spurgeon, the great English nineteenth century preacher, a similar book of Bible teachings to this one, saying, 'This is like chapter 37 of Ezekiel's valley of dry bones – very many and very dry!' But Spurgeon wisely replied, " Be a prophet and they will live!" Spiritual teachers not only need the power of the Holy Spirit; they also need to be able to teach the fundamental truths of the Bible as well.

i) The Lord Jesus Christ taught his disciples

The Gospels were written by those who heard his teaching and wrote down what he taught them. Luke is the exception and used written sources for his gospel. Jesus sent out his disciples to preach and teach all that he had taught them. It took him three years to teach them by word and by example before they were ready to be left to do this work on their own.

ii) The apostle Paul taught the churches

For example, he spent over two years in Ephesus teaching the Word of God every day in the School of Tyrannus (Acts 19:9-10). He not only taught the church publicly; he also went to believers' homes to teach them 'the whole counsel of God' (Acts 20:27). What was this? If we read his letter to the Ephesians we can see that he taught them all the major Christian doctrines. Do we today teach 'the whole counsel of God'?

iii) The apostle Paul commanded church elders to teach the Word

He tells Timothy to read the Scriptures to the congregation, to exhort them and to teach them (1 Timothy 4:13). He also tells him that those elders who work hard at teaching God's Word should be properly remunerated, because teaching requires much study and diligence.

> Let the elders who rule well be counted worthy of double honour, especially those who labour in the word and doctrine (1 Timothy 5:17).

> Let him who is taught the word share in all good things with him who teaches (Galatians 6:6).

> And the things that you have heard from me among many witnesses, commit these to faithful men who will be able to teach others also (2 Timothy 2:2).

iv) The apostle Paul also taught the churches by his letters

These letters prove that the Church needs to be taught Christian truths. From them we can see how important it is for these to be taught to Christians at all times. If we fail to teach doctrine what will happen? Let the apostle Paul tell us:

> And He Himself gave some to *be* apostles, some prophets, some evangelists, and some pastors and teachers, for the equipping of the saints for the work of ministry, for the edifying of the body of Christ ... that we should no longer be children, tossed to and fro and carried about with every wind of doctrine ... (Ephesians 4:11-12,14).

Christians who are ill taught are unstable and will inevitably be blown about by every wind of teaching. If we do not teach properly we will have weak, ignorant and carnal churches, easily confused by the cults and led astray by the devil.

b) The Church must have a teaching plan

The two-year programme given at the back of this book is only a suggestion. Some prefer to work Sunday by Sunday through a book of the Bible or a special theme. Whatever method is chosen must be suitable for each individual church. It is important that some method, some programme of teaching is put into operation by the elders of the church or else there will be no regular teaching. In this scheme 46 Sundays are covered each year, leaving six for special occasions.

It will need much preparation and hard work by those who teach, but there is no other way for believers to learn and to grow in an understanding of their faith and their Lord.

CHAPTER ONE

HOW DID RELIGION BEGIN?

1 The nature of man

2 The centre of religion in man

    a) Mind
    b) Heart
    c) Will

3 The origin of religion

    a) Witch-doctors
    b) Fetishes
    c) Natural forces
    d) Psychological cause
    e) An opiate

1 The nature of religion

How can we define religion? It is the belief in an unseen personal and supernatural being who controls the universe and to whom worship and obedience are due. Christians believe that God has revealed himself to man and that these revelations have been written down and collected together in a book that we call the Bible – the only true source of religion. The Old Testament defines true religion as 'the fear of the Lord'. Solomon said 'The fear of the Lord is the beginning of wisdom' (Proverbs 1:7).

The Bible tells us that man was made in the image of God and for fellowship with him but then fell into sin and as a consequence became estranged from God and his ways.

Man, although now a fallen creature, has not completely lost the image of God in which he was made. Some knowledge of God remains in him. The seed of religion is still there, even though his sinful nature constantly reacts against it. Some have even called man a worshipping animal.

Archaeologists have found evidence of religious rites and symbols in all past civilisations, and Christian missionaries from all parts of the world have found some form of religion even among the most depraved and primitive tribes. True religion is the greatest of blessings, but false religion due to the influence of Satan and the wickedness of man can be the cruellest bondage.

And now Israel, what does the LORD your God require of you but to fear the LORD your God, to walk in all His ways, and to love Him, to serve the LORD your God with all your heart and with all your soul (Deuteronomy 10:12).

The fear of the LORD *is* the beginning of wisdom; A good understanding have all those who do *His commandments*. His praise endures forever (Psalm 111:10).

But this fear is not a feeling of terror, such as a child might feel towards a cruel father, but of reverence, awe and willing obedience which expresses itself in worship and praise. In the New Testament, religion is a response to the gospel of Christ rather than to the law of Moses, and which expresses itself in acts of daily repentance, faith, kindness and godliness.

The Bible teaches us that the essence of true religion is based on a relationship with God in which man is conscious not only of his own sinfulness and helplessness but also of God's great grace and goodness. The fruit of this relationship is found in the offering of true and sincere worship, and of good deeds to all men prescribed not by man and his ideas but by God and his Word.

2 The centre of religion in man

There are several wrong ideas about where the origin or seat of religion should be.

a) Mind. Some think of religion mainly as a matter of knowledge and place its centre in the intellect.

b) Heart. Others see it as a matter of our feelings and place its centre in the emotions.

c) Will. Lastly, there are those who believe it is primarily a matter of good deeds and place its centre in the will.

All these opinions are one-sided and fail to meet the biblical standard which teaches that the centre of true religion involves the whole man – mind, heart and will. Jesus proved this to be the case when he said:

> ... The LORD our God, the LORD is one. And you shall love the LORD your God with all your heart, with all your soul, with all your mind, and with all your strength (Mark 12:29-30).

3 The origin of religion

During the early years of the twentieth century several attempts were made to explain how religion first began and to find a natural explanation for it.

a) Witch-doctors. Some thought it began through cunning and deceitful witch-doctors or priests pretending to have magic powers, who were able to deceive primitive and superstitious people in order to rule them or make money out of them. This explanation is no longer accepted.

b) Fetishes. Others thought religion began with the worship of lifeless objects (fetishes), or with the worship of spirits which were believed to exist either in natural objects, such as trees, or in the unseen spirit-world of departed ancestors.

c) Natural forces. Another theory is that religion originated with man worshipping the life-giving forces of nature, the sun, moon and stars or the seas, rivers, winds and weather. Through his ignorance he attributed a supernatural origin to everything he could not explain.

d) Psychological cause. Some have sought to explain religion in psychological terms saying that man needs to believe in Someone or Something greater than himself and that this arises in the subconscious soon after birth. When we were infants we were totally dependent on our parents for everything. Belief in God is therefore just a projection of our earliest need for our parents; this remains in our subconscious and expresses itself in a belief in some kind of father-figure.

e) An opiate. Karl Marx (1818-1883) saw the origin of religion as the result of the cruel exploitation of servants by their masters. In order to relieve the misery of this present life the oppressors invented a mythical after-life in which the poor would be comforted by gods and angels. Religion is therefore an illusion and an opiate, drugging people into accepting their miserable conditions.

But all these theories do not explain how in all parts of the world there is this universal belief in some form of religion among all types of races of mankind. These theories are ultimately not capable of proof because they all start by having to investigate someone who is already religious. It is impossible therefore to prove that at the dawn of history man had no religion and later acquired one; rather the very opposite is true, for from earliest recorded time we have evidence from man's religious practices and beliefs that he had some consciousness of God.

The Bible gives the only reliable account of the origin of religion by informing us of the existence of God, infinite and yet personal, the only object worthy of worship, who revealed himself to man and created him in his own image:

> In the beginning God created the heavens and the earth. ... so God created man in His *own* image, in the image of God He created him, male and female He created them (Genesis 1:1,27).

The Bible describes how God, whom man could never discover with his own natural powers, revealed himself in creation and especially in his Word, so that man could know how to worship and serve him. God has made man with the ability to respond to his Creator, to have fellowship with him and to glorify him. As Augustine of Hippo (354-430) said, 'You have made us for yourself and our hearts are restless until they find their rest in you.'

Questions

1 What is the source of true religion?

2 Where is the centre of true religion in man?

3 According to the opponents of Christianity how did religion begin?

CHAPTER TWO

THE WORD OF GOD

1 How can we learn about God?

    a) The Book of Nature
    b) The Voice of Conscience
    c) The Book of God – the Bible

2 Men spoke from God

3 The Old Testament as God's Word

    a) Jesus Christ believed it
    b) Why God caused it to be written down
    c) The New Testament writers believed it
    d) Parts of it are now superseded by the New Testament
    e) How God inspired the Prophets
    f) The harmony of the Old and New Testaments

4 Modern scepticism about the Bible

5 Christ's view of the Bible

    a) Christ's use of the Old Testament
    b) Obedience to Christ's authority

6 The New Testament as God's Word

    a) The testimony of apostolic eye-witnesses
    b) The recognition of apostolic writings by the Church

7 Conclusion: The Bible is God's revelation about himself

    a) How are we to interpret the Bible?
    b) How should we study the Bible?

1 How can we learn about God?

In 1510, a young German monk named Martin Luther
visited Rome. A marble staircase, now called the Scala Sancta,
had been brought from Jerusalem to Rome in the 4th century
AD because it was believed to be the staircase that Christ
descended after his trial before Pilate. The Roman Catholic
Church taught that if anyone climbed these stairs, kissing each
step and praying the Lord's Prayer on each one, it would help
deliver a soul from purgatory. Luther climbed these stairs
on his knees, kissing them and praying but when he got to
the top he asked himself, "Who knows whether these things
please God?" Today many people are asking themselves
the same question: how can we know the truth about God?
Where can we look for answers to our questions? God has
given us two books to read and to study, one is the book of
nature and the other is the book of God, the Bible.

a) The book of nature. What is the book of nature? It is the
world and the universe in which we live. There are no words
in this book, yet all the things we see in it have a story to tell.
The sun, moon and stars, the birds, animals and insects, the
mountains, fields and rivers, the trees, flowers and fruit and
finally, Man himself with all his amazing powers, proclaims
that there is a wonderful Person we call God who made all
these things long ago. This is what the Bible says:

> In the beginning God created the heavens and the earth
> (Genesis 1:1).

> The heavens declare the glory of God; and the firmament
> shows His handiwork. Day unto day utters speech and
> night unto night reveals knowledge. *There* is no speech nor
> language *where* their voice is not heard (Psalm 19:1-3).

Because what may be known of God is manifest in them, for God has shown it to them. For since the creation of the world His invisible *attributes* are clearly seen, being understood by the things that are made, *even* His eternal power and Godhead, so that they are without excuse (Romans 1:19-20).

The human brain, though so very small, is in reality a powerful little computer able to do all kinds of complicated calculations very quickly and to remember and store what it learns in a data-base carrying hundreds of thousands of pieces of information during a life-span of seventy years or more. Who made such a wonderful piece of equipment? This is the work of God the great and super-intelligent Creator. However, we also see many terrible things in the world, animals eating each other in order to survive, dreadful diseases killing millions of people every year, wars, murders, famines, earthquakes, hurricanes and tidal waves devastating countries in some parts of the world. Why is this if an all-wise God made the world and everything in it? The Bible ascribes these disasters to God's judgement on the first man and woman when they fell into sin by disobeying God their Creator. The entry of sin and evil into the world had cosmic results: God cursed the earth for their sake. Creation has been spoilt as a consequence but not totally ruined, so we can still see enough of the wonder and beauty of creation to realise that it has been made by God.

Then to Adam God said, 'Because you have heeded the voice of your wife, and have eaten from the tree of which I commanded you saying, "You shall not eat from it": Cursed is the ground for your sake; in toil you shall eat *of* it all the days of your life. Both thorns and thistles it shall bring forth for you, and you shall eat the herb of the field' (Genesis 3:17-18).

b) The voice of conscience. The Bible tells us that since human beings were made in God's image, man still has some awareness of God, and in some respects still resembles him:

> Then God said, 'Let Us make man in Our image, according to Our likeness; let them have dominion over the fish of the sea, over the birds of the air, and over the cattle, over all the earth and over every creeping thing that creeps on the earth' (Genesis 1:26).

What does this mean? It means that man reflects and has some awareness of some of the very same qualities and capacities as God himself. God made man with an intellect, emotions and a will of his own. He made him to be immortal, pure and righteous. This means that man has both a sense of eternity, telling him that death is not the end of everything and also a deep sense of right and wrong: he is a moral being. God has given man a conscience which tells him when he ought to do certain things and when he ought not to do others. In spite of wide cultural differences throughout the world even the most primitive tribes have this innate sense of right and wrong – all men have a conscience that can be appealed to even though it has been damaged by habitual sinful behaviour. But even with the book of nature open before us and with some sense of eternity within us, we still have a very inadequate and incomplete knowledge of God. For example, how would we know that God is a Trinity of Persons, Father, Son and Holy Spirit or how would we know what is his holy and perfect will unless he first revealed it to us? Man is like a lost traveller walking at night through the countryside. Suddenly there is a flash of lightning and he sees where he is, but just as suddenly he is back in darkness again and cannot find his way. Thank God he has not left us to walk in darkness, but he has given us his own book, the Bible, which sheds a bright and enduring light on our pathway!

c) **The Book of God – the Bible**. What is the Bible? It is a collection of sixty-six books written originally in Hebrew, Aramaic and Greek over a period of about 1600 years. Its writers included prophets (Moses and Isaiah), Kings (David and Solomon), a farmer (Amos), a tax collector (Matthew), a doctor (Luke) and many others. In total, God used about forty different men to give us his word so that we might come to know him and his great salvation. This alone of all the religious books in the world is God's book. We cannot add anything to it (like the Catholics, Mormons and Moslems try to do) nor can we take anything from it:

> You shall not add to the word which I command you, nor take *anything* from it, that you may keep the commandments of the LORD your God which I command you (Deuteronomy 4:2).

> For I testify to everyone who hears the words of the prophecy of this book: If anyone adds to these things, God will add to him the plagues that are written in this book; and if anyone takes away from the words of the book of this prophecy, God shall take away his part from the Book of Life, from the holy city, and *from* the things which are written in this book (Revelation 22:18-19).

In the Gospel of Mark our Lord Jesus Christ condemned the Pharisees for daring to add their own rules and regulations to the Bible (Mark 7:1-13). The Bible does not claim to tell us all that can be known about God and his ways; for example, it does not tell us exactly how and at what precise date God made the universe, or the earth and the myriad forms of life upon it – it simply gives us the order in which he created everything and saw that it was very good. The Bible is not given to satisfy our curiosity about all scientific, philosophical or theological questions; it is given to show us who God is and how we can come to know, love and please him:

> The secret *things belong* to the LORD our God, but those *things which are* revealed *belong* to us and to our children forever, that *we* may do all the words of this law (Deuteronomy 29:29).

> And truly Jesus did many other signs in the presence of His disciples, which are not written in this book, but these are written that you may believe that Jesus is the Christ, the Son of God, and that believing you may have life in His name (John 20:30-31).

If we read the Bible in this way with reverence and with understanding then we shall find that God speaks through it to us today.

2 Men spoke from God

The Bible is God's book through which he speaks to us clearly and unmistakably, but as we have already seen he has spoken through all kinds of different men:

> Knowing this first, that no prophecy of Scripture is of any private interpretation, for prophecy never came by the will of man, but holy men of God spoke *as they were* moved by the Holy Spirit (2 Peter 1:20-21).

Each book of the Bible therefore has two authors, the Holy Spirit who is the primary author and the person who wrote the book! We must recognize therefore both the human and the divine elements throughout the Bible. We can see that the different authors each have their own style – Isaiah is mighty and majestic, while Solomon is more quiet and reflective. In the New Testament, Luke writes very good Greek while Mark writes in a very rough style. The Holy Spirit did not use the authors like some managers do their secretaries, dictating every word that they should say and leaving no room for their own style and personality. For

example, when a man is driving a horse and cart he guides
the horses in the direction he wants them to take by holding
the reins, but the horses are allowed to trot and pull the cart
along by themselves in their own particular manner. In much
the same way the Holy Spirit guided the biblical authors in
what he wanted them to say, but never so as to destroy their
own unique gifts, cultural background or personality. On the
human side, we see the author of the Book of Proverbs collect-
ing and arranging his material, while in the New Testament
Luke has to research and gather together the material for his
gospel and the Book of Acts just as an historian might do
today. Again, the reasons for books being written were various: to provide historical records, laws, psalms for worship,
proverbs for godly living, prophecies concerning present
situations and those predicting events in the future, Gospels
of the life, ministry and teaching of Jesus and finally letters
to the churches. The biblical authors spoke to all these needs
and left the imprint of themselves and their times on their
writings. We nevertheless believe that God preserved both
the Old and the New Testament authors from making errors
either in doctrine or in matters of historical fact.

3 The Old Testament as God's Word

a) Jesus Christ believed it. The Lord Jesus Christ fully
believed the Old Testament and often quoted passages from
it to prove a point. Here are some examples;

> And He [Jesus] was handed the book of the prophet
> Isaiah ... He found the place where it was written: [Isaiah
> 61:1-2]. Then He closed the book ... and He began to say
> to them, 'Today this Scripture is fulfilled in your hearing.'
> (Luke 4:17,20-21).

> For if you believed Moses you would have believed Me; for
> he wrote about Me. But if you do not believe his writings
> how will you believe My words? (John 5:46-47).

> Then He [Jesus] said to them, 'These are My words which I spoke to you while I was still with you, that all things must be fulfilled which were written in the Law of Moses and *the* Prophets and *the* Psalms concerning Me' (Luke 24:44).

The coming of Christ and his kingdom as recorded in the New Testament is seen as the fulfilment of Old Testament prophecy. The two therefore fit perfectly and harmoniously together as Jesus himself said:

> Do not think that I came to destroy the Law or the Prophets. I did not come to destroy but to fulfil (Matthew 5:17).

b) Why God caused it to be written down. God took great care to see that his Word was written down very accurately so that it could be handed down from one generation to another. In this way his will would be made known and preserved for the future. We can see how this was done both in the life of Moses and in the prophets who lived several hundred years after him:

> So Moses came and told the people all the words of the LORD and all the judgements. And all the people answered with one voice and said, 'All the words which the LORD has said we will do.' And Moses wrote all the words of the LORD ... (Exodus 24:3-4).

> Moreover the LORD said to me, 'Take a large scroll and write on it with a man's pen ... Now go, write it before them on a tablet, and note it on a scroll, that it may be for time to come, forever and ever' (Isaiah 8:1; 30:8).

> So I will bring on that land all My words which I have pronounced against it, all that is written in this book, which Jeremiah has prophesied concerning all the nations (Jeremiah 25:13).

For further study look up Deuteronomy 17:18; 31:24-39; Joshua 24:26; 1 Samuel 10:25; Jeremiah 36:4, 45:1; Habakkuk 2:2.

God's Word is very precious because it shows us the truth about God, about ourselves and the way to everlasting life. It teaches us how God wants us to live and it preserves us from sin and from temptation.

> ... The judgements of the LORD *are* true *and* righteous altogether. More to be desired *are they* than gold, yea, than much fine gold; sweeter also than honey and the honeycomb. Moreover by them Your servant is warned, *and* in keeping them *there is* great reward (Psalm 19:9-11).

Later in the history of Israel there were two notable occasions when the nation, having lost the books containing God's Law, was brought to repentance and reformation as the result of the word of God being rediscovered and read to them. The first was in the days of King Josiah, and the second after the return from Babylon under the leadership of Nehemiah during the rebuilding of Jerusalem. (2 Kings 22:8 - 23:2; Nehemiah 8-10).

c) The New Testament writers believed it. There are many examples where New Testament writers quote from the Old Testament, showing their full acceptance of it as the word of God. Throughout his writings Paul continually quotes from the Old Testament to prove various points. For example:

> And we declare to you glad tidings – that promise made to the fathers. God has fulfilled this for us their children, in that He has raised up Jesus. As it is also written in the second Psalm: '*You are my Son, Today I have begotten You*' (Acts 13:32-33).

See also Romans 15:4; 1 Corinthians 2:9; Galatians 3:6 -13. The

writer to the Hebrews, James, Peter and Jude all do the same
(Hebrews 1:5 -13; James 2:8 -11; 1 Peter 2:6 -10; Jude 7, 11, 14).

d) Parts of it are now superseded by the New Testament.
The Old Testament worship and sacrifices were temporary
and pointed forward to the coming of the Messiah, our Lord
Jesus Christ. This is explained very fully in the Letter to the
Hebrews. This means that parts of the law given to Moses
were of a temporary nature to be observed only until Jesus
came. The law can be divided into three sections, firstly
the *civil law* for regulating the life of the nation of Israel,
secondly the *ceremonial law* for the worship of the Jewish
Temple and thirdly the *moral law*. The moral law is summed
up in the Ten Commandments (Exodus 20) and because it
is taught in various parts of the New Testament it is to be
obeyed as the will of God for all time (Matthew: 5:17-20;
Luke 16:16-18). Since the destruction of Jerusalem in AD 70
and the dispersal of the Jews throughout the world, both
the civil and ceremonial laws have ceased to apply. This
does not mean that there is no longer any point in reading
the Books of Moses because God's word to Israel is full of
instruction for us today:

> For whatever things were written before were written for
> our learning, that we through the patience and comfort of
> the Scriptures might have hope (Romans 15:4).

The historical books of the Old Testament covering many
centuries narrate the fortunes of God's people with bad
men and evil days outnumbering righteous men and good
days. What is the value of reading them? These books are all
about men and women like ourselves. We see how weak they
often were, how some succeeded while others failed, and as
we read we are instructed either to follow their example or
to be warned by their failure. Paul reminds us about this in
1 Corinthians 10:1-13:

Now all these things happened to them as examples, and they were written for our admonition, on whom the ends of the ages have come (verse 11).

e) How God inspired the Prophets. Another large section of the Old Testament (28%) is devoted to the Prophets (four major and twelve minor) who spoke as messengers of God, not speaking their own words or thinking their own thoughts but simply passing on to the people the messages they were given. The phrase, 'Thus says the Lord', occurs almost 2,000 times in the Old Testament! See how God called Jeremiah to be his prophet:

> Then the LORD put forth His hand and touched my mouth and the LORD said to me, 'Behold I have put my words in your mouth. See I have this day set you over the nations and over the kingdoms, to root out and to pull down, to destroy and to throw down, to build and to plant' (Jeremiah 1:9-10).

The same happened with some variation to all the prophets when God called them to leave their occupations to serve him. For example, Amos was an ordinary farmer when God called him and told him what to say:

> Surely the Lord GOD does nothing, unless He reveals His secret to His servants the prophets. A lion has roared! Who will not fear? The Lord GOD has spoken! Who can but prophesy? (Amos 3:7-8).

Therefore the worst judgement that could come upon the people of Israel was for God to withdraw his word from them, and leave them without any prophet to point them back to himself.

> 'Behold, the days are coming,' says the Lord GOD, 'That I will send a famine on the land, not a famine of bread, nor

a thirst for water, but of hearing the words of the LORD.
They shall wander from sea to sea, and from north to east;
they shall run to and fro, seeking the word of the LORD, but
shall not find it' (Amos 8:11-12).

But there were also false prophets in those days, just as there
are today, who dream up their own ideas and speak from
their own imaginations, wanting to please those in power, or
seeking to obtain either money or influence for themselves.
These men often opposed Gods prophets as we can see in
several places throughout the Old Testament. For example,
both Jeremiah and Ezekiel had to contend against these
enemies of the truth (Jeremiah 14:13-6; 23:16-40; Ezekiel
13:3-16). But the true prophet waited for God to speak and
only then would he say, "Thus says the Lord". And because
his message was unpopular the prophet often had to suffer
persecution and sometimes even death itself for being true
to God and faithful to his calling.

God also used the prophets to foretell the coming of his
Son into the world; this was many hundreds of years before
he was born in Bethlehem. They also speak of things yet to
be fulfilled and their writings are therefore very important
for us today. They foretold that Christ would be born in
Bethlehem (Micah 5:2) of a virgin (Isaiah 7:14), would be the
Son of God (Isaiah 9:6), be crucified on a cross (Psalm 22:16),
and suffer for the sins of the world (Isaiah 53:4-6).

f) The harmony of the Old and New Testaments. The Old
and New Testaments form one unified book. Both our Lord
and his apostles regarded the Old Testament as the Word
of God. The apostles believed that what they wrote was
the truth about God as it had been revealed to them by the
Lord Jesus Christ. Not only did Isaiah say that the word of
the Lord abides forever (Isaiah 40:6-8), but so also did Peter
when referring to the apostolic preaching of the gospel. His
readers have –

... been born again, not of corruptible seed but incorruptible, through the word of God which lives and abides
forever, because '*All flesh is as grass, and all the glory of
man as the flower of the grass. The grass withers, and its
flower falls away, but the word of the* LORD *endures forever.*'
Now this is the word which by the gospel was preached
to you (1 Peter 1:23-25).

The New Testament frequently quotes the Old Testament
as the word of God. In 1 Timothy 5:18 Paul quotes from
two scriptures, one from the Old Testament (Deuteronomy
25:4 and one from the Gospel of Luke (10:7) in the New
Testament and calls them both Scripture! It is worthy
of note that the Book of Revelation calls itself a book of
prophecy just like the books of prophecy in the Old Testament. Paul sometimes writes, 'The Scripture says to Pharaoh', when what he really means is, 'God says to Pharaoh'
(Romans 9:17). To Paul, Scripture is God's word written.

4 Modern scepticism about the Bible

In the nineteenth century some scholars questioned the
authenticity of many books of the Bible and developed
sceptical theories about their authorship, date and literary
form. The movement began in Germany and soon spread to
England and America penetrating all the major Protestant
denominations mainly through their theological seminaries.
It was known in those days as, 'Higher Criticism', but today
it is called Liberalism; sadly it is still the dominant view
of the Bible in the Western world and in some theological
seminaries in China. It believes the Bible is not inspired by
God, but it can inspire genuine religious experiences in those
who read it. It is only a book like any other book and its
authors reflect the ideas and values of their times. The Higher
Critical Movement reflected nineteenth century rationalistic
ideas about the origin of the world and of civilisation. It
did not believe in miracles or supernaturalism, and it held

evolutionary ideas about the physical world, the history of man and the history of Israel. Its scholars produced sceptical theories about the origin and composition of the books of the Bible based on these assumptions. Modern Liberalism has much the same attitude to the Bible, believing that its own theories of scientific historical enquiry must precede faith. It asserts in effect that only theological scholars know what is true in the Bible and what is false; the ordinary Christian is dependent upon their findings and must take his faith from them. Liberalism denies that the Bible is the infallible word of God and that Christianity is the only true religion in the world.

5 Christ's view of the Bible

a) Christ's use of the Old Testament. When we look at Christ's view of the Old Testament we immediately move into a totally different world from that of liberal theology. In John 10:35 Jesus says, 'The Scripture cannot be broken,' and in his prayer to the Father he says, 'Sanctify them by Your truth. Your word is truth' (John 17:17). This shows that Jesus' view of the Bible is very different from that of Liberalism and of many contemporary western theologians. When he was tempted three times by the devil in the desert (Matthew 4:1-11), on each occasion Jesus used texts from the book of Deuteronomy to reject the devil's temptations. Clearly he believed God's word was true! When the Sadducees denied the resurrection of the body, Jesus said to them, 'You are mistaken, not knowing the Scriptures nor the power of God' (Matthew 22:29).

He then quoted another Scripture, Exodus 3:6, to settle this point of theological dispute. In a similar dispute with the Pharisees, over claims that their traditions were of equal authority with the law of Moses, Jesus replied that the commandments which Moses had written were the commandments of God (Mark 7:6-13), and must therefore be obeyed.

On another occasion Jesus emphasised that his mission was not to destroy the Old Testament but to fulfil it; therefore even the smallest parts of Hebrew lettering found in the Scriptures were not to be altered.

> Do not think that I came to destroy the Law or the Prophets. I did not come to destroy but to fulfil. For assuredly, I say to you, till heaven and earth pass away, one jot or one tittle will by no means pass from the law till all is fulfilled (Matthew 5:17-18).

Again, he said to the Pharisees, 'It is easier for heaven and earth to pass away than for one tittle of the Law to fail' (Luke 16:17). Jesus frequently referred to the things that he was doing as fulfilling prophecies made in the Old Testament many hundreds of years before:

> For I say to you that this which is written must still be accomplished in Me: *'And He was numbered with the transgressors.'* For the things concerning Me have an end (Luke 22:37).

See also Matthew 26:24; Mark 9:12; 12:10-11; 14:27; John 13:18.

Several matters in the Old Testament that are dismissed by liberal theologians as myths were accepted by Christ as being factual and true. For example, Adam and Eve (Matthew 19:4-5), Sodom and Gomorrah (Luke 17:28-30), Noah (Matthew 24:37-39), Jonah and the great fish (Matthew 12:39-41), and Lot's wife being turned into a pillar of salt (Luke 17:31-32). Although liberal scholars admit that Jesus appeared to believe in the historicity of these events, they suggest that he only pretended to believe them so as not to shock the Jews. Others suggest that when Jesus became man, he laid aside his divine wisdom and knowledge to such an extent that he could be mistaken about many things, just like any other man! This tells us nothing about Jesus but quite a lot about modern liberal theologians and what a low opinion they have of God's only begotten Son! Jesus not only placed a high value on the Scriptures of the past; he also wished to preserve for posterity the record of his own life and ministry. For this reason he said to his followers:

> These things I have spoken to you while being present with you. But the Helper, the Holy Spirit, whom the Father will send in My name, He will teach you all things, and bring to your remembrance all things that I said to you (John 14:25-26).

See also Matthew 24:25; 26:13 and 28:20

b) Obedience to Christ's authority. For the Christian there is no higher obligation, no more sacred duty than to follow Jesus Christ as Master, Lord and God.

> ... I am the light of the world. He who follows me shall not walk in darkness but have the light of life (John 8:12).

The believer not only follows Jesus' example but also obeys Jesus' words. If Jesus says the Old Testament is true and reliable and should be believed as the word of God, then the Christian will obey and believe what his Lord commands. The Christian must follow Christ in all things including what he says about the Bible. If he is not Lord of all then he is not Lord at all.

6 The New Testament as God's Word

The writers of the New Testament, mostly apostles chosen by Christ to be eye-witnesses of his glory and resurrection (see Acts 1:21-22), were conscious that they were commissioned by him to preserve and explain the truths which Christ himself had revealed to them. We need to understand that the Lord Jesus selected a special group from among his disciples whom he called apostles. In the Greek this word means 'sent ones':

> Then He appointed twelve, that they might be with Him and that He might send them out to preach, and to have power to heal sicknesses and to cast out demons (Mark 3:14-15).

a) The testimony of apostolic eye-witnesses. This group of men were eyewitnesses of all that Jesus said and did, as John said: 'The Word became flesh and dwelt among us, and we beheld His glory, the glory as of the only begotten of the Father, full of grace and truth' (John 1:14). As we have already seen, Jesus promised to give them the Holy Spirit after he had died and risen again. The Holy Spirit would glorify Christ, guide them into all truth, teach them, help them to remember all he had said, reveal the things of Christ to them, and tell them what was to happen in the future (John 14:25-26; 15: 26-27; 16:12-15).

What were the special qualifications of the twelve apostles?

• They were personally chosen by Christ (Mark 3:13-19)
• They had to be eye-witnesses of his ministry and of his physical resurrection (Acts 1:21-26).
• They were given miraculous powers (Matthew 10:1,8; Acts 2:43; 2 Corinthians 12:12).
• They were given universal authority (Matthew 28:18-20; Acts 26:16-18).

It is very clear that Jesus also chose Paul to be an apostle not to the Jews only but more especially to the Gentiles (1 Corinthians 1:1; 9:1-2; Romans 11:13; 2 Corinthians 12:12). This is proved by the fact that all four of these qualifications were personally given by the risen Christ to Paul. These men not only told the good news of Christ by word of mouth; some of them also wrote about it and did so under the influence of the Holy Spirit. So Paul could say that the words that he wrote came from the Holy Spirit (1 Corinthians 2:13) and that they were therefore to be obeyed as the commands of the Lord (1 Corinthians 14:37). He was certain that not even an angel from heaven could teach a different gospel (Galatians 1:6-9). Paul did not issue commands on every subject (Romans 14:5-6) but whenever he knew that he should do so he wrote very clearly and authoritatively (2 Thessalonians 3:6,12). Paul knew that the message he had received was not the word of man but the word of God (1 Thessalonians 2:13). The apostle Peter said that he regarded Paul's writings as having the same authority as other Scripture:

> ... as also our beloved brother Paul, according to the wisdom given to him, has written to you, as also in all his epistles, speaking in them of these things, in which are some things hard to understand, which those who *are* untaught and unstable twist to their own destruction, as *they do* also the rest of the Scriptures (2 Peter 3:15-16).

b) The recognition of apostolic writings by the Church. When the Apostles had died the early Church collected together their Gospels, letters and other writings to form what we now call 'The New Testament'. Four tests were applied to distinguish which were Apostolic and which were not;
i)   Apostolic authorship
ii)   From the Apostolic period
iii) Apostolic doctrine
iv)   Received by the great majority of the Churches

Roman Catholic and Russian Orthodox Churches claim that it was the Church which gave the New Testament to the world at the Synod of Hippo in AD 393 but this is not true. The early Church did not write these twenty-seven books; they did not produce them, they only recognised in them the authentic teaching of the apostles. When we say that Isaac Newton discovered the law of gravity we do not mean that he invented or produced it; he only found something in nature that was already there and he understood how it worked. It is just the same with the apostolic writings; the early Church councils did not invent or produce the Scriptures, they merely recognised them for what they already were. So it is wrong to say that the Church gave us the Bible – God inspired it and caused it to be written down, so it was God alone who gave it to us, not the Church.

7 Conclusion: The Bible is God's revelation about himself

From all that has been said in this chapter about the word of God it must be very plain that the Bible gives full and ample testimony to itself when it claims to speak authoritatively as the voice of God to man. This is why theologians speak of Scripture as being 'self-authenticating', – it bears witness to itself in hundreds of verses as speaking the words of God himself.

We began this chapter with Luther asking himself the question, 'Who knows whether these things please God?' Many people today are asking themselves another important question, 'How can we know the truth about God?' We can now answer that question. We can know about him through reading his Word, the Bible. This does not mean that simply by reading and understanding the Bible a person automatically knows God and will go to heaven. We need the help of God the Holy Spirit to enable us to understand and believe spiritual things; only then can we know what he is saying to us personally. 'But the natural man does not receive the things of the Spirit of God, for they are foolishness to him; nor can he know them because they are spiritually discerned' (1 Corinthians 2:14). In order to know God we not only need God's word but we need God's Spirit too.

a) How are we to interpret the Bible?

i) Because all Scripture is inspired (2 Timothy 3:16) it does not contradict itself. The best way to understand the Bible is to compare one part with another: the Scripture is self-interpreting (1 Corinthians 2:13). Ask older Christians to help you if you have difficulty, but remember, no human being or church is infallible.

ii) The Bible is to be understood literally except where a figurative sense is obviously intended. There is symbolic language, poetical, allegorical and prophetic language; all are used in the Bible and we need to understand when each author is using these different types of language.

• Firstly, the **symbolic** – Jesus said, 'I am the door', 'I am the vine', 'I am the light', and 'I am the good shepherd'. He is speaking symbolically. Each of these sayings represent or illustrate an important truth about his relationship to us; the door speaks of him being the entrance into eternal life; the vine speaks of his life-giving relationship to the believer; the light speaks of his power to dispel the darkness of our ignorance, the good shepherd speaks of his care for us as his sheep.

• The Bible also uses **poetic** language. David says, 'the trees of the woods shall rejoice before the Lord' (1 Chronicles 16:33) and Solomon says, 'the sun… rises and the sun goes down' (Ecclesiastes 1:5). In both places the author is using language poetically not literally.

• In his ministry Jesus also spoke to people in **parables,** which were word pictures from everyday life used to explain spiritual truths. For example, a tiny seed growing into a big tree illustrates how the kingdom of God, although it has small and humble origins, grows to be the greatest of all the kingdoms.

• The Bible also uses **prophetic** language; Isaiah speaks of a suffering servant who will come into the world to bear the sins of God's people (Isaiah 53). This was fulfilled by the Lord Jesus Christ (Acts 8:32-35) almost 800 years later.

iii) We should always interpret the difficult and obscure parts of the Bible by the obvious and clear parts, e.g. the Gospels help us to understand the events in the Book of Revelation, not the other way round!

b) How should we study the Bible?

Read it reverently:	God is speaking to you, Christ has died for you (Luke 24:25-27, 32)
Read it sincerely:	God promises to bless those who seek him with all their hearts (Jeremiah 29:13)
Read it prayerfully:	God promises to answer honest prayers (Matthew 6:6)
Read it regularly:	God feeds our souls by his word (1 Peter 2:2) just as we feed our bodies with food.
Believe what you read:	Without faith it is impossible to please God (Hebrews 11:6).
Practise what you read:	God has promised, "Obey my voice and I will be your God." (Jeremiah 7:23)
Understand what you read:	Jesus said that we can only do his will when we know what it is. (Matthew 13: 19-23).
Discuss what you read:	Other Christians are given to us for mutual help and encouragement.

Questions

1 Why did God give us the Bible?

2 How does the New Testament help us to understand the purpose of the Old Testament?

3 What is theological Liberalism and why does it deny that the Bible is truly God's Word?

4 Why did Christ choose twelve Apostles and what is their importance for the formation of the New Testament?

5 We are to understand the Bible literally except where it uses figurative language – what are the four categories of figurative language?

CHAPTER THREE

THE TRINITY

1 What is God like?

    a) God's divine qualities

2 What is the Trinity?

    a) We must be careful to avoid four common mistakes

3 What does the Old Testament teach about the Trinity?

    a) References to God in the plural
    b) The Angel of the Lord
    c) Theophanies

4 The Father is God

5 The Son is God

    a) Christ is the image of the invisible God
    b) Christ does things that only a divine person is able to do
    c) Old Testament references to Christ as God

6 The Holy Spirit is God

7 Conclusion

1 What is God like?

Ever since the beginning of time, men have tried to find out what God is like. Some have made idols, others have tried to make contact with him through spirits, mediums and witch doctors, while others, such as the Hindus, think that God is in everything and everybody and therefore there is no distinction between the Creator and his creation. If we really want to know God we must turn to the book he has given us, the Bible. As we saw in the previous chapter, nature can tell us something about God as Creator (Romans 1:20) and so can our conscience (Romans 2:14-16), but in the Bible God gives us the clearest revelation of himself. One day the Lord Jesus strongly attacked the Pharisees because they were teaching that their own traditions were more important than the word of God in the Old Testament (Matthew 15:1-14). It is the Word of God that is our only guide in matters of faith, not human traditions however old they may be. Some churches teach that Scripture and tradition are equal in authority, but Jesus taught that everything including church tradition must be tested by the word of God, not the other way round.

The foundation of all true knowledge of God must be a clear understanding of his perfections as revealed in the Scriptures. An unknown God can neither be trusted, worshipped nor served. In this chapter we have listed the principal perfections of God's divine character. But if we are to profit spiritually from reading about them we need to ask God to bless our study and to apply the truth to our hearts and consciences. God is only truly known to our souls as we surrender ourselves to him, submit to his authority and regulate our lives by what we learn from his Word. A mere theoretical knowledge of God is useless. We must never forget that the devil knows a lot about God; he is not an atheist, but his knowledge neither helps nor saves him (James 2:19).

Some theologians have divided God's divine qualities into two parts. Firstly those qualities which belong uniquely to God, and secondly those qualities which in his grace he also communicates to man in redemption. In the first we are reminded of his deity (his Godness) and that he is totally different to man. In the second we are reminded that God created man in his own image and therefore we bear in measure a resemblance to our Creator

1 In the first group of divine qualities:

i) God is Spirit
ii) Infinite
iii) Perfect
iv) Omnipresent
v) Transcendent
vi) Eternal
vii) Glorious
viii) Unchanging
ix) Omnipotent
x) Omniscient
xi) Sovereign

2 In the second group:

xii) God is Holy
xiii) Righteous
xiv) Love
xv) Merciful
xvi) Gracious
xvii) Patient

He is the only true God. There are many different religions in the world, all with different ideas about God. Some worship many gods and goddesses and practise evil and cruel rites as part of their religion. Today, some people are teaching that although there are many religions, they are all really worshipping the same God, one God under many names. But when you compare what they each teach about God, you can soon see how different they are. For example, the God of the Koran is very different to the God of the Bible; 'the God and Father of our Lord Jesus Christ'.

Thus says the LORD, the King of Israel, and His Redeemer, the LORD of hosts: 'I *am* the First and I *am* the Last; besides Me *there* is no God' (Isaiah 44:6).

And this is eternal life, that they may know You, the only true God, and Jesus Christ whom You have sent (John 17:3).

a) God's divine qualities.

i) He is Spirit. This means that he has no form or shape or body as we do. A spirit, though invisible and non-material, is also personal and capable of thought, feeling and action. He is without the limitations of both time and space that belong to our own existence as human beings:

[Jesus said], 'God *is* Spirit, and those who worship Him must worship in spirit and in truth' (John 4:24).

[Paul said that God is], ... the King eternal, immortal, invisible... the blessed and only Potentate, the King of kings and Lord of Lords, who alone has immortality, dwelling in unapproachable light, whom no man has seen or can see ... (1 Timothy 1:17; 6:15-16).

ii) He is infinite. You cannot measure or weigh God because he is totally without any limitation either in himself, his divine qualities or his measureless abilities and powers. His presence is not confined to the world for he existed before it was created and he will be there after it has finished.

In relation to himself	–	he is **perfect**
In relation to space	–	he is **omnipresent** (everywhere)
In relation to creation	–	he is **transcendent** (above all)
In relation to time	–	he is **eternal**

iii) He is perfect. God alone in the universe is free from sin and all imperfection. We can therefore trust him completely because he is without any defect either in his essence, character, thoughts or works.

> [Jesus said], 'Be ... perfect, even as your Father which is in heaven is perfect' (Matthew 5:48, AV).

> Who is like You, O LORD, among the gods? Who is like You, glorious in holiness, fearful in praises, doing wonders? (Exodus 15:11)

> Every good and perfect gift is from above, and comes down from the Father of lights, with whom there is no variation or shadow of turning (James 1:17).

iv) He is omnipresent. God is in every place in heaven and in earth knowing all that happens everywhere.

> If I ascend into heaven, You *are* there; If I make my bed in hell, behold, You *are there*. *If* I take the wings of the morning, *and* dwell in the uttermost parts of the sea, even there Your hand shall lead me, and Your right hand shall hold me (Psalm 139:8-10).

> For the eyes of the LORD run to and fro throughout the whole earth, to show Himself strong on behalf of *those* whose heart is loyal to Him ... (2 Chronicles 16:9).

> 'Can anyone hide himself in secret places, so I shall not see him?' says the LORD. 'Do I not fill heaven and earth?' says the LORD (Jeremiah 23:24).

v) He is transcendent. God is not dependent on anything that he has made; he reigns far above his creation, dwelling in eternity, supreme and pre-eminent. He fills all things and his Being knows no limitations either in time or space.

Before the mountains were brought forth, or ever You had formed the earth and the world, even from everlasting to everlasting, You *are* God (Psalm 90:2).

To whom then will you liken God? Or what likeness will you compare to Him?… *It is* He who sits above the circle of the earth, and its inhabitants *are* like grasshoppers, who stretches out the heavens like a curtain, and spreads them out like a tent to dwell in (Isaiah 40:18, 22).

vi) He is eternal. God is without beginning or end – he eternally is. His essence cannot grow old or decay. He remains gloriously constant and everlasting. 'The eternal God is your refuge and underneath are the everlasting arms' (Deuteronomy 33:27).

Your throne *is* established from of old; You *are* from everlasting (Psalm 93:2).

For thus says the High and Lofty One Who inhabits eternity, whose name is Holy: 'I dwell in the high and holy *place*, with him *who* has a contrite and humble spirit, to revive the spirit of the humble, and to revive the heart of the contrite ones' (Isaiah 57:15).

vii) He is glorious. In the Old Testament when God revealed his presence and his power it was a manifestation, a shining forth of his essential being and excellence. His radiance and holiness were far above and beyond the brightest shining of the sun.

Now the glory of the LORD rested on Mount Sinai, and the cloud covered it six days. And on the seventh day, He called to Moses out of the midst of the cloud. The sight of the glory of the LORD *was* like a consuming fire on the top of the mountain… (Exodus 24:16-17)

> And he [Moses] said, 'Please, show me Your glory.' Then He said, 'I will make all My goodness pass before you, and I will proclaim the name of the LORD before you. I will be gracious to whom I will be gracious, and I will have compassion on whom I will have compassion.' But He said, 'You cannot see My face… and live' (Exodus 33:18-20).

In the New Testament, the glory of God is seen in the revelation of the character and presence of God in the person and work of Jesus Christ. 'We beheld His glory, the glory of the only begotten of the Father, full of grace and truth' (John 1:14).

> And [Jesus] was transfigured before them. His face shone like the sun, and His clothes became as white as the light (Matthew 17:2).

> [God] has in these last days spoken to us by *His* Son, whom He has appointed heir of all things, through whom also He made the worlds; who being the brightness of *His* glory and the express image of His person, and upholding all things by the word of His power, when He had by Himself purged our sins, sat down on the right hand of the Majesty on high (Hebrews 1:2-3).

viii) He is unchanging. Because God is perfect and everlasting he cannot improve or deteriorate. He is constant. As he was in eternity past, so he is now and will forever be in the future. This means he is not unpredictable but is always consistent and therefore reliable. His excellence is perpetual. We can trust him to be always the same and to act in accordance with what he says in his Word.

> For I *am* the LORD, I do not change; therefore you are not consumed, O sons of Jacob (Malachi 3:6).

> But You *are* the same and Your years will have no end (Psalm 102:27).

Jesus Christ *is* the same yesterday, today, and forever (Hebrews 13:8).

ix) He is omnipotent. God made the universe, the distant galaxies, the stars, our solar system and the planet on which we live called earth. He also created life and all living creatures from the microscopic in size to the great whales. He not only created all these things by his great power but he also controls and sustains them day by day. What tremendous power is needed to create and sustain all these things! The angel Gabriel said, 'For with God nothing will be impossible' (Luke 1:37).

God has spoken once, twice I have heard this; that power *belongs* to God (Psalm 62:11).

Lift up your heads, O you gates! And be lifted up, you everlasting doors! And the King of glory shall come in. Who *is* this King of glory? The LORD strong and mighty, the LORD mighty in battle (Psalm 24:7-8).

He has made the earth by His power; He has established the world by His wisdom, and stretched out the heaven by His understanding (Jeremiah 51:15).

[That you may know] ... what is the exceeding greatness of His power toward us who believe, according to the working of His mighty power which He worked in Christ when He raised Him from the dead ... (Ephesians 1:19-20).

x) He is omniscient. By observing all the things in this vast universe which God has made, by considering the wisdom of his Laws, his control of history, and by understanding his plan of salvation past, present and future we realise that God is a super-intelligent being whose words and ways far exceed all that we can say or even think. His wisdom in every aspect of all these things is unsearchable. He knows everything about us:

> O LORD, how manifold are Your works! In wisdom have You have made them all ... (Psalm 104:24).

> ... Blessed be the name of God forever and ever, for wisdom and might are His and He changes the times and the seasons; He removes kings and raises up kings; He gives wisdom to the wise and knowledge to those who have understanding (Daniel 2:20-21).

> Oh, the depth of the riches both of the wisdom and knowledge of God! How unsearchable *are* His judgements and His ways past finding out! *'For who has known the mind of the LORD? Or who has become His counsellor? Or who has first given to Him and it shall be repaid to him?'* For of Him and through Him and to Him *are* all things, to whom *be* glory forever. Amen (Romans 11:33-36).

xi) He is sovereign. This means God not only knows all that happens in history but as king of the universe he has planned it all and knows everything that will happen in the future. Even Satan cannot deceive God or do anything outside of his will. Satan's works are allowed by God but they are not approved by him. This does not make God the author of sin; it means God knows in advance all that evil men and the devil will do, and makes his own redemptive plans so that evil is made eventually to serve good (Genesis 50:20). God is the great king over all and this includes both the devil and all his wicked servants. This is seen supremely in the crucifixion of Christ by the hands of evil men (Acts 2:23). God, knowing what evil men would do to his Son, used the crucifixion to accomplish his redemptive purposes. God never loses control of his world; he is our king and the supreme ruler of all things:

> ... Jesus of Nazareth ... Him, being delivered by the determined counsel and foreknowledge of God, you have taken by lawless hands, have crucified, and put to death (Acts 2:22-23).

Yours, O LORD, *is* the greatness, the power and the glory, the victory and the majesty; For *all that* is in heaven and in earth *is Yours*; Yours *is* the Kingdom, O LORD, and You are exalted as head over all. Both riches and honour *come* from You, and You reign over all. In Your hand *is* power and might; in Your hand *it is* to make great and to give strength to all (1 Chronicles 29:11-12).

Whatever the LORD pleases He does, in heaven and in earth, in the seas and in all deep places (Psalm 135:6).

The LORD has made all *things* for Himself, Yes, even the wicked for the day of doom (Proverbs 16:4).

See also Genesis 15:16; Daniel 4:34, 35.

xii) He is holy. God is totally and absolutely holy. By his very nature he can have nothing to do with sin and evil. His purity burns more brightly than the sun. But his holiness is not something negative; it is positive, excellent, morally perfect, beautiful, clean and pure: therefore everything God is and does in thought word and deed is holy. In order to have fellowship with a holy God we too must be holy.

For thus says the High and Lofty One who inhabits eternity, whose name is Holy: 'I dwell in the high and holy *place*, with him *who* has a contrite and humble spirit' ... (Isaiah 57:15).

Who *is* like You, O LORD, among the gods? Who *is* like You, glorious in holiness, fearful in praises, doing wonders? (Exodus 15:11).

But as He who called you *is* holy, you also be holy in all *your* conduct, because it is written, '*Be holy, for I am holy*' (1 Peter 1:15-16).

xiii) He is righteous. Because God is perfect and holy it follows that everything that he thinks and does will also be perfect and holy. When he gave his laws to Moses these were an expression of his righteousness. His holy laws show us the kind of righteous God he is. We see that in all his dealings with men he behaves in a way that is always totally consistent with his law. He is always just and right and true in himself – he is a God of righteousness. There is no sin in him.

> Righteous *are* You, O LORD, and upright *are* your judge -ments. Your testimonies, *which* You have commanded, *are* righteous and very faithful (Psalm 119:137-138).

> For the LORD *is* righteous, He loves righteousness; His countenance beholds the upright (Psalm 11:7).

> Clouds and darkness surround Him; righteousness and justice *are* the foundation of His throne (Psalm 97:2).

xiv) He is love. Unlike human love, which is stimulated by beauty, admiration and respect in the object of our affection, God's love saw nothing beautiful, excellent or virtuous in man but just the very opposite! God's love, which arises out of his very nature, seeing the plight of man, desired his highest good. In his love he gave his own Son as a costly sacrifice to save sinners and to bring them into fellowship with himself (John 3:16).

> But when the kindness and love of God our Saviour toward man appeared, not by works of righteousness which we have done, but according to His mercy He saved us, through the washing of regeneration and renewing of the Holy Spirit (Titus 3:4-5).

> In this is love, not that we loved God, but that He loved us and sent His Son *to be* the propitiation for our sins (1 John 4:10).

And we have known and believed the love that God has for us. God is love, and he who abides in love abides in God and God in him (1 John 4:16).

xv) He is merciful. This means God is full of compassion and pitying love towards those who have sinned against him and broken his holy laws. Mercy is an active not a passive virtue, for God delights in mercy and acts in kindness towards those who are in the wrong in order to rescue and help them. Mercy is the active out-flowing of the love of God to man, who deserves no mercy.

And the LORD passed before him and proclaimed, 'The LORD, the LORD God, merciful and gracious, long-suffering, and abounding in goodness and truth, keeping mercy for thousands, forgiving iniquity and transgression and sin ...' (Exodus 34:6-7).

Then a leper came to Him, imploring Him, kneeling down to Him and saying to Him, 'If you are willing, You can make me clean.' And Jesus, moved with compassion, put out *His* hand and touched him, and said to him, 'I am willing; be cleansed' (Mark 1:40-41).

Indeed, we count them blessed who endure. You have heard of the perseverance of Job and seen the end *intended by* the Lord – that the Lord is very compassionate and merciful (James 5:11).

xvi) He is gracious. Grace is the undeserved, unmerited favour of God, which he gives freely, generously, and spontaneously to all who feel and confess their sinfulness and who call on the name of the Lord for salvation. Grace is the sole source of salvation. The grace of God saw nothing in man but sin and rebellion. It is therefore entirely of his wonderful loving-kindness and goodness that he intervenes to give his salvation freely to poor, helpless, wicked men and women on their way to hell.

> They refused to obey, and they were not mindful of Your wonders that You did among them. But they hardened their necks, and in their rebellion they appointed a leader to return to their bondage. But You *are* God, ready to pardon, gracious and merciful, slow to anger, abundant in kindness, and did not forsake them (Nehemiah 9:17).

The grace of God is freely given:

> For all have sinned and fall short of the glory of God, being justified freely by His grace through the redemption that is in Christ Jesus (Romans 3:23-24).

The grace of God is eternal:

> Who has saved us and called *us* with a holy calling, not according to our works, but according to His own purpose and grace which was given us in Christ Jesus before time began (2 Timothy 1:9).

The grace of God is sovereign:

> Then He said, 'I will make all My Goodness pass before you, and I will proclaim the Name of the LORD before you. I will be gracious to whom I will be gracious, and I will have compassion on whom I will have compassion' (Exodus 33:19).

Christ, the Son of God, by coming into the world for our salvation, is the greatest manifestation of God's grace:

> And the Word became flesh and dwelt among us, and we beheld His glory, the glory as of the only begotten of the Father, full of grace and truth... And of His fullness have all we received, and grace for grace. For the law was given through Moses *but* grace and truth came through Jesus Christ (John 1:14,16-17).

xvii) He is patient. God's patience with humanity is insepa-
rable from his mercy and his goodness. His patience is that
great power of control that he exercises over his holiness and
justice. It causes him to bear long with the wicked and their
evil ways and prevents him from destroying them from the
face of the earth. In the Old Testament God's patience is
called 'slow to anger'.

> The LORD is gracious and full of compassion, slow to
> anger and great in mercy (Psalm 145:8).

Before the Flood God gave the world plenty of time to
repent while Noah preached to them and prepared the ark
(1 Peter 3:20; see also 2 Peter 2:5):

> Who formerly were disobedient, when once the long-
> suffering of God waited in the days of Noah, while *the* ark
> was being prepared, in which a few, that is, eight souls,
> were saved through water (1 Peter 3:20).

It was God's patience that gave Israel so many opportunities
throughout their long history to repent and return to God
(Nehemiah 9:17; Jeremiah 7:25-26). God always gives men
time to repent and this is solely due to his patience and mercy:

> *What* if God, wanting to show *His* wrath and to make
> His power known, endured with much long-suffering the
> vessels of wrath prepared for destruction (Romans 9:22).

> But beloved, do not forget this one thing, that with the
> Lord one day is as a thousand years, and a thousand
> years as one day. The Lord is not slack concerning *His*
> promise, as some count slackness, but is long-suffering
> towards us, not willing that any should perish but that all
> should come to repentance (2 Peter 3:8-9).

The apostle Paul had been a hater of Christ and a militant persecutor of the Church. He was amazed at how patient God had been towards him during those years when he was doing all he could to destroy the work of Christ:

> However, for this reason I obtained mercy, that in me first Jesus Christ might show all long-suffering, as a pattern to those who are going to believe on Him for everlasting life (1 Timothy 1:16).

We have tried to answer the question, what is Almighty God like? As the one and only true God he is Spirit, infinite, perfect, omnipresent, transcendent, everlasting, glorious, unchanging, omnipotent, omniscient and sovereign. He is also holy, righteous, loving, merciful, gracious and patient. 'This is God, our God forever and ever; He will be our guide even to death' (Psalm 48:14).

2 What is the Trinity?

When Christians speak of God, they often speak of the Trinity – Father, Son and Holy Spirit. You will not find the word 'Trinity' in the Scriptures, but you will find the teaching that God is one Being in three Persons. Although it does not use the word Trinity, the Bible teaches that God is three Persons in the one essence (or substance). This sounds very difficult, and we must admit that no one can understand it completely, but we can grasp something of the doctrine of the Trinity if we keep very closely to the Bible.

a) We must be careful to avoid four common mistakes.

i) Sometimes people have spoken as if there were three Gods, but this is a very serious error. There is only one God. 'Hear O Israel, the Lord our God, the Lord is one' (Deuteronomy 6:4). Look up also Isaiah 44:6, Mark 12:29, 32; and 1 Corinthians 8:4.

ii) Some treat the Father as if he were the one true God, but the Son and the Spirit as if they were not really God at all. The modern sect called Jehovah's Witnesses, and many modern theologians, make this tragic mistake. Jesus spoke of equality between the three persons of the Godhead: he said, 'Go therefore and make disciples of all nations, baptizing them in the name of the Father and the Son and the Holy Spirit' (Matthew 28: 19). Look up also Colossians 2:9 and Matthew 12:31-32 where Christ and the Holy Spirit are shown to be equal with God.

iii) Some have thought of the three Persons in the Godhead as being only one Person but appearing in three different forms, just as water can appear as liquid, ice or steam. However, the three Persons are distinct from one another. The Father was not crucified on the cross and the Son was not poured out on men and women on the Day of Pentecost. 'And Jesus crying out with a loud voice said, "Father into your hands I commit my spirit"' (Luke 23:46). This shows that Jesus is an individual person. Look up Matthew 3:16-17; 27:46; and Acts 2:1-4, 17.

iv) Sometimes you may see illustrations that are supposed to help you to understand the Trinity. For example, you might see a circle divided into three parts. Each part is supposed to represent one Person of the Holy Trinity. This may appear to be helpful, but it will give you a wrong idea of God. The circle has three parts and if you remove one part it is no longer a circle! However this cannot be true of the Trinity because the Father, Son and Holy Spirit are not each one-third of the Godhead. Each is fully God. Perhaps the best illustration is drawn from mathematics. God is not to be envisaged as $1+1+1=3$ but as $1+1+1=1$. In the second series each 1 is equal to each other 1, but in total they are 1 not 3. The doctrine of the Trinity remains a great mystery because our finite minds can never understand God completely – only God can understand himself, 'All things have been handed over to me by my Father and no one knows the Son except the Father, nor does anyone know the Father except the Son and he to whom the Son wills to reveal Him' (Matthew 11:27). But we can believe that he is one God manifested in three Persons. (Look up 1 Corinthians 2:11).

3 What does the Old Testament teach about the Trinity?

Although the main teaching about God as Trinity comes from the New Testament, God nevertheless prepared the way for this teaching by giving his people hints of it in the Old Testament. We can find these hints in many places:

a) References to God in the plural. Sometimes God speaks of himself in the plural. For example, in Genesis 1:26 he says, 'Let us make man in our image.' You would expect God to have said, 'I will make man in my image,' but he did not. Every word of Scripture is precious (Matthew 4:4; 5:18), so there must have been a reason for God to have spoken in the plural. We now know that God was preparing his people for the time when he would reveal himself more clearly as one God in three Persons. There are other passages where God speaks in the plural, for example: 'Also I heard the voice of the Lord saying: "Whom shall I send and who will go for us?"' (Isaiah 6:8). See also Genesis 3:22; 11:5-7.

b) The Angel of the Lord. In Old Testament times God often spoke to his people through an angel called 'the angel of the Lord' ('the angel of Jehovah'). Yet in many places the angel of the Lord is also called 'the Lord'. In Genesis 16, for example, we read of Hagar running away from Sarai. In verse 7 the angel of the Lord finds her and begins to speak to her. At the end of his speech, however, Hagar says that she had actually seen God (v. 13). The angel of the Lord was undoubtedly the Lord Jesus. We can see this in other passages too;

> And the Angel of the LORD appeared to him [Moses] in a flame of fire from the midst of a bush ... Moreover He said, 'I *am* the God of your father – the God of Abraham, Isaac and Jacob.' ... (Exodus 3:2,6).

See also Genesis 18:1-33; and Judges 6:11-16; 13:3, 9,22.

c) **Theophanies (manifestations of God to man)**. There are other places also which indicate that there is more than one Person in the Godhead. Just before the Israelites attacked Jericho, Joshua saw a man who is described as the commander of the Lord's army (Joshua 5:13-15). But this man (5:13) is also described as Jehovah himself (6:2). Much later, Isaiah described the coming Messiah as both, 'a child', and 'the Mighty God' (Isaiah 9:6). Other passages which ought to be studied are Psalm 44:7-8; 109:1; Isaiah 48:16; Jeremiah 23:5-6; Daniel 3:25; and Hosea 1:7. If we look carefully in the Old Testament we can see how wonderfully God was preparing his people to receive the truth about the Trinity. In fact, one of the Hebrew words for 'God' is 'Elohim', which though plural in form, always goes with a verb in the singular (e.g. Genesis 1:1,3,4).

4 The Father is God

This section will be very short because even the heretical cults such as the Mormons and Jehovah's Witnesses agree that the Father is God. Their mistake is to think that only the Father is God.

In the Lord's Prayer, Jesus taught Christians to pray, 'Our Father in heaven' (Matthew 6:9). Later Jesus promised that the Father would give the Holy Spirit to those who ask him (Luke 11:13). Jesus described the Temple in Jerusalem as 'my Father's house' (Luke 2:49; John 2:16). Jesus also declared that he was the Son of Man on whom God the Father had set his seal (John 6:27). In the High-Priestly prayer in John chapter 17, Jesus looked towards heaven and called upon the Father, describing him as, 'the only true God' (verses 1-3). On the cross, Jesus' last words were, 'Father, into Your hands I commit my spirit' (Luke 23:46). You will find that in the New Testament the Father is referred to as God over 250 times.

The Father is God, the first Person of the Holy Trinity. When we pray, we normally pray to him. Only occasionally in Scripture do we read of prayers to Christ (e.g. Acts 7:59) or to the Holy Spirit (e.g. Ezekiel 37:9).

It is important that we understand the difference between an earthly father and God the Father. An earthly father only becomes a father when a child is born to him. But God never became a Father; he was always God the Father, because God the Son was always his Son.

5 The Son is God

When Christ first appeared to his disciples after his resurrection Thomas was not among them. When they told him the thrilling news that Jesus was alive and risen from the dead he refused to believe them and said:

> Unless I see in His hands the print of the nails, ... and put my hand into His side, I will not believe (John 20:25).

Eight days later when the disciples were together and Thomas with them Jesus suddenly appeared in their midst and said to Thomas,

> Reach your finger here, and look at My hands; and reach your hand *here*, and put it into My side. Do not be unbelieving but believing (John 20:27).

What could doubting Thomas do when face to face with the one whose physical resurrection he had stubbornly refused to believe? He simply replied to Jesus,

> ... My Lord and My God! (John 20:28).

For an orthodox Jew this was a very strange thing to say, for the Jews believed that there is only one God and he is a Spirit, not a mere mortal man. To say that a man is God is either blasphemy or it is the truth; Jesus was either God or else he was not. Shortly before his crucifixion the High Priest, Caiaphas, demanded that Jesus should say whether or not he was the Son of God. When Jesus admitted that he was then Caiaphas replied, 'He has spoken blasphemy!' (Matthew 26:65)

Jesus accepted Thomas' confession that he was truly God, and it seems that Jesus made this special resurrection appearance to him in particular to banish his doubts and confirm his faith. That Christ is the Son of God was an essential part of the gospel preached by the apostles to both Jews and Gentile alike. Peter's closing words of his sermon on the day of Pentecost in Jerusalem were:

> Therefore let all the house of Israel know assuredly that God has made this Jesus, whom you crucified, both Lord and Christ. (Acts 2:36)

The Scriptures bear witness in several places to the deity of Christ as the Son of God:

> In the beginning was the Word, and the Word was with God and the Word was God. He was in the beginning with God. All things were made through Him and without Him nothing was made that was made (John 1:1-3).

> No one has seen God at any time. The only begotten Son who is in the bosom of the Father, He has declared *Him* (John 1:18).

Therefore the Jews sought all the more to kill Him, because He not only broke the Sabbath, but also said that God was His Father, making Himself equal with God (John 5:18).

Of whom are the fathers and from whom, according to the flesh, Christ *came* who is over all *the* eternally blessed God. Amen (Romans 9:5).

See also John 5:17,18, 23; Philippians 2:6; Titus 2:13; Hebrews 1:8; 2 Peter 1:1; 1 John 5:20.

a) Christ is the image of the invisible God. The Scriptures say that Christ shares the very same nature as God the Father.

He is the image of the invisible God, the firstborn over all creation (Colossians 1:15).

i) *God is eternal: Christ is also eternal*

Then the Jews said to Him 'You are not yet fifty years old, and have You seen Abraham?' Jesus said to them ... 'Before Abraham was, I AM' (John 8:57-58).

'I am the Alpha and Omega, *the* Beginning and *the* End,' says the Lord 'who is and who was and who is to come, the Almighty.' ... And when I saw Him I fell at His feet as dead. But He laid His right hand upon me saying to me, 'Do not be afraid; I am the First and the Last' (Revelation 1:8,17).

ii) *God is omnipresent: so is Christ*

For where two or three are gathered together in My name, there am I in the midst of them (Matthew 18:20).

Go therefore and make disciples of all nations baptizing them in the name of the Father and of the Son and of the Holy Spirit, teaching them to observe all things that I have commanded you; and lo, I am with you always, even to the end of the age. Amen (Matthew 28:19-20).

iii) *God is immutable: so is Christ*

Who being the brightness of *His* glory and the express image of His person and upholding all things by the word of His power, when He had by Himself purged our sins, sat down at the right hand of the Majesty on high (Hebrews 1:3).

Jesus Christ is the same yesterday, today and forever (Hebrews 13:8).

iv) *God is omniscient: so is Christ*

But Jesus did not commit Himself to them, because he knew all *men* and had no need that anyone should testify of man, for He knew what was in man (John 2:24-25).

And I will kill her children with death. And all the churches shall know that I am He who searches the minds and hearts. And I will give to each one of you according to your works (Revelation 2:23).

v) *God is omnipotent: so is Christ*

For our citizenship is in heaven, from which we also eagerly await the Saviour the Lord Jesus Christ, who will transform our lowly body that it may be conformed to His glorious body, according to the working by which He is able even to subdue all things to Himself (Philippians 3:20-21).

Who being the brightness of *His* glory and the express image of His person, and upholding all things by the word of His power, when He had by Himself purged our sins, sat down at the right hand of the Majesty on high (Hebrews 1:3).

b) Christ does things that only a divine person is able to do

i) *Christ created the world*

He was in the beginning with God. All things were made through Him, and without Him nothing was made that was made (John 1:2-3).

For by Him all things were created that are in heaven and that are on earth, visible and invisible, whether thrones or dominions or principalities or powers. All things were created through Him and for Him (Colossians 1:16).

God, who at various times and in different ways spoke in past times to the fathers by the prophets, has in these last days spoken to us by *His* Son, whom He has appointed heir of all things, through whom also He made the worlds (Hebrews 1:1-2).

ii) *Christ forgave sins*

When Jesus saw their faith, He said to the paralytic, 'Son, your sins are forgiven you' ... 'Which is easier, to say to the paralytic, "*Your* sins are forgiven you," or to say, "Arise, take up your bed and walk?" But that you may know that the Son of Man has power on earth to forgive sins...' (Mark 2:5,9-10).

And He said to her, 'Your sins are forgiven.' And those who sat at table with Him began to say to themselves, 'Who is this who even forgives sins?' (Luke 7:48-49).

iii) *Christ is the Judge of all men*

When the Son of Man comes in His glory and all the holy angels with Him, then He will sit on the throne of His glory. All the nations will be gathered before Him, and He will separate them one from another as a shepherd divides his sheep from the goats (Matthew 25:31-32).

For as the Father has life in Himself, so He has granted the Son to have life in Himself, and has given Him authority to execute judgement also, because He is the Son of Man (John 5:26-27).

For we must all appear before the judgement seat of Christ, that each one may receive the things *done* in the body, according to what he has done, whether good or bad (2 Corinthians 5:10).

iv) *Christ gives everlasting life*

My sheep hear My voice, and I know them, and they follow Me. And I give them eternal life and they shall never perish; neither shall anyone snatch them out of My hand (John 10:27-28).

Most assuredly, I say to you, he who believes in Me has everlasting life. I am the bread of life ... I am the living bread which came down from heaven. If anyone eats of this bread he will live forever; and the bread that I will give is My flesh, which I shall give for the life of the world (John 6:47,48,51).

c) Old Testament references to Christ as God

i) *When Isaiah had a vision of God in the temple it was actually Christ whom he saw:*

> In the year that King Uzziah died, I saw the Lord sitting on a throne, high and lifted up, and the train of His *robe* filled the temple ... Then I said, 'Woe is me for I am undone! Because I *am* a man of unclean lips and I dwell in the midst of a people of unclean lips; for my eyes have seen the King, the LORD of hosts.' (Isaiah 6:1,5) [read verses 1-10].

> These things Isaiah said when he saw His glory and spoke of Him (John 12:41) [read verses 37-41].

ii) *The Psalmist speaks of God creating the world, but the New Testament applies this statement to Christ*

> I said, 'O my God, do not take me away in the midst of my days; Your years *are* throughout all generations. Of old You laid the foundation of the earth, and the heavens *are* the work of Your hands.' (Psalm 102:24-25).

Hebrews 1:10-12 applies these verses to the Son of God.

iii) *The prophet Joel speaks of those who call on God to save them. The New Testament quotes this as referring to Christ:*

> And it shall come to pass *that* whoever calls on the name of the LORD shall be saved ... (Joel 2:32) [read verses 28-32].

Peter in his sermon on the day of Pentecost quotes Joel (Acts 2:16-21). Then he says:

> Men of Israel, hear these words: Jesus of Nazareth, a Man attested by God to you by miracles, wonders and signs which God did through Him in your midst, as you yourselves know ... Therefore let all the house of Israel know assuredly that God has made this Jesus, whom you crucified, both Lord and Christ (Acts 2:22,36).

iv) *Isaiah refers to the Lord as a stumbling stone but the New Testament applies this description to Christ:*

> The LORD of hosts, Him you shall hallow; *let* Him *be* your fear, and *let* Him *be* your dread. He will be as a sanctuary, but a stone of stumbling and a rock of offence to both the houses of Israel ... (Isaiah 8:13-14).

Peter quotes this verse as applying to Christ (1 Peter 2:8). He also quotes Isaiah 28:16 (1 Peter 2:6):

> ... *Behold, I lay in Zion a chief cornerstone, elect, precious, and he who believes on Him will by no means be put to shame* (1 Peter 2:6).

Paul applies the same quotation to Christ (Romans 9:33).

v) *Christ quotes the Messianic Psalm 110 as referring to himself:*

> The LORD said to my Lord, 'Sit at My right hand until I make Your enemies Your footstool' (Psalm 110:1).

> While the Pharisees were gathered together, Jesus asked them, saying, 'What do you think about the Christ? Whose Son is he?' They said to Him, '*The Son* of David.' He said to them, 'How then does David in the Spirit call Him, "Lord", saying: "*The LORD said to my Lord, sit at My right hand, till I make Your enemies Your footstool?*"' (Matthew 22:41-44)

6   The Holy Spirit is God

Because many of the cults and some modern theologians think that the Holy Spirit is only a force or power and not a Person, we must first show that he is a Person before showing that he is God. For example, we can see this in the following passages: the Holy Spirit teaches (Luke 12:12; John 14:26), testifies (John 15:26), guides and speaks (John 16:13), sends (Acts 13:4) and forbids (Acts 16:6-7). We can lie to him (Acts 5:3), tempt him (Acts 5:9), grieve him (Ephesians 4:30) and even blaspheme him (Matthew 12:31). All these things can only be true if the Spirit is a Person.

In addition, there are many passages which show clearly that the Holy Spirit is God:

- A lie to the Holy Spirit is the same as a lie to God (Acts 5:3-4).
- The Spirit raises the dead (Romans 8:11).
- He knows all things; he knows 'the depths of God' (Isaiah 40:13-14; 1 Corinthians 2:10-11), for he himself is a divine Person.
- He is everywhere at the same time (Psalm 139:7-10). Because of this, he is able to be with all Christians at the same time (1 Corinthians 3:16; 6:19).
- He is eternal (Hebrews 9:14).
- He created the world (Genesis 1:2; Psalm 104:30).

The Father is God, the Son is God, and the Spirit is God, yet there is only one God. No wonder the apostle Paul asked, 'Who has known the mind of the Lord?' (Romans11: 34). Augustine (AD 354-430) said, 'If you are able to comprehend him, he is not God.' We cannot understand ourselves (Jeremiah 17:9), let alone God, but even if we cannot fully understand him we can still worship and serve 'God in three Persons, blessed Trinity'.

7   Conclusion

There are many places in the New Testament where the three Persons in the Trinity are seen to act together.

Then Jesus when He had been baptized, came up immediately from the water; and behold, the heavens were
opened to Him, and He saw the Spirit of God descending
like a dove and alighting upon Him. And suddenly a voice
came from heaven saying, 'This is My beloved Son, in
whom I am well pleased' (Matthew 3:16-17).

See also 1 Corinthians 12:4-6; 2 Corinthians 13:14; Galatians
4:6; and 1 Peter 1:2.

Perhaps the best text to quote is Matthew 28:19. When the
Lord Jesus was about to leave his disciples and return to his
Father in heaven, he left them with some final instructions.
One of these was to baptize believers in the name of the
Father and of the Son and of the Holy Spirit. Three Persons
are mentioned here, but Jesus only spoke of one name, to
show that the three are One. Back in the fourth century, a
Christian writer named Gregory of Nazianzus wrote of the
Trinity, 'I cannot think of the One without quickly being
encircled by the splendour of the Three; nor can I discern the
Three without being straightway carried back to the One.'
    We close this chapter with praise to the Trinity in the words
of an ancient hymn:

'Praise and honour to the Father,
Praise and honour to the Son,
Praise and honour to the Spirit,
Ever Three and ever One,
One in power, and One in glory,
While unending ages run.'

(an early Greek hymn, author unknown)

Questions

1 Which of God's divine qualities should be reflected in the life of a Christian?

2 Since the Bible does not use the word 'trinity' why do we use the word today?

3 Where in the Bible does it say that Jesus is God and the Holy Spirit is God?

CHAPTER FOUR

SIN AND THE FALL OF MAN

1 What is the Fall?

2 What is the origin of sin and evil?

3 What are the results of the Fall?

   a) Man lost his original righteousness
   b) Man lost communion with God and was banished from
      his presence
   c) Man's whole nature was affected – mind, heart, and
      will
   d) Man is now conscious of guilt and shame
   e) Man became subject to physical death
   f) Man became subject to spiritual death

4 What is sin?

   Seven truths to be remembered

5 The effects of sin

   Five results of sin

1 What is the Fall?

The Bible says that God created Adam and Eve perfect yet with freedom to choose between good and evil. Before the creation of the world some of the angels had rebelled against God and fallen from heaven. Here is the origin of sin and evil. Although God had created a perfect environment for the man and the woman to live in, called the Garden of Eden, one of the fallen angels named Satan tempted them to disobey God. As a consequence they fell into sin and under the judgement of God their creator. He turned them out of the Garden and into a world which itself, as part of creation, was now under judgement as the result of their sin and disobedience (Genesis 3:1-24). They had fallen from a state of innocence into a state of sin and rebellion.

2 What is the origin of sin and evil?

Even secular thinkers acknowledge that the origin of evil is one of the profoundest problems both of philosophy and theology. It forces itself on man's attention because of its devastating power and its universality. Some say that evil is part of the natural constitution of things, whilst others say it has a voluntary origin in the free choice of man. The Bible does not explain why God allowed evil to enter his universe; it only tells us how it happened and what God has done to help us overcome it.

The biblical view is that sin originated in the angelic world. Satan, the leader of a host of angels, aspired to usurp the place of God in heaven and as a consequence was thrown out.

> And the angels who did not keep their proper domain, but left their own habitation, He has reserved in everlasting chains under darkness, for the judgement of the great day ... Yet Michael the archangel, in contending with the devil, when he disputed about the body of Moses, dared not bring against him a reviling accusation but said, 'The Lord rebuke you!' (Jude 6,9)

See also Isaiah 14:12-14; Ezekiel 28:12-15; Matthew 13:36-43; 1 Timothy 3:6.

Satan by tempting him caused Adam to fail the test of pure obedience to God. Adam believed that by choosing his own way he could be like God himself. Adam thus became the servant of sin. Because he was the representative of the whole human race he transmitted to his descendants the pollution and guilt of sin (Romans 5:12, 18-19). We therefore inherit our fallen and sinful human natures from Adam our earthly head.

3 What are the results of the Fall?

The biblical doctrines of sin and redemption are founded upon the doctrine of the fall. If we have a defective or deficient understanding of the fall it will inevitably affect our understanding both of the extent of sin and our need of redemption. The fall of mankind into sin was a catastrophe of such magnitude that only the cross of Christ was a sufficient remedy.

The main consequences of the fall were the following:

a) Man lost his original righteousness

> ... There is none righteous, no, not one. There is no one who understands; there is no one who seeks after God. They have all gone out of the way; they have together

become unprofitable; there is none who does good, no, not one... For all have sinned and fall short of the glory of God (Romans 3:10-12,23).

b) Man lost communion with God and was banished from his presence

Therefore the LORD God sent him out of the garden of Eden to till the ground from which he was taken. So He drove out the man; and He placed cherubim at the east of the garden of Eden, and a flaming sword which turned every way, to guard the way to the tree of life (Genesis 3:23-24).

c) Man's whole nature was affected – mind, heart, and will

Then the LORD saw that the wickedness of man *was* great in the earth, and *that* every intent of the thoughts of his heart *was* only evil continually (Genesis 6:5).

And have put on the new *man* who is renewed in know-ledge according to the image of Him who created him (Colossians 3:10).

The LORD looks down from heaven upon the children of men, to see if there are any who understand, who seek God. They have all turned aside, they have together become corrupt; *there* is none who does good, no,not one (Psalm 14:2-3).

d) Man is now conscious of guilt and shame

So he [Adam] said, 'I heard Your voice in the garden, and I was afraid because I was naked; and I hid myself' (Genesis 3:10).

e) Man became subject to physical death

> In the sweat of your face you will eat bread till you return to the ground, for out of it you were taken; for dust you *are*, and to dust you shall return (Genesis 3:19).

f) Man became subject to spiritual death

> And you *He made alive* who were dead in trespasses and sins ... But God, who is rich in mercy, because of His great love with which He loved us, even when we were dead in trespasses, made us alive together with Christ (by grace you have been saved) (Ephesians 2:1, 4-5).

4   What is sin?

Seven truths to be remembered

i) Sin is not something passive. It is not just an absence of good qualities or a little moral weakness. It is not some kind of spiritual sickness or a mere lack of goodness for which we are not responsible.

ii) Sin is a force, something living and active. It expresses itself positively as rebellion against God, a hatred of his holy laws and an instinctive desire to be independent of God and to express ourselves in whatever way we like:

> Against You, You only, have I sinned, and done this evil in Your sight – that You may be found just when You speak *and* blameless when You judge (Psalm 51:4; see Romans 1:18-32.

iii) Sin so infects us that we sin by nature and become evil in God's sight. We are not in a neutral position, somewhere between good and evil. In God's sight, so far as human morality is concerned, someone is either good or bad.

iv) The only adequate concept of sin is one that understands it as affecting our relationship with God. When man sinned he had to leave the immediate presence of God in the Garden of Eden – sin had broken his relationship with God.

v) Sin involves not only moral guilt but also the pollution of our natures as well. These two aspects of sin are:

- Guilt: because of breaking God's commandments.
- Pollution: being unclean and defiled in God's sight.

   And He [Jesus] said, 'What comes out of a man, that defiles a man. For from within, out of the heart of men, proceed evil thoughts, adulteries, fornications, murders, thefts, covetousness, wickedness, deceit, licentiousness, an evil eye, blasphemy, pride, foolishness. All these evil things come from within and defile a man' (Mark 7:20-23).

vi) Sin has its seat deep within us, in our hearts, in the very nerve-centre of the human soul.

   The heart is deceitful above all *things* and desperately wicked; Who can know it? (Jeremiah 17:9)

   Behold, I was brought forth in iniquity, and in sin my mother conceived me (Psalm 51:5).

vii) Sin is therefore a lack of conformity to the will of God as revealed in his Word, either in thought, word or deed.

   Whoever commits sin also commits lawlessness, and sin is lawlessness (1 John 3:4).

In the Old Testament a number of words are used to describe what sin is. There are four main terms.

i) The most common is the verb *chata* and the related noun *chataah*. These convey the idea of missing the mark, whether in respect of man (Genesis 20:9), or God (Lamentations 5:7). The noun is frequently used of a sin-offering (e.g. Leviticus 4:20,24,29,33), but its basic meaning is that of deviation from the law or will of God (Hosea 13:2).

> And Moses said to the people, 'Do not fear; for God has come near to test you, that his fear may be before you, so that you may not sin' (Exodus 20:20).

ii) The term *pesha* indicates that sin involves a breach of relationship, 'rebellion'. It indicates that sin is *rebellion* against God, *defiance* of his holy rule.

> The destruction of transgressors and of sinners *shall be* together, and those who forsake the LORD *shall be* consumed (Isaiah 1:28; see also 1 Kings 8:50)

iii) The verb *awah* is used to describe sin as *deliberate wrongdoing*, whereas the related noun *awon* emphasises the idea of the guilt that stems from deliberate wrongdoing.

> We have sinned and committed iniquity, we have done wickedly and rebelled, even by departing from Your precepts and Your judgments (Daniel 9:5).

> My punishment (iniquity, *awon*) *is* greater than I can bear (Genesis 4:13).

iv) To be wicked, to act *wickedly*, is indicated by the verb *rasa*.

> I have kept the ways of the LORD, and have not wickedly departed from my God (2 Samuel 22:22).

> You have dealt faithfully, but we have done wickedly (Nehemiah 9:33).

It is clear from this brief survey that in the Old Testament sin is multifaceted in its meaning. It is missing the mark (as defined by God); the breaking of our relationship with God; deliberate wrongdoing as well as unintentional going astray (Leviticus 4:13) and acting wickedly.

In the New Testament the following words are used to describe sin.

- *Harmartia* is equivalent in meaning to *chata*. It is the general term for sin as the *violation* of God's law.

  'Which of you convicts Me of sin?' [says Jesus] (John 8:46).

  Then, when desire has conceived, it gives birth to sin; and sin, when it is full-grown, brings forth death (James 1:15).

- *Paraptoma* expresses sin as *trespass*, unlawful intrusion into God's domain.

  And you *He made alive*, who were dead in trespasses and sins (Ephesians 2:1; see also verse 5).

- A closely related term is *parabasis* – 'going beyond the norm'.

  And Adam was not deceived, but the woman being deceived, fell into transgression (1Timothy 2:14).

- *Asebeia* is perhaps the profoundest New Testament term for sin. It implies active ungodliness or impiety that issues in a thoroughly ungodly life-style.

  For the wrath of God is revealed from heaven against all ungodliness and unrighteousness of men, who suppress the truth in unrighteousness (Romans 1:18).

(The ungodly life-style is described in verses 24-32).

- *Anomia, lawlessness,* has in view contempt for God's law.

  Depart from Me, you who practise lawlessness (Matthew 7:23). See also 2 Corinthians 6:14.

- Both *kakia* and *ponēria* are general terms expressing moral and spiritual *depravity*. An example of the first word is 1 Peter 2:16:

  As free, yet not using liberty as a cloak for vice [i.e. wickedness], but as bondservants of God.

An example of the second word is Acts 8:22:

  Repent therefore of this your wickedness, and pray God if perhaps the thought of your heart may be forgiven you (Acts 8:22).

- *Adikia* indicates wrong done to our fellow humans. It is variously translated in the NKJV.

  What shall we say then? *Is there* unrighteousness with God? Certainly not! (Romans 9:14).

  But shun profane *and* idle babblings, for they will increase to more ungodliness (2 Timothy 2:16).

The fundamental feature of sin in all its aspects is that it is always against God (see Psalm 51:4; Romans 8:7). It is not adequate to speak of it as selfishness, for that is to downplay its seriousness. Sin is contrary to God's glory, a contradicting of God himself.

5 The effects of sin.

Five results of sin

i) Sin is universal and affects all men at all times and in all places.

> All have sinned and fall short of the glory of God (Romans 3:23).

ii) Sin affects the whole personality – mind, heart and will.

- **The mind:**

> For since, in the wisdom of God, the world through wisdom did not know God, it pleased God through the foolishness of the message preached to save those who believe (1 Corinthians 1:21).

> This I say, therefore, and testify in the Lord, that you should no longer walk as the rest of the Gentiles walk, in the futility of their mind, having their understanding darkened, being alienated from the life of God, through the ignorance that is in them, because of the hardening of their heart (Ephesians 4:17-18).

- **The heart:**

> Therefore God also gave them up to uncleanness, in the lusts of their hearts, to dishonour their bodies among themselves (Romans 1:24).

> For the love of money is a root of all *kinds of* evil, for which some have strayed from the faith in their greediness, and pierced themselves through with many sorrows (1 Timothy 6:10).

- **The will:**

    Jesus answered them, 'Most assuredly I say to you who-
    ever commits sin is a slave of sin' (John 8:34).

    For the good that I will *to do*, I do not do; but the evil I will
    not *to do*, that I practise. Now if I do that I will not *to do*, it
    is no longer I who do it but sin that dwells in me (Romans
    7:19-20).

iii) Because sin affects our minds, hearts and wills man's
condition is described as one of 'total depravity'.

This does *not* mean:
- Man has no conscience.
- Man does not admire virtue and cannot be virtuous.
- Man is as wicked as he can possibly be.
- Man loves to indulge every kind of sin.

But it *does* mean:
- Sin has affected every part of man's nature.
- Sin has rendered man unclean in God's sight.

    The carnal mind *is* enmity against God; for it is not subject
    to the law of God, nor indeed can be. So then, those who
    are in the flesh cannot please God (Romans 8:7-8).

    To the pure all things are pure, but to those who are de-
    filed and unbelieving is nothing pure; but even their mind
    and conscience are defiled (Titus 1:15; see also Romans
    1:28-32; 3:19; Ephesians 2:1-3; 4:18).

iv) If we accept that the Bible teaches total depravity, it
follows that left to himself man is powerless to save himself.
He cannot please God and is therefore totally dependent on
God's grace.

The sinner's dilemma is that he cannot keep God's law, nor can he change either his rebellious attitude towards God, or his preference for sin and for self-will; he is totally dependent on God's grace. Only the liberating power of Christ can set him free.

> Most assuredly, I say to you, whoever commits sin is a slave of sin... therefore if the Son makes you free, you shall be free indeed (John 8:34, 36).

> But God, who is rich in mercy, because of His great love with which He loved us, even when we were dead in trespasses, made us alive together with Christ (by grace you have been saved) (Ephesians 2:4-5).

> All that the Father gives Me will come to Me, and the one who comes to Me I will by no means cast out ... No one can come to Me unless the Father who sent Me draws him; and I will raise him up at the last day (John 6:37, 44). See also Romans 7:18, 24; 8:7-8; 1 Corinthians 2:14; Ephesians 2:8-10.

v) The sin of man has brought judgement, not only on himself but also upon his environment. Even nature and the animals are subject to destruction and death.

> Cursed *is* the ground for your sake; in toil you shall eat of it all the days of your life. Both thorns and thistles it shall bring forth for you, and you shall eat the herb of the field. In the sweat of your face you shall eat bread till you return to the ground, for out of it you were taken; for dust you *are,* and to dust you shall return (Genesis 3:17-19).

> Because the creation itself also will be delivered from the bondage of corruption into the glorious liberty of the children of God. For we know that the whole creation groans and labours with birth pangs together until now (Romans 8:21-22).

Questions

1 Where did sin originate?

2 What were the main consequences of the fall for man kind?

3 Has sin affected all parts of man's nature?

4 What do theologians mean by 'total depravity'?

CHAPTER FIVE

THE PERSON OF CHRIST

1 Twelve examples of how he fulfils Old Testament prophecies

2 His incarnation

3 His virgin birth

4 His deity

    a) Fifteen names which ascribe deity to Jesus Christ
    b) His divine attributes
    c) Divine powers attributed to God and to Jesus Christ
    d) References to God in the Old Testament ascribed to Christ in the New Testament
    e) Names of God and Jesus Christ are coupled together
    f) Christ accepts worship from men
    g) Christ was conscious of his own deity

5 Christ's humanity

Ten evidences

6 Two natures in one person:

His manhood is essential
    a) That he might bear our sins
    b) That he might be a sympathetic High Priest
    c) That he might be our pattern and example

His Godhead is essential

1　He fulfils the following Old Testament prophecies

i) As the Seed of the woman. When Satan had brought about the fall of man in the Garden of Eden, God promised to send a deliverer who would crush Satan:

> And I will put enmity between you and the woman, and between your seed and her Seed; He shall bruise your head, and you shall bruise His heel (Genesis 3:15).

The New Testament speaks of Christ as the promised Seed:

> Now to Abraham and to his Seed were the promises made. He does not say, 'And of seeds,' as of many, but as of one, 'And to your Seed,' who is Christ (Galatians 3:16).

Christ came into the world to defeat Satan and to save mankind from his power and dominion:

> He who sins is of the devil, for the devil has sinned from the beginning. For this purpose the Son of God was manifested, that He might destroy the works of the devil (1 John 3:8; see also Hebrews 2:14).

ii) As the Seed of Abraham. God promised Abraham that blessing was going to come to the whole world through his descendants:

> In your seed all the nations of the earth shall be blessed (Genesis 22:18; see also 12:3).

Paul says that this Seed was Christ (Galatians 3:16) and that he would bring the blessing of salvation to all the peoples of the world.

iii) Being born in Bethlehem, Judah. God revealed this to the prophet Micah more than 700 years before Christ was born in this little town in Judah:

> But you, Bethlehem Ephrathah, *though* you are little among the thousands of Judah, *yet* out of you shall come forth to Me the One to be Ruler in Israel, whose goings forth *are* from of old, from everlasting (Micah 5:2).

The wise men from the east came to Jerusalem to find the newborn King of the Jews;

> And he [Herod] sent them to Bethlehem and said, 'Go and search diligently for the young Child' ... And when they had come into the house, they saw the young Child with Mary His mother, and fell down and worshipped Him (Matthew 2:8,11; see also Luke 12:11-12; Hebrews 1:6)

iv) As the Son of David. The Messiah is referred to in prophecy as being a direct descendant or branch of the tree of David,

> 'Behold, the days are coming,' says the LORD, 'that I will raise to David a Branch of righteousness; A King shall reign and prosper, and execute judgement and righteousness in the earth. In His days Judah will be saved, and Israel will dwell safely; Now this is His name by which He will be called: THE LORD OUR RIGHTEOUSNESS' (Jeremiah 23:5-6; see also 33:16).

See also Isaiah 11:1-10; a Branch will grow out of the root of Jesse (David's father).

Matthew at the beginning of his gospel uses a genealogy to show the descent of Joseph, the husband of Mary, through David:

> The book of the genealogy of Jesus Christ, the Son of David, the Son of Abraham (Matthew 1:1).

Luke records the same thing in his Gospel:

> Joseph also went up from Galilee, out of the city of
> Nazareth, into Judea, to the city of David, which is called
> Bethlehem, because he was of the house and lineage of
> David (Luke 2:4).

See also Acts 13:22-23.

v) That the throne of King David would continue for ever. It
seemed that with the fall of Jerusalem in 587 BC and the exile
of the Jews to Babylon that King Zedekiah was the last king
of Judah, and that with his death in Babylon the royal line of
the house of David had come to an end. But God through his
prophets had promised that the throne of King David would
be an enduring one and that his royal line would never come to
an end. The prophet Nathan had said to David, about 1000 BC:

> When your days are fulfilled and you rest with your
> fathers, I will set up your seed after you, who will come
> from your body, and I will establish his kingdom. He shall
> build a house for My name, and I will establish the throne
> of his kingdom forever (2 Samuel 7:12-13).

> Once I have sworn by My holiness; I will not lie to David:
> His seed shall endure forever and his throne as the sun
> before Me (Psalm 89:35-36).

See also Psalm 72:17; Isaiah 9:6-7; Amos 9:11; Acts 15:16.

These prophecies are fulfilled in the Lord Jesus Christ. When
the angel Gabriel was sent by God to tell Mary that she would
have the greatest of all honours in being the mother of Christ,
he also told her that her son would be King David's royal son.
In this way the throne of David would be an everlasting one
because Christ is the eternal Son of God. Jesus is therefore
the promised King according to God's appointment:

> He will be great, and will be called the Son of the Highest, and the Lord God will give Him the throne of His father David (Luke 1:32).

> Men *and* brethren, let *me* speak freely to you of the patriarch David, that he is both dead and buried, and his tomb is with us to this day. Therefore, being a prophet, and knowing that God had sworn with an oath to him that of the fruit of his body, according to the flesh, He would raise up the Christ to sit on his throne ... spoke concerning the resurrection of the Christ (Acts 2:29-31).

See also John 12:13-15; 18:33-39.

vi) As the One chosen by God to bring gospel light to the Gentiles. Isaiah had prophesied that in a coming day God's blessing was going to fall not just upon the Jews but also on the Gentile nations. These prophecies are called 'messianic' because it is understood that they will be fulfilled only with the appearance on the Earth of God's messiah, Jesus Christ:

> ... In Galilee of the Gentiles. The people who walked in darkness have seen a great light; those who dwelt in the land of the shadow of death, upon them a light has shined (Isaiah 9:1-2).

> And in that day there shall be a Root of Jesse, who shall stand as a banner to the people; for the Gentiles shall seek Him and His resting place shall be glorious (Isaiah 11:10).

> Behold! My Servant whom I uphold, my Elect One *in whom* My soul delights! I have put My Spirit upon Him; He will bring forth justice to the Gentiles (Isaiah 42:1).

See also Isaiah 9:1-6; 11:1-10; 42:1-6; Hosea 1:10; 2:23)

In his Gospel Matthew (Chapter 12:15-21) says that the Person of Christ and his ministry are a direct fulfilment of Isaiah's prophecy (42:1-6). Christ, when referring to himself as the Good Shepherd, said he had come to lay down his life for the sheep:

> As the Father knows Me, even so I know the Father; and I lay down My life for the sheep. And other sheep I have which are not of this fold; them also I must bring, and they will hear My voice; and there will be one flock *and* one shepherd (John 10:15-16).

Jesus is referring to two groups of sheep whom he is soon going to unite together as one; these are Jews and Gentiles who will become members together of the Church of Christ. Caiaphas the high priest also prophesied about the purpose of Christ's death:

> Now this he did not say on his own *authority*; but being high priest that year he prophesied that Jesus would die for the nation, and not for that nation only, but also that He would gather in one the children of God who were scattered abroad (John 11:51-52).

Paul in his writings rejoices in the fact that Christ sent him to be the apostle to the Gentiles, and says that Christ came to fulfil God's promises to save the Gentiles:

> Jesus Christ has become a servant to the circumcision for the truth of God, to confirm the promises made to the fathers, and that the Gentiles might glorify God for *His* mercy (Romans 15:8-9).

When Simeon met the parents of Jesus in the temple he recognised Jesus, though still an infant, as God's promised Messiah and he said:

> Lord, now You are letting Your servant depart in peace, according to Your word; for my eyes have seen Your salvation which You have prepared before the face of all peoples, a light to *bring* revelation to the Gentiles, and the glory of Your people Israel (Luke 2:29-32).

vii) By his birth. Isaiah had prophesied eight hundred years before Christ came that God's promised deliverer would first appear as a child. In other words, that the deliverer, the Messiah, would be a person both human and divine:

> For unto us a Child is born, unto us a Son is given; and the government will be upon His shoulder. And His name will be called Wonderful, Counsellor, Mighty God, Everlasting Father, Prince of Peace (Isaiah 9:6).

> The Lord Himself will give you a sign: Behold the virgin shall conceive and bear a Son, and shall call His name Immanuel (Isaiah 7:14).

Matthew quotes this verse when describing the events leading up to the birth of Jesus (Matthew 1:23); Jesus is God's Immanuel.

As we have already seen in paragraph (iii) the birth of the promised Messiah would take place in the town of Bethlehem (Micah 5:2). The New Testament writers see the birth of Jesus and the events that accompanied it as the fulfilment of ancient prophecies that pointed to the coming of God's Messiah:

> Then the angel said to her, 'Do not be afraid, Mary, for you have found favour with God. And behold, you will conceive in your womb and bring forth a Son, and shall call His name JESUS. He will be great, and will be called the Son of the Highest; and the Lord God will give Him the throne of His father David' (Luke 1:30-32).

Do not be afraid, for behold, I bring you good tidings of
great joy which will be to all people. For there is born to
you this day in the city of David a Saviour, who is Christ
the Lord (Luke 2:10-11).

viii) By his triumphal entry into Jerusalem. The spontaneous popular acclaim with which the crowds welcomed
Jesus into Jerusalem (Matthew 21:1-11) was to be a fulfilment of prophecy, though his disciples did not realise it at
the time:

Rejoice greatly O daughter of Zion! Shout, O daughter
of Jerusalem! Behold, your King is coming to you; He *is*
just and having salvation, lowly and riding on a donkey, a
colt, the foal of a donkey (Zechariah 9:9).

The news that Jesus had raised Lazarus from the dead at
Bethany, a village very close to Jerusalem, had spread to
the city so that people believed a great prophet had arisen
in Israel. In the same way, some time earlier, a tremendous
impression had been made on the whole region of Judea
by the raising of a young man from the dead when Jesus
visited the town of Nain. This and many other miracles
that Jesus had been doing all over the country in healing
hundreds of sick people gave him the reputation of being a
great prophet and a man of God. It was no wonder therefore
that the crowds gave him such an enthusiastic welcome
and acclaim usually given only to kings and princes. They
also greeted him with words from Psalm 118:25-26 ascrib-
ing to him a royal status and therefore someone worthy
to receive honour and glory. The significance of using this
Psalm may not have been fully understood by the crowds
because the previous verses also speak of the death and
exaltation of Christ:

The stone *which* the builders rejected has become the
chief cornerstone. This was the LORD's doing; it *is* marvellous in our eyes (Psalm 118:22-23).

It seems certain that Jesus was well aware of the significance of his entry into Jerusalem and that it would be a fulfilment of the prophecy of Zechariah. This is confirmed by Matthew (21:4) when he wrote about this important event in his gospel;

> Then the multitudes who went before and those who followed cried out, saying: 'Hosanna to the Son of David! Blessed is He who comes in the name of the LORD! Hosanna in the highest!' (Matthew 21:9).

ix) By the price of his betrayal. The Scriptures not only predicted that Messiah would be betrayed by a close friend but also the price of that betrayal,

> Even my own familiar friend in whom I trusted, who ate my bread, has lifted up *his* heel against me (Psalm 41:9).

> ... So they weighed out for my wages thirty *pieces* of silver. And the LORD said to me, 'Throw it to the potter' — that princely price they set on me. So I took the thirty *pieces* of silver and threw them into the house of the LORD for the potter (Zechariah 11:12-13).

Judas Iscariot was one of the twelve apostles; he was also the one who kept their common finances and so occupied a special position of trust. He betrayed Jesus with a kiss:

> Then one of the twelve, called Judas Iscariot, went to the chief priests and said, 'What are you willing to give me if I deliver Him to you?' And they counted out to him thirty pieces of silver (Matthew 26:14-15).

x) By his substitutionary death on the cross. The prophets predicted that the Messiah, the Servant of the Lord, would suffer and die to atone for the sins of the people:

Surely He has borne our griefs and carried our sorrows;
yet we esteemed Him stricken, smitten by God, and
afflicted. But He *was* wounded for our transgressions, *He
was* bruised for our iniquities; the chastisement for our
peace was upon Him, and by His stripes we are healed ...
and the LORD has laid on Him the iniquity of us all (Isaiah
53:4-6).

A number of important details in connection with his death
on the cross were also predicted:

His side would be pierced	Zechariah 12:10; John 19:34
His hands and feet would be pierced	Psalm 22:6-8; John 20:25
His clothing parted by lots	Psalm 22:18; Matthew 27:35
Given vinegar to drink	Psalm 69:21; Matthew 27:48
Forsaken by God	Psalm 22:1; Matthew 27:46
He died with sinners	Isaiah 53:12; Matthew 27:38
Mocked by the people	Psalm 22:7-9; Matthew 27:39-44
Prayed for his enemies	Isaiah 53:12; Luke 23:34
Buried in rich man's grave	Isaiah 53:9; Matthew 27:57-60

**xi) That Messiah would have a threefold ministry – as
*Prophet, Priest and King.***

• As *Prophet* he reveals the will of God to his people for
their salvation and edification:

God, who at various times and in different ways spoke
in time past to the fathers by the prophets, has in these
last days spoken to us by *His* Son, whom He has
appointed heir of all things, through whom also He made
the worlds (Hebrews 1:1-2).

See also Deuteronomy 18:18, where God promises Israel a
Prophet like Moses.

• As *Priest* he offered himself once for all as a sacrifice for
sin to make reconciliation for his people:

> But Christ came *as* High Priest of the good things to come
> ... not with the blood of goats and calves, but with His own
> blood He entered the Most Holy Place once for all, having
> obtained eternal redemption (Hebrews 9:11-12).

• As *King* he rules over the world and his church,
rewarding his people's obedience and correcting their sins:

> Jesus answered, 'My kingdom is not of this world. If My
> kingdom were of this world, My servants would fight, so
> that I should not be delivered to the Jews; but now My
> kingdom is not from here.' Pilate therefore said to Him,
> 'Are you a king then?' Jesus answered, 'You say *rightly*
> that I am a king. For this cause was I born, and for this
> cause I have come into the world, that I should bear wit-
> ness to the truth. Everyone who is of the truth hears My
> voice' (John 18:36-37).

xii) By rising from the dead. The Old Testament predicted
that the Messiah would rise from the dead. When Peter
preaches at Pentecost he tells the Jews that Christ's resurrection was foretold by David;

> For You will not leave my soul in Sheol, nor will you allow
> your Holy One to see corruption (Psalm 16:10; Acts 2:27).

2 His incarnation

In his Gospel John tell us, 'In the beginning was the Word,
and the Word was with God, and the Word was God ...
and the Word became flesh and dwelt among us, and we
beheld His glory, the glory as of the only begotten of the
Father, full of grace and truth' (John 1:1,14). John says that
in some sense God, without ceasing to be God, became man.

It appears to mean that the Divine Creator actually became one of his own creatures! How did such an amazing and seemingly contradictory belief that Jesus of Nazareth was God incarnate arise in the early Church? The only explanation that covers the facts is that the impact of Jesus' own life, ministry, death and resurrection convinced his disciples of his personal deity even before he ascended to heaven. All this shows that, even if the deity of Jesus was not at first clearly stated in words (and the Book of Acts gives no clue that it was), it was nevertheless a major part of the faith by which the first Christians lived, worked and prayed. The full theological formulation of Christian belief came later at Chalcedon in 451 AD, but the belief was there in the Church from the beginning.

The New Testament writers do not try to explain the meta-physical and psychological problems of the doctrine of the incarnation. Their interest in the person of Christ is not philosophical or speculative but religious and evangelistic. They speak of Christ not as a metaphysical problem, but as a divine Saviour. They were prompted to do so by their desire to declare his salvation and to proclaim the centrality of his redemptive work in the purposes of God. For them he was at one and the same time perfect God and perfect man, two natures in one person without mixture or confusion, truly God and truly man yet without sin:

> But when the fulness of the time had come, God sent forth His Son, born of a woman, born under the law, to redeem those who were under the law, that we might receive the adoption as sons (Galatians 4:4-5).

> He was in the world, and the world was made through Him, and the world did not know Him. He came to His own and His own did not receive Him (John 1:10-11).

> Of whom are the fathers and from whom, according to the flesh, Christ *came*, who is over all, *the* eternally blessed God (Romans 9:5).

3 His virgin birth

According to the prophecies already referred to Christ was to be the 'Seed of the woman' (Genesis 3:15) who would defeat Satan. He was also the child who according to Isaiah 9:6 would be called 'the Mighty God'. Clearly the Coming One was to be no mere man!

> Therefore the Lord Himself will give you a sign: Behold, the virgin shall conceive and bear a Son and shall call His name Immanuel (Isaiah 7:14; see also Matthew 1:21-23).

Since he had to be sinless, if he was to take the sins of the world upon him and die in our place, Christ could not inherit a sinful human nature and be born of natural human parentage. God would have to bring 'a clean thing out of an unclean.' In other words he would have to work a miracle of reproduction:

> Then Mary said to the angel, 'How can this be, since I do not know a man?' And the angel answered and said to her, '*The* Holy Spirit will come upon you, and the power of the Highest will overshadow you; therefore, also, that Holy One who is to be born will be called the Son of God' (Luke 1:34-35).

Those who do not believe in the miraculous scoff at the doctrine of the Virgin Birth, but those who believe both in God and in his mighty power will agree with the angel when he said to Mary:

> For with God nothing will be impossible (Luke 1:37).

4 His deity

a) The following fifteen names ascribe deity to Jesus Christ:

i) *Son of God:* Matthew 14:33; 16:16; Mark 1:1, 14:61-62; 15:39; Luke 1: 32-35; John 1: 34 & 49; 5:25-26; 10:36; 11:4, 27; 19:7; 20:31; Acts 8:37; 9:20; Romans 1:4; 2 Corinthians 1:19; Galatians 2:20; Ephesians 4:13; Hebrews 4:14; 6:6; 7:3; 10:29; 1 John 3:8; 4:15; 5:5,10,12,13,20; 2 John 3; Revelation 2:18

ii) *My beloved Son:* Matthew 3:17; 17:5; Mark 1:11; 9:7; Luke 3:22; 9:35; 2 Peter 1:17

iii) *The only begotten Son:* John 1:18; 3:16 & 18; Acts 13:33 (quoting Psalm 2:7); 1 John 4:9

iv) *The Son:* Matthew 11:27; 22:42, 45; 28:19; John 3:35-36; 5:20-23, 26; 6:40; 8:35-36; 14:13; 17:1; 1Corinthians 5:28; Hebrews 1:8; 7:28; 1 John 2: 22-23; 5:12; 2 John 9

v) *His Son:* John 3:17; Romans 1:3,9; 5:10; 8:3, 29,32; 1 Corinthians 1:9; Galatians 1:16; 4:4-6; Colossians 1:13; 1 Thessalonians 1:10; Hebrews 1:2; 1 John 1:3, 7; 3:23; 4:10; 5:9-11,20

vi) *Your Holy Servant Jesus:* Acts 4:27,30

vii) *The Holy and Just One:* Acts 3:14

viii) *The Lord:* Matthew 24:42; Mark 16:20; Luke 2:11; 6:5; 20:44; 24:34; John 9:38; 20:28; Acts 2:36; 7:59-60; 9:5; 10-17; 10:36; Romans 1:4; 1 Corinthians 1:9; 2:8; 4:5; 6:14; 12:3; Philippians 2:11; Revelation 19:16

ix) *Lord Jesus Christ:* This title occurs 130 times from Acts to Revelation

x) *The Lord of glory:* 1 Corinthians 2:8

xi) *Emmanuel, God with us:* Matthew 1:23

xii) *The great God and our Saviour Jesus Christ:* Titus 2:13

viii) *God blessed for ever:* Romans 9:5

xiv) *King of Kings and Lord of Lords:* Revelation 19:16

xv) *The First and the Last:* Revelation 1:17

b) His divine attributes show that he is more than just a man

Omnipotence	Hebrews 1:3
Omniscience	John 2:23-25; Matthew 11:27
Omnipresence	Matthew 18:20; 28:20
Eternity	John 1:1; 8:58
Immutable	Hebrews 13:8
Pre-existence	John 17:5; Philippians 2:6; Colossians 1:17; 2:9

c) Divine powers attributed to God are also attributed to Jesus Christ

Creating the world	John 1:10; Colossians 1:16
Preserving the world	Hebrews 1:3; Colossians 1:17
Forgiving sins	Mark 2:5-10
Raising the dead	John 6:39-40; 11:38-44
Changing our bodies	Philippians 3:21
Judging the world	2 Timothy 4:1; Matthew 25:31-32
Giving eternal life	John 17:2

d) References to God in the Old Testament ascribed to Christ in the New Testament

Psalm 102:25-28	Hebrews 1:10-12
Isaiah 40:3-4	Matthew 3:3; Luke 1:68-69
Isaiah 61:1-2	Luke 4:17-19
Isaiah 8:13-14	1 Peter 2:7-8
Isaiah 45:23	Philippians 2:9-11

e) The names of God and Jesus Christ are coupled together

> Go therefore and make disciples of all the nations, baptizing them in the name of the Father and of the Son and of the Holy Spirit (Matthew 28:19).

> The grace of the Lord Jesus Christ, and the love of God, and the communion of the Holy Spirit *be* with you all (2 Corinthians 13:14).

> So that He may establish your hearts blameless in holiness before our God and Father at the coming of our Lord Jesus Christ with all His saints (1 Thessalonians 3:13).

See also Romans 1:7 and James 1:1.

f) The second commandment prohibits the worship of anything or anybody except God, but Jesus accepted worship from men

> [Jesus said] 'Do you believe in the Son of God?' ... He said, 'Lord, I believe!' And he worshipped Him (John 9:35-38).

> And when they got into the boat, the wind ceased. Then those who were in the boat came and worshipped Him, saying, 'Truly You are the Son of God' (Matthew 14:32-33).

See also Matthew 2:11; 8:2; 9:18; 28:9, 17; John 5: 22-23; Philippians 2:10.

g) Christ was conscious of his own deity

* *As a child in the temple*

> So when they saw Him, they were amazed; and His mother said to Him, 'Son, why have You done this to us? Look,

Your father and I have sought you anxiously.' And He said to them, 'Why *is it* that you sought Me? Did you not know that I must be about My Father's business?' (Luke 2:48-49).

- *At his baptism by John*

  Then Jesus, when He had been baptized, came up immediately from the water; and behold, the heavens were opened to Him, and He saw the Spirit of God descending like a dove and alighting upon Him. And suddenly a voice *came* from heaven, saying, 'This is My beloved Son, in whom I am well pleased' (Matthew 3:16-17).

- *In his temptation in the wilderness*

  Then Jesus said to him, 'Away with you, Satan! For it is written, "You shall worship the LORD your God and Him only shall you serve."' Then the devil left Him, and behold, angels came and ministered to Him (Matthew 4:10-11).

- *In his authoritative teaching*

  And so it was, when Jesus had ended these sayings, that the people were astonished at His teaching, for He taught them as one having authority, and not as the scribes (Matthew 7:28-29).

- *In giving his power to the disciples to heal and cast out demons*

  Behold, I give you authority to trample on serpents and scorpions, and over all the power of the enemy, and nothing shall by any means hurt you. Nevertheless do not rejoice in this, that the spirits are subject to you, but rather rejoice because your names are written in heaven (Luke 10:19-20).

- *In his ability to save mankind*

  All things have been delivered to Me by My Father, and no one knows the Son except the Father. Nor does anyone know the Father except the Son and *he* to whom the Son wills to reveal *Him*. Come to Me all *you* who labour and are heavy laden, and I will give you rest (Matthew 11:27-28).

- *In his ability to heal and to forgive sin*

  But that you may know that the Son of Man has power on earth to forgive sins – He said to the man who was paralysed, 'I say to you, arise, take up your bed, and go to your house' ... And they were all amazed, and they glorified God and were filled with fear, saying, 'We have seen strange things today!' (Luke 5:24, 26).

5 Christ's humanity – ten evidences

i) The Virgin Birth. As described in paragraph 3 the Holy Spirit supernaturally enabled Mary to conceive a male child (Luke 1:34-35), free from the inherited sin of Adam (Romans 5:12). Therefore Christ was born a sinless human being (Hebrews 7:26-27).

ii) The Son of Man. Jesus used this title more than any other (76 times) when referring to himself and his work. Although it has strong Messianic connections in the Old Testament (Daniel 7:13-14) Jesus frequently used it in close association with his suffering and death:

  The Son of Man did not come not to be served, but to serve, and to give His life a ransom for many (Mark 10:45).

This was because he was identifying himself with guilty humanity, appearing in the form of a servant (Luke 22:27; Philippians 2:6-8). See also Mark 8:31; 9:31; 10:33; 14:21-41.

iii) A real man. The New Testament sometimes refers to Christ simply as a man without further qualification. For example the apostle John said of Christ that he was a person, 'which we have heard, which we have seen with our eyes, which we have looked on and our hands have handled ... ' (1 John 1:1). He is emphasising the point that Jesus was not some kind of angel or spirit but a real man whom he knew as a personal friend.

> A Man called Jesus made clay and anointed my eyes and said to me, 'Go to the pool of Siloam and wash ...' (John 9:11).

See also Acts 2:22 and 1 Timothy 2:5.

iv) He was subject to human growth. His physical and mental development appears to have been the same as that of any normal human being:

> And the Child grew and became strong in spirit, filled with wisdom; and the grace of God was upon Him (Luke 2:40)

> And Jesus increased in wisdom and stature, and in favour with God and men (Luke 2:52).

> Though He was a Son, *yet* He learned obedience by the things which He suffered (Hebrews 5:8).

v) Certain limitations in knowledge. Although Jesus often had a supernatural insight into the lives of people he met (John 1:48; 4:18; Matthew 9:4), as well as being aware of future events (Luke 22:10-13; Matthew 24:1-31), there were some things he did not know (Luke 7:9; Mark 11:13).

> But of that day and hour no one knows, neither the angels in heaven, nor the Son, but only the Father (Mark 13:32).

vi) Physical limitations. As a man Christ knew the same limitations as ourselves, even though at times he was enabled to rise above them by the power of the Holy Spirit – fasting for forty days in the desert (Matthew 4:1-2), and walking on the water (Matthew 14:25). At other times he was weary (John 4:6); needed food (Mark 11:12); drink (John 4:7); sleep (Matthew 8:24); wanted prayer support (Matthew 26:38-40); experienced agony (Luke 22:44) and grief (John 11:33-35).

vii) He was tempted. The devil was constantly attacking him and attempting to discourage him and trying to get him to adopt earthly policies. (Matthew 4:3-11; 16:23; Luke 22:31; John 13:2). The presence of evil, personified by the devil, was a burden to him:

> For in that He Himself has suffered, being tempted, He is able to aid those who are tempted (Hebrews 2:18; see also 4:15).

viii) He needed to pray. In the greatest crisis of his life, facing the prospect of Calvary in Gethsemane he prayed (Matthew 26:36-44), 'with loud cries and tears', (Hebrews 5:7). He would retire to the wilderness to pray (Luke 5:16); before choosing the twelve he prayed all night (Luke 6:12); he prayed at his baptism (Luke 3:21); he prayed alone (Luke 9:18); he prayed with his disciples (Luke 9:28) and he prayed for them (John 17:6-19). We can say that his prayer life showed his dependence on his heavenly Father for the spiritual resources of his earthly ministry.

ix) He was given the power of the Holy Spirit. At his baptism the Holy Spirit came upon him in the form of a dove (John 1:32-33) and it was on that day that his public ministry began, a ministry empowered by the Holy Spirit. Peter said that:

God anointed Jesus of Nazareth with the Holy Spirit and with power, who went about doing good and healing all who were oppressed by the devil, for God was with Him (Acts 10:38). See also John 3:34; Luke 4:1.

x) He was fully human yet sinless. Jesus did not inherit a sinful nature from Adam since he was conceived by the Holy Spirit (Luke 1:35). His enemies could find no sin in him (John 8 : 46). He said that he always pleased his Father (John 8:29). Satan had no power over him (John 14:30) because he always kept his Father's commandments (John 15:10). He was able to say, 'I and the Father are one' (John 10:30). Christ had to be sinless in order to be the sacrifice for our sins, as a lamb without blemish and without spot (1 Peter 1:19). As Paul said:

For He [God] made Him who knew no sin *to be* sin for us, that we might become the righteousness of God in Him (2 Corinthians 5:21).

See also Hebrews 4:15; 7:26; 1 Peter 2:22; 1 John 3:5.

6 The two natures in one person

John describes Jesus as the Word made flesh:

In the beginning was the Word, and the Word was with God, and the Word was God ... And the Word became flesh and dwelt among us, and we beheld His glory, the glory as of the only begotten of the Father, full of grace and truth (John 1:1,14).

The divine and the human natures of Christ were not mixed together. They existed without confusion in one Person in complete harmony with each other. His deity was not diminished (John 1:14; Philippians 2:6-7) and neither was his humanity. His human nature was complete —body, soul and spirit — which he derived from the Virgin Mary. He is therefore truly the promised seed of Abraham and David (Matthew1:1) and truly God.

He said that he was subordinate to the Father for the work he had been given to do by the Father: 'I have glorified You on the earth. I have finished the work You gave Me to do' (John 17:4). Jesus said, 'I live by the Father' (John 6:57); 'My Father is greater than I' (John14:28); 'the Father does the works' (John 14:10).

His manhood is essential:

a) **That he might bear our sins.** If Jesus had not been truly man he could not have died in our place and paid the penalty that was due to us for having broken God's law:

> Therefore, in all things He had to be made like *His* brethren, that He might be a merciful and faithful High Priest ... (Hebrews 2:17).

Further, because we were alienated from God by sin we needed someone to come between God and ourselves to bring us back to Him. The perfect man Christ Jesus was the only person who was qualified to do this. Not only is he our mediator, he is also our sin-bearer, the one who can take our sins upon himself as though they were his own:

> Behold! The Lamb of God who takes away the sin of the world (John 1:29).

> But we see Jesus, who was made a little lower than the angels, for the suffering of death crowned with glory and honour, that He, by the grace of God, might taste death for everyone (Hebrews 2:9).

> Inasmuch then as the children have partaken of flesh and blood, He Himself likewise shared in the same, that

through death He might destroy him who had the power of death, that is, the devil (Hebrews 2:14).

b) That he might be a sympathetic High Priest. If Jesus had not been a real man he would never have been able to know by personal experience what it is like to feel the power of Satan's temptations, to be tired, hungry, homeless, misunderstood by family and friends, persecuted, mocked, beaten and forsaken by everyone. Only by sharing our life could he know all these things as we know them:

> Therefore, in all things He had to be made like *His* brethren, that He might be a merciful and faithful High Priest in things *pertaining* to God, to make propitiation for the sins of the people. For in that He Himself has suffered, being tempted, He is able to aid those who are tempted (Hebrews 2:17-18).

c) That He might be our pattern and example

Paul tells us that we who are children of God have been "predestined to be conformed to the image of His Son that he might be the first-born among many brethren" (Romans 8:29). It is the will of God that as followers of Christ our thoughts, words and behaviour should in every way resemble that of our Saviour. John says that the aim of every Christian should be to be like Christ. 'He who says he abides in Him ought himself also to walk even as He walked' (1 John 2:6). Peter says that especially in suffering for Christ we should remember his example, 'For Christ also suffered for us leaving us an example that we should follow His steps' (1 Peter 2:21).

> Take My yoke upon you and learn from Me, for I am gentle and lowly in heart, and you will find rest for your souls (Matthew 11:29).

For I have given you an example, that you should do as I have done to you...A new commandment I give to you, that you love one another; as I have loved you, that you also love one another (John 13:15,34).

His Godhead is essential:

Though He was a Son, *yet* He learned obedience by the things which He suffered. And having been perfected, He became the author of eternal salvation to all who obey Him, called by God as High Priest 'according to the order of Melchizedek' (Hebrews 5:8-10).

God was manifested in the flesh (1 Timothy 3:16).

Questions

1 What do the Old Testament prophecies reveal about the Person of Christ?

2 What does the word 'incarnation' mean?

3 What are the main biblical reasons for believing that Jesus is God?

4 What are the main biblical reasons for believing that Jesus is also a real man?

5 Why is it essential that Jesus was both God and man?

CHAPTER SIX

THE WORK OF CHRIST

1 Christ as a prophet

a) The prophet's role
b) Before his incarnation
c) After his incarnation

2 Christ as a priest

a) The High Priest in the Old Testament
b) In order to be our Great High Priest, Christ fulfils seven conditions
c) Why do we need Christ to be our Great High Priest?

Four reasons

3 Christ as a king

a) Why is Christ a King?
b) When did Christ begin his mediatorial kingship?
c) What is God's kingdom?
d) When did Christ take his throne?
e) The twofold aspect of Christ's kingdom – present and future
f) How does Christ exercise his kingship?

Christ came into the world as Prophet, Priest and King.

• **Prophet** As a prophet Christ is God's messenger to men. He represents God to men by being his spokesman. He delivers us from the ignorance of God that sin has brought into our lives.

• **Priest** As a priest Christ is the only intermediary between God and men. He represents men to God. He delivers us from the guilt of our sin through the sacrifice of himself.

• **King** As a king Christ rules over men and leads them. He delivers us from the rule of sin and Satan in our lives. He is the head of the new humanity that God is forming out of all nations, tribes and tongues.

1 Christ as a prophet

a) **The Prophet's role**. What is a Prophet? The work of the prophet is twofold: proclamation of God's Word for today and prediction of God's plan and purpose for the future.

Proclamation: Telling men what God wants them to hear today.
Prediction: Telling men what God wants them to know about the future.

Moses promised Israel that one day God would send them another Prophet-leader like himself. God said through Moses:

> I will raise up for them a Prophet like you from among their brethren, and will put My words in His mouth, and He shall speak to them all that I command Him (Deuteronomy 18:18).

When Christ had risen Peter told the crowds in the temple at Jerusalem that Jesus Christ was this Prophet, the fulfilment of Moses' prophecy. See Acts 3:22-23; Luke 24:19.

Jesus told men very plainly that he was a prophet and that God himself had given him his message to proclaim:

> I have many things to say and to judge concerning you, but He who sent Me is true; and I speak to the world those things which I heard from Him (John 8:26).

See also Luke 13:33; John 12:49-50.

How does Christ exercise his prophetic function?

b) Christ's prophetic role before his incarnation. He was the true light of morality and knowledge (the Word) that has influenced the world since its creation (John 1:4, 5, 9).

He was active in the Old Testament on many occasions as the angel of the Lord:

> Now the Angel of the LORD found her (Hagar) by a spring of water in the wilderness ... (Genesis 16:7; see also verses 9,13; 32:24-30)

As the Messiah one of his roles was to be 'Counsellor' (Isaiah 9:6), and this is part of his prophetic ministry.

c) Christ's prophetic role after his incarnation –
i) On earth Christ came to reveal the Father by preaching and teaching the love of God, the true meaning of the law of God and the way of salvation. He claimed that the salvation he had come to bring was the fulfilment of all the promises and prophecies recorded in the Old Testament about the Messiah.

> No one has seen God at any time. The only begotten Son, who is in the bosom of the Father, He has declared *Him* (John 1:18).

> I have called you friends, for all things that I heard from
> My Father I have made known to you (John 15:15).

Not only by his teaching but also by his person, his example and his life people could see the truth in action. Jesus preached to the people everywhere, in houses, in synagogues and in the open air. His was no academic ministry confined to intellectuals and doctors of the law but it was for all men everywhere. Jesus could rightly say to the Jews:

> He who has seen Me has seen the Father (John 14:9).

> I am the light of the world (John 8:12).

> And behold, a leper came and worshipped Him, saying,
> 'Lord, if You are willing, You can make me clean.' Then
> Jesus put out *His* hand and touched him, saying, 'I am
> willing; be cleansed.' And immediately his leprosy was
> cleansed (Matthew 8:2-3).

ii) In heaven After his ascension Christ exercises his prophetic ministry on the earth through the Holy Spirit. Christ promised to send the Helper, the Spirit of truth, who would lead his disciples into all truth. The Holy Spirit would reveal to them things to come and enable them to bear witness to Christ in the world:

> But the Helper, the Holy Spirit, whom the Father will send
> in My name, He will teach you all things, and bring to your
> remembrance all things that I said to you (John 14:26)

See also 15:26-27; 16:13-15.

The Holy Spirit was instrumental in guiding the apostles and others to write the scriptures of the New Testament so that Christ's teaching would be preserved for future generations (John 14:26; 2 Peter 3:15-16).

The Holy Spirit is at work in the Church (Acts 13:2) and in the lives of individual believers to make Christ and his truth known (Romans 8:15-16).

2 Christ as priest

a) **The High Priest in the Old Testament**. What is a priest? A priest represents men to God; he functions as an intermediary between them. He offers sacrifices to God on their behalf and intercedes for them.

In Old Testament times, the high priest played a very important role. Chapter 16 of Leviticus describes how, on the annual Day of Atonement, it was his solemn duty to go alone into the Most Holy Place to make atonement for the whole nation of Israel. Before entering it he had to wash his whole body and then put on special vestments for the occasion (v.4). First he had to sacrifice a bull for his own sins and collect its blood in a bowl. Then with a burning censer in one hand and the bowl of blood in the other he would go through the curtain of the Tabernacle and into the Most Holy Place. With the censer he would make a cloud of incense to cover the mercy-seat where God's presence resided, to protect him from dying in that awesome place (v.13). Next he would sprinkle some of the blood on the mercy seat and in front of it (v.14). Returning to the tabernacle the high priest sacrificed a goat for the sins of the people and to cleanse the tabernacle and all its services. He then brought the blood of the goat into the Most Holy Place and sprinkled it in the same manner as before. After this the High Priest took a second goat, laid his hand on its head, and confessed the sins of the nation of Israel over it (v.21). The goat was then driven far away into the wilderness and banished for ever from the nation of Israel. In this way the sins of the nation were covered for another year. Only the high priest was allowed to perform all these duties on behalf of the people of Israel.

In the epistle to the Hebrews (5:1-5) the main features of the high priest's ministry are summarized as follows:

- He offers gifts and sacrifices for the sins of the people
- He can have sympathy with sinners like himself
- He must offer sacrifice for his own sins
- He can only be appointed by God

b) In order to be our Great High Priest Christ had to be:

i) made like his brethren

Inasmuch then as the children have partaken of flesh and blood, He Himself likewise shared in the same, that through death He might destroy him who had the power of death, that is, the devil (Hebrews 2:14).

ii) the propitiation for our sins

Therefore, in all things He had to be made like *His* brethren, that He might be a merciful and faithful High Priest in things *pertaining* to God, to make propitiation for the sins of the people (Hebrews 2:17).

iii) appointed a priest like Melchizedek

So also Christ did not glorify Himself to become High Priest, but it was He who said to Him: 'You are My Son, today I have begotten You.' As *He* also *says* in another *place*: '*You are a priest for ever according to the order of Melchizedek*' (Hebrews 5:5-6).

iv) an eternal priest

But He, because He continues forever, has an unchangeable priesthood. Therefore He is also able to save to the uttermost those who come to God through Him, since He ever lives to make intercession for them (Hebrews 7:24-25).

v) holy and sinless

For such a High Priest was fitting for us, who is holy, harmless, undefiled, separate from sinners, and has become higher than the heavens; who does not need daily, as those high priests, to offer up sacrifices, first for His own sins and then for the people's, for this He did once for all when He offered up Himself (Hebrews 7:26-27).

vi) a priest continually in heaven

But Christ came *as* High Priest of the good things to come, with the greater and more perfect tabernacle not made with hands, that is, not of this creation. Not with the blood of goats and calves, but with His own blood He entered the Most Holy Place once for all, having obtained eternal redemption (Hebrews 9:11-12).

vii) the spotless sacrifice for our sins

But this Man, after He had offered one sacrifice for sins forever, sat down at the right hand of God, from that time waiting till His enemies are made His footstool. For by one offering He has perfected forever those who are being sanctified (Hebrews 10:12-14).

c) Why do we need Christ to be our Great High Priest?

i) To render satisfaction to an offended God. Paul says that 'the wrath of God is revealed from heaven against all ungodliness and unrighteousness of men' (Romans 1;18; 5:9). The wrath of God is his natural reaction against all wickedness. Sin against God has to be propitiated. To propitiate someone we must turn away their anger by offering restitution. The Bible says that Christ makes propitiation for us by offering himself as the substitute for our sins.

And if anyone sins, we have an Advocate with the
Father, Jesus Christ the righteous. And He Himself is the
propitiation for our sins, and not for ours only but also for
the whole world (1 John 2:1-2)

See also Romans 3:25; Hebrews 2:17 and 1 John 4:10.

ii) To offer himself for our sins. In Old Testament times it
was necessary for those who sought forgiveness of their sins
to offer an animal to die in their place; for God said, 'The
soul who sins shall die' (Ezekiel 18:20) The one bringing the
sacrifice had to lay his hand upon its head before killing it at
the door of the tabernacle in the presence of the priest. The
guilt of the penitent sinner was thus symbolically transferred
to the animal who died as a substitute in his place.

He shall bring the bull to the door of the tabernacle of
meeting before the LORD, lay his hand on the bull's head,
and kill the bull before the LORD(Leviticus 4:4).

When John the Baptist saw Jesus coming to him to receive
baptism he said:

Behold! The Lamb of God that takes away the sin of the
world! (John 1:29).

When Isaiah prophesied of Christ as the One who would bear
the sins of God's people he said:

He was oppressed and He was afflicted yet He opened
not his mouth; He was led as a lamb to the slaughter, and
as a sheep before its shearers is silent, so He opened not
His mouth (Isaiah 53:7; see also Acts 8:31-35).

When Peter spoke of the redemption price that was paid by
Christ for us he said:

> You were not redeemed with corruptible things, *like* silver or gold, from your aimless conduct *received* by tradition from your fathers, but with the precious blood of Christ, as of a lamb without blemish and without spot (1 Peter 1:18-19).

Just as in Old Testament times the guilt of the sinner was transferred to the animal sacrifice, so in New Testament times the guilt of the penitent sinner is laid upon Christ, the Lamb of God:

> For Christ also suffered once for sins, the just for the unjust, that He might bring us to God, being put to death in the flesh but made alive by the Spirit (1 Peter 3:18).

> For He made Him who knew no sin *to be* sin for us, that we might become the righteousness of God in Him (2 Corinthians 5:21).

Therefore Christ combines in himself the function both of sacrificial offering and of High Priest. Instead of offering to God the blood of bulls and goats in an earthly tabernacle, he offered his own blood in the heavenly tabernacle:

> But Christ came *as* High Priest of the good things to come, with the greater and more perfect tabernacle not made with hands, that is, not of this creation. Not with the blood of goats and calves, but with His own blood He entered the Most Holy Place once for all, having obtained eternal redemption (Hebrews 9:11-12).

This offering of himself by Christ upon the cross is a once and for all offering. It can never be repeated or re-enacted, because he has presented his sacrifice to God in heaven where it has been accepted:

> For Christ has not entered the holy places made with hands, *which are* copies of the true, but into heaven itself, now to appear in the presence of God for us; not that He should offer Himself often, as the high priest enters the Most Holy Place every year with blood of another – He then would have had to suffer often since the foundation of the world; but now, once at the end of the ages, He has appeared to put away sin by the sacrifice of Himself (Hebrews 9:24-26).

iii) To reconcile God to man. In the Garden of Eden man lived in complete harmony with God. By taking upon himself the guilt of man's sin, Christ removes the wrath of God so that man can be restored to fellowship with God:

> Therefore, in all things He had to be made like *His* brethren, that He might be a merciful and faithful High Priest in things *pertaining* to God, to make propitiation for the sins of the people (Hebrews 2:17).

iv) To make continual intercession for us . Christ has entered into the Holiest of All with his own blood, now to appear in the presence of God for us (Hebrews 9:12, 24; see also 7:25)). He is there as the Lamb of God (Revelation 5:6), in his Father's presence, in the merit of his obedience and sacrifice, declaring it his will to have his saving work applied to all believers:

> For Christ has not entered the holy places made with hands, *which are* copies of the true, but into heaven itself, now to appear in the presence of God for us (Hebrews 9:24).

> But He, because He continues forever, has an unchangeable priesthood. Therefore He is also able to save to the uttermost those who come to God through Him, since He ever lives to make intercession for them (Hebrews 7:24-25).

> For if when we were enemies we were reconciled to God
> through the death of His Son, much more, having been
> reconciled, we shall be saved by His life (Romans 5:10).

3 Christ as King

Perhaps we do not find it easy to think of our Lord Jesus
Christ as a King. When he came into the world and lived
among men he possessed none of the usual marks of
royalty. He had no palace, no throne, no crown, no riches,
no courtiers, no army, in short, nothing that we usually
associate with earthly power. This was because he had not
come to rule but to serve (Luke 22:27). One day he would
rule but this was still in the future.

a) Why is Christ a king? The angel Gabriel had told Mary
that her Son would inherit the throne of David (Luke 1:32).
But first he would have to die upon the cross. The Bible tells
us that Christ's atoning death was planned before the foundation of the world, for he is

> The Lamb slain from the foundation of the world (Rev
> elation 13:8).

The Father, the Son and the Holy Spirit in foreknowledge
of the fall of man took counsel together to save mankind.
Christ agreed to be the One who should redeem the lost by
dying for them, and by becoming the head and King of a new
humanity – the Church. Christ is therefore not only our
Mediator, Saviour and Redeemer, but also our King. This was
prophesied in the Old Testament:

> Yet I have set my King on My holy hill of Zion. I will
> declare the decree: the LORD has said to Me, 'You *are* My
> Son, today I have begotten You. Ask of Me, and I will give
> You the nations *for* Your inheritance, and the ends of the
> earth *for* Your possession ...' (Psalm 2:6-8)

See also Acts 4:25-27; Luke 1:31-33; John 18:37-39; 19:15.

b) When did Christ begin his mediatorial kingship? As soon as man fell into sin God's plan went into action (Genesis 3:15). From that moment Christ began his mediatorial work as Prophet, Priest and King, the One through whom all God's redemptive plans would be put into effect. Throughout the Old Testament period under the form of the Angel of the Lord and other theophanies, Christ was in control of God's purposes. Paul confirms this when he says that Christ was with the Jews in their deliverance from Egypt and journey through the wilderness:

> All were baptized into Moses in the cloud and in the sea, all ate the same spiritual food, and all drank the same spiritual drink. For they drank of that spiritual Rock that followed them, and that Rock was Christ (1 Corinthians 10:2-4).

c) What is God's kingdom? When Christ began preaching his gospel he always did so in the context of 'The kingdom', referring to it either as the kingdom of God or the kingdom of heaven:

> 'Repent, for the kingdom of heaven is at hand' ... Jesus went about all Galilee, teaching in their synagogues, preaching the gospel of the kingdom, and healing all kinds of sickness and all kinds of disease among the people (Matthew 4:17,23).

The kingdom of God is that kingdom which has God as its king and his will as its rule. Christ's preaching was to persuade men to confess their sin and recognize him as the anointed king of God's new kingdom. Isaiah had foretold the coming of Christ as the Son who would occupy the throne of David, whose kingdom would last for ever and ever (Isaiah 9:6-7). Daniel prophesied of a kingdom yet to come which would overcome and outlast all earthly kingdoms. This was the kingdom that Christ himself would set up and which will last for ever:

> And in the days of these kings the God of heaven will set up a kingdom which shall never be destroyed; and the kingdom shall not be left to other people; it shall break in pieces and consume all these kingdoms, and it shall stand forever (Daniel 2:44-45).

In modern times both Hitler and Stalin sought to build anti-Christian kingdoms, but their kingdoms have been destroyed while Christ's kingdom continues to grow and prosper.

d) When did Christ take his throne? Although his media-torial reign and rule had begun with the fall of man, the Bible says that it was not until he had completed his atoning sacrifice on Calvary and ascended to heaven that he took his throne. Peter said that David had prophesied that God would raise up Christ to sit on his throne (Acts 2:29-33):

> But we see Jesus, who was made a little lower than the angels, for the suffering of death crowned with glory and honour, that He, by the grace of God, should taste death for everyone (Hebrews 2:9)

See also Matthew 16:28; Acts 5:31; Ephesians 1:20-21; Philip-pians 2:9-11.

e) The twofold aspect of Christ's kingdom – present and future

i) At present: concealed – an inward and spiritual king-dom. Jesus spoke to people personally saying that they should repent, believe his gospel, and receive him as their Saviour and their King (Matthew 21:28-32). For example he told Nicodemus that unless he was born again he could not receive or understand the kingdom of God (John 3:3-6). He told a scribe who answered wisely that he was not far from the kingdom of God (Mark 12:34). At this present time Christ's kingdom is not an earthly and visible kingdom but it is established by God in the hearts of those who accept and receive him by faith (John 1:12):

> Jesus answered, 'My kingdom is not of this world. If My kingdom were of this world, My servants would fight, so that I should not be delivered to the Jews: but now My kingdom is not from here' (John 18:36).

> Now when He was asked by the Pharisees when the kingdom of God would come, He answered them and said, 'The kingdom of God does not come with observation: nor will they say, "See here!" or "See there!" For indeed, the kingdom of God is within you' (Luke 17:20-21.)

> For the kingdom of God is not food and drink, but righteousness and peace and joy in the Holy Spirit (Romans 14:17)

See also Luke 16:16; Colossians 1:3-13.

ii) In the future: revealed – a visible and universal kingdom. The second coming of Christ will reveal to the world of men and of angels that Christ is the King of Kings and Lord of Lords. It will be the greatest international event that the world has ever seen for every eye will see him. Then Christ will deliver up the kingdom to God the Father and crush all his enemies under his feet (1 Corinthians 15:24-28). Then the King and the kingdom will be victorious, visible, universal and eternal:

> When the Son of Man comes in His glory, and all the holy angels with Him, then He will sit on the throne of His glory ... Then the King will say to those on His right hand, 'Come,

you blessed of My Father, inherit the kingdom prepared for you from the foundation of the world' (Matthew 25:31, 34).

I charge *you* therefore before God and the Lord Jesus Christ, who will judge the living and the dead at His appearing and His kingdom (2 Timothy 4:1)

See also 2 Thessalonians 1:5-10; 2 Peter 3:10-13; Revelation 1:5-8.

f) How does Christ exercise his kingship? Wherever there are those who accept him as King and submit to his reign over their lives, there is the kingdom of Christ. Christ administers his kingdom through the Holy Spirit whom he sent to take his place in the lives of believers after his resurrection. God has given his Son control over all creation. He rules it in the interests of his Church and kingdom.

And He put all *things* under His feet, and gave Him *to be* head over all *things* to the church (Ephesians 1:22).

All authority has been given to Me in heaven and on earth. Go therefore and make disciples of all the nations ... I am with you always, *even* to the end of the age (Matthew 28:18-20).

According to Paul, Christ is now seated at God's right hand in the heavenly places far above all spiritual or human authority. He is there for ever ruling over everything in the interests of his Church (Ephesians 1:20-23). Because of his dominion over Satan, the world, and even creation itself, he is able to control them all on behalf of his Church. For this reason Paul is able to say,

We know that all things work together for good to those who love God, to those who are the called according to *His* purpose (Romans 8:28).

When Christians suffer for Christ, and sometimes lay down their lives for his sake, it is not because Christ has no power to prevent it. It is because, as his followers, we are called to suffer for his name's sake:

> Do not fear any of those things which you are about to suffer. Indeed, the devil is about to throw *some* of you into prison, that you may be tested, and you will have tribulation ten days. Be faithful until death, and I will give you the crown of life (Revelation 2:10).

> So that we ourselves boast of you among the churches of God for your patience and faith in all your persecutions and tribulations that you endure (2 Thessalonians 1:4).

However, we need to remember that Christ can also deliver us from suffering and even from death if it suits his plan and purpose. He has all power in heaven and in earth, even the devil is subject to him.

> But the Lord stood with me and strengthened me, so that the message might be preached fully through me, and *that* all the Gentiles might hear. And I was delivered out of the mouth of the lion (2 Timothy 4:17).

Questions

1 The work of Christ can be seen from three perspectives: what are they?

2 Explain how each of these three roles is essential to our salvation

3 What aspect of Christ's work has yet to be fulfilled?

CHAPTER SEVEN

THE ATONEMENT

1 The need for the Atonement

2 The words used

   a) Atonement
   b) Propitiation
   c) Reconciliation
   d) Ransom and redemption

3 Christ saves us by his death

4 Christ died as our substitute

   Seven statements about the cross

5 What motivated God to plan the Atonement?

   a) His desire to save the lost
   b) His love for the lost
   c) His justice which demanded that the law must be fulfilled

6 Two reasons why the Atonement was necessary

   a) Because man has broken God's law and the demands
       of the law must be honoured
   b) Because death is the penalty for sin

7 Seven fruits of Christ's Atonement

For if when we were enemies we were reconciled to God
through the death of His Son, much more, having been
reconciled, we shall be saved by His life. And not only *that,*
but we also rejoice in God through our Lord Jesus Christ,
through whom we have now received the reconciliation
(Romans 5:10-11).

1 The need for the Atonement

God and man need to be reconciled. They have become
alienated from one another due to the sin and rebellion of
man. From man's side there is no way back to God, but in
his grace God provides the way of reconciliation. In the Old
Testament atonement was provided by animal sacrifices.
There was no inherent value in these sacrifices; it was the
death of the victim that was important. Why? Because sin in
God's sight is so serious that it not only needs to be repented
of but also atoned for. The life of the animal in place of the
life of the sinner provided the way of reconciliation:

For the life of the flesh *is* in the blood, and I have given it
to you upon the altar to make atonement for your souls;
for it *is* the blood *that* makes atonement for the soul
(Leviticus 17:11).

Sacrifice was the divinely appointed way of securing atonement; it was the death of the victim that was important.

There are references to atonement in the Old Testament
by other means than animal sacrifices. For example Moses
seeks to make atonement for the sin of the people by asking God to punish him instead, and blot his name out of the
book of life (Exodus 32:30-32). Phinehas makes atonement for
Israel by killing the ringleaders of an idolatrous rebellion
(Numbers 25:6-8,13). It is clear that in the Old Testament death

was the recognized penalty for sin (Ezekiel 18:20), but God graciously permitted animal sacrifices as a substitute for the death of the sinner.

The New Testament says that animal sacrifices were not truly sufficient. They were only prefiguring the death of Christ whose sacrifice would redeem transgressions not only under the New Testament, but under the Old Testament also:

> And for this reason He is the Mediator of the new covenant, by means of death, for the redemption of transgressions under the first covenant ... (Hebrews 9:15).

> For *it is* not possible that the blood of bulls and goats could take away sins (Hebrews 10:4).

The cross is therefore vital not only to the New Testament but to the Old as well: everything that happened before the cross looks forward to it, and everything after the cross looks back to it. The need for the death of Christ, as an atonement for the sin of man, was planned by God before the foundation of the world:

> You were not redeemed with corruptible things, *like* silver or gold ... but with the precious blood of Christ, as of a lamb without blemish and without spot. He indeed was foreordained before the foundation of the world, but was manifest in these last times for you (1 Peter 1:18-20).

See also Revelation 13:8.

2 The words used

a) **Atonement**. In the Old Testament the word atonement means reconciliation by the covering of sin. Sin needs to be buried out of sight. This is the thought in Psalm 32:

Blessed is *he whose* transgression is forgiven, *whose* sin is covered. Blessed *is* the man to whom the LORD does not impute iniquity, and in whose spirit *there* is no guile (Psalm 32:1-2).

Why does sin have to be covered so that it is no longer visible to God? Because he abominates all wickedness, it spoils and disfigures his creation and he has to react against it. Although he is 'slow to anger' (Nehemiah 9:17), there is abundant evidence in the Old Testament of the wrath of God and of his anger at the sin of his people:

He, *being* full of compassion, forgave *their* iniquity, and did not destroy *them*. Yes, many a time He turned His anger away, and did not stir up all His wrath (Psalm 78:38).

The averting of God's wrath is not something that man can bring about, only God can do that. The wrath of God is thus a solemn fact to be reckoned with.

b) Propitiation. In the Greek version of the Old Testament, called the Septuagint, the Hebrew word for atonement is translated by a Greek word hilasterion which occurs in the following places in the New Testament: Luke 18:13 (literally, 'God be propitiated to me, the sinner'); Romans 3:25; Hebrews 2:17; 9:5 ('the mercy seat' is the place of propitiation [hilasterion]); 1 John 2:2; 4:10. This word is rendered propitiation in the AV and the NKJV — the removal of wrath by the offering of a sacrifice.

In this is love, not that we loved God, but that He loved us and sent His Son *to be* the propitiation for our sins (1 John 4:10).

Paul wrote that 'the wrath of God is revealed from heaven against all ungodliness and unrighteousness of men.' (Romans 1:18). In the following two chapters he shows that

Jew and Gentile are equally sinners before God. Christ's sacrifice alone can satisfy God's holiness and save men from God's wrath against sin:

> Being justified freely by His grace through the redemption that is in Christ Jesus, whom God set forth *to be* a propitiation by His blood, through faith, to demonstrate His righteousness ... (Romans 3:24-25).

Because of our sin we need Christ to be our advocate with the Father and to be the propitiation for our sins:

> My little children, these things I write to you, that you may not sin. And if anyone sins, we have an Advocate with the Father, Jesus Christ the righteous. And He Himself is the propitiation for our sins, and not for ours only but also for the whole world (1 John 2:1-2).

Since Christ alone can do this for us it shows how very serious our plight must be. It also shows that the wrath of God against sin is a reality that has to be reckoned with. The death of Christ as 'the Lamb of God who takes away the sin of the world' reminds us of those lambs and animal sacrifices in the Old Testament that were offered as an atonement for sin. It is also a proof of the continuity that exists between the Old and the New Testaments.

c) Reconciliation. In the New Testament the word reconciliation means the effect of an action that changes a hostile relationship to one of friendship. For example, a person must put right the wrong he has done to his friend before they can be reconciled:

> If you bring your gift to the altar, and there remember that your brother has something against you, leave your gift there before the altar, and go your way. First be reconciled to your brother, and then come and offer your gift (Matthew 5:23-24).

God has graciously taken the initiative to reconcile man to himself by providing his own Son as the means whereby sin can be both judged and forgiven:

> For if when we were enemies we were reconciled to God through the death of His Son, much more, having been reconciled, we shall be saved by His life. And not only *that*, but we also rejoice in God through our Lord Jesus Christ, through whom we have now received the reconciliation (Romans 5:10-11).

See also Romans 11:15; 2 Corinthians 5:18-21; Ephesians 2:16; Colossians 1:20-21.

From these verses we can see that God has reconciled us to himself:

- By the death of Christ.
- While we were his enemies
- As a free gift

d)   Ransom and redemption. The Bible often speaks of, 'the redemption that is in Christ Jesus' (Romans 3:24), and also of those who believe in Christ as being 'redeemed by his precious blood' (1 Peter 1:18-19). Christ also spoke of his coming into the world 'to give His life as a ransom for many' (Matthew 20:28), and the apostles continued the same idea by saying that believers have been 'bought with a price' (1 Corinthians 6:20). These words, 'redemption, redeemed, ransom, bought', convey the idea of deliverance achieved by the payment of a price. At the time they were written it was common practice for prisoners of war to be released on the payment of a ransom price. Slaves too could purchase their freedom by the payment of a sum of money to their masters. The name given to this process was redemption – freedom secured by the payment of a price. This raises two questions:

i) Why is it necessary for believers to be bought with a price? It is necessary because the Bible speaks of sin as slavery. Jesus said, 'Whoever commits sin is the slave of sin' (John 8:34). He also said that Satan is like a strong man who rules over his kingdom so effectively that none of his captives can escape unless God himself rescues them (Luke 11:14-22). Paul says that at one time we were all slaves to sin (Romans 6:17), under the controlling power of Satan (Ephesians 2:1-3), from whose dark kingdom only Christ could deliver us (Colossians 1:12-14). This means that we were captives needing to be rescued. This was no easy matter, because it cost the death of God's own Son to release us, by bearing our sins and the judgement that we deserved.

ii) What is the ransom price? The Bible says that Christ is the ransom price. He said he had come to give his life as a ransom for many (Mark 10:45) and Paul says that believers are, 'justified freely by His grace through the redemption that is in Christ Jesus: whom God has set forth to be propitiation through faith in His blood' (Romans 3:24). Christ purchased our salvation by laying down his life in our place. Because he was both God and sinless man he was the only one who could take upon himself the punishment our sins deserved. The whole point of using the word ransom is to show that salvation is a costly matter to God. How can God be just and the justifier of him who believes in Jesus? Only through Christ paying the penalty for our sin by shedding his precious blood for us. That was the great price that the holiness of God and his law required for our deliverance.

However, we must be careful not to press the term too far. Ransom emphasises the costliness of our salvation, and our inability to free ourselves from sin's slavery. It does not mean that a price was paid to Satan whose slaves we are by nature, or to God whose slaves we are not until he saves us. It is, therefore, unhelpful to ask to whom the ransom was paid.

(See also 1 Corinthians 1:30; 7:23; Galatians 3:13; 4:5; Ephesians 1:7, 14; 4:30; 1 Timothy 2:6; Titus 2:14; 2 Peter 2:1; Revelation 5:9; 14:3-4).

We can therefore say that

- Christ is the *propitiation* for our sins
- Christ is the *reconciliation* for our sins
- Christ is the *ransom* for our sins

3 Christ saves us by his death

We have already seen that Christ said he had come into the world in order to give his life as a ransom for many (Mark 10:45), and that redemption could only be secured by Christ shedding his blood for us (Romans 3:24). In the last week of his earthly life some Greeks, who had come to Jerusalem for the Passover, asked to see him. Jesus regarded this as some kind of divine signal for he said:

> ...The hour has come that the Son of Man should be glorified ... Now My soul is troubled, and what shall I say, 'Father save Me from this hour?' But for this purpose I came to this hour ... Now is the judgement of this world; now the ruler of this world will be cast out. And I, if I am lifted up from the earth, will draw all *peoples* to Myself. This He said, signifying by what death He would die (John 12:23,27,31-33).

It is clear from this scripture that Jesus knew in advance about his crucifixion, and that his mission to save the world was to be fulfilled by suffering this terrible death. As the Good Shepherd he also said that he would die for his sheep:

> ...I lay down My life for the sheep ... no one takes it from Me, but I lay it down of Myself. I have power to lay it down, and I have power to take it again. This command I have received from My Father (John 10:15,18).

On the Mount of Transfiguration Moses and Elijah, representing the Law and the Prophets, came especially from heaven to speak with Christ. What about? 'And they spoke of His decease (literally, his exodus) which He would accomplish at Jerusalem' (Luke 9:31). His death was central to his mission and this vivid experience taught the disciples as much.

See also Romans 5:6-10; 1 Corinthians 5:7; Galatians 1:4; Ephesians 2:13; Hebrews 9:11-14; 10:10-14; 1 Peter 1:18-19; 3:18.

4 Christ died as our substitute

The heart of the gospel is that 'Christ died for our sins according to the Scriptures' (1 Corinthians 15:3). In other words he died on our behalf and in our place, taking upon himself the punishment due to us. In theological terms this is known as penal substitution. As our High Priest Christ did not offer animal sacrifices to God for our sins, but instead he offered himself and presented his precious blood to God in the heavenly temple (Hebrews 9:11-14). He therefore combines in himself the role of Priest and of sacrifice. It is in fulfilling this role, so clearly described in Mosaic sacrificial worship, that we have the most powerful evidence for the penal and substitutionary death of Christ. Further evidence from the Old Testament comes from the prophet Isaiah, who spoke of God's Servant bearing our sins:

> All we like sheep have gone astray; we have turned, every one, to his own way; and the LORD has laid on Him the iniquity of us all ... Yet it pleased the LORD to bruise Him; He has put *Him* to grief. When You make His soul an offering for sin, He shall see *His* seed, He shall prolong *His* days, and the pleasure of the LORD shall prosper in His hand (Isaiah 53:6,10).

In addition to the substitutionary character of Christ as our ransom and redemption, in which he paid the price to rescue us, Paul says that God made Christ responsible for our sins as though they were his own:

> For He [God] made Him who knew no sin *to be* sin for us, that we might become the righteousness of God in Him (2 Corinthians 5:21).

Paul also says that Christ actually took upon himself the penalty and the curse that we deserved for having broken God's law:

> For as many as are of the works of the law are under the curse; for it is written, 'Cursed is everyone who does not continue in all things which are written in the book of the law, to do them' (Galatians 3:10).

> Christ has redeemed us from the curse of the law, having become a curse for us, (for it is written, 'Cursed is everyone who hangs on a tree') (Galatians 3:13).

See also John 11:50-52; Romans 5:8; Hebrews 9:28; 1 Peter 2:24; 1 John 2:2

The cross was the appointed way by which Christ became our substitute:

i) Christ predicted that he would die on a cross

> 'Now is the judgement of this world; now the ruler of this world will be cast out. And I, if I am lifted up from the earth, will draw all *peoples* to Myself.' This He said, signifying by what death He would die (John 12:31-33).

> And as Moses lifted up the serpent in the wilderness, even so must the Son of Man be lifted up, that whoever

believes in Him should not perish but have eternal life (John 3:14-15).

ii) Christ told his disciples that he would die by crucifixion

Behold, we are going up to Jerusalem, and the Son of Man will be betrayed to the chief priests and to the scribes; and they will condemn Him to death, 'and deliver Him to the Gentiles to mock and to scourge and to crucify. And the third day He will rise again' (Matthew 20:18-19).

Then Jesus said to His disciples, 'If anyone desires to come after Me, let him deny himself, and take up his cross, and follow Me. For whoever desires to save his life will lose it, and whoever loses his life for My sake will find it' (Matthew 16:24-25).

iii) Christ prayed for strength to endure the cross

Then He said to them, 'My soul is exceedingly sorrowful, even to death. Stay here and watch with Me.' He went a little farther and fell on His face, and prayed saying, 'O My Father, if it is possible, let this cup pass from Me; never-theless not as I will, but as You *will*' (Matthew 26:38-39).

iv) The cross is central to our salvation

For Christ did not send me to baptize, but to preach the gospel, not with wisdom of words, lest the cross of Christ should be made of no effect. For the message of the cross is foolishness to those who are perishing, but to us who are being saved it is the power of God (1 Corinthians 1:17-18).

[Christ] having wiped out the handwriting of requirements that was against us, which was contrary to us. And He has taken it out of the way, having nailed it to the cross. Having disarmed principalities and powers, He made a public spectacle of them, triumphing over them in it (Colossians 2:14-15).

v) Christ bore the curse of the law on the cross

Christ has redeemed us from the curse of the law, having become a curse for us, (for it is written, 'Cursed is everyone who hangs on a tree') (Galatians 3:13).

For as many as are of the works of the law are under the curse; for it is written, 'Cursed is everyone who does not continue in all things which are written in the book of the law, to do them' (Galatians 3:10).

vi) The cross and the shedding of Christ's blood are inseparable

In Him we have redemption through His blood, the forgiveness of sins, according to the riches of His grace (Ephesians 1:7).

And by Him to reconcile all things to Himself, by Him, whether things on earth or things in heaven, having made peace through the blood of His cross (Colossians 1:20).

vii) Christ's cry of dereliction on the cross was from the psalm predicting his death by crucifixion

My God, My God, why have you forsaken Me? *Why are You so* far from helping Me, *and from* the words of My groaning? (Psalm 22:1).

For dogs have surrounded Me; the assembly of the wicked has enclosed Me. They pierced My hands and My feet; I can count all My bones. They look *and* stare at Me. They divide My garments among them, and for My clothing they cast lots (Psalm 22:16-17).

5 What motivated God to plan the Atonement?

a) His desire to save the lost

All we like sheep have gone astray; we have turned, every-one, to his own way; and the LORD has laid on Him the iniquity of us all (Isaiah 53:6).

Grace to you and peace from God the Father and our Lord Jesus Christ, who gave Himself for our sins, that He might deliver us from this present evil age, according to the will of our God and Father (Galatians 1:3-4).

b) His love for the lost

In this the love of God was manifested towards us, that God sent His only begotten Son into the world, that we might live through Him. In this is love, not that we loved God, but that He loved us and sent His Son *to be* the propitiation for our sins (1 John 4:9-10).

But God, who is rich in mercy, because of His great love with which He loved us, even when we were dead in trespasses, made us alive together with Christ (by grace you have been saved) (Ephesians 2:4-5).

c) His justice which demanded that the law must be fulfilled

Being justified freely by His grace through the redemption that is in Christ Jesus, whom God set forth *to be* a propitiation by His blood, through faith, to demonstrate His righteousness, because in His forbearance God had passed over the sins that were previously committed, to demonstrate at the present time His righteousness, that He might be just and the justifier of the one who has faith in Jesus (Romans 3:24-26).

6 Two reasons why the Atonement was necessary.

a) Because man has broken God's law and the demands of the law must be honoured

- Scripture says that God will not overlook sin

  The LORD is longsuffering and abundant in mercy, forgiving iniquity and transgression; but He by no means clears *the guilty,* visiting the iniquity of the fathers on the children to the third and fourth *generation* (Numbers 14:18).

(See also Exodus 34:7 and Nahum 1:2-3).

- The holiness of God reacts against sin and condemns it:

  For You *are* not a God who takes pleasure in wickedness, nor shall evil dwell with You. The boastful shall not stand in Your sight; You hate all workers of iniquity. You shall destroy those who speak falsehood; the LORD abhors the bloodthirsty and deceitful man (Psalm 5:4-6).

  For the wrath of God is revealed from heaven against all ungodliness and unrighteousness of men, who suppress the truth in unrighteousness (Romans 1:18).

- God has to be just in the way he justifies the ungodly:

  Whom God set forth *to be* a propitiation by His blood, through faith, to demonstrate His righteousness, because in His forbearance God had passed over the sins that were previously committed, to demonstrate at the present time His righteousness, that He might be just and the justifier of the one who has faith in Jesus (Romans 3:25-26).

b) Because death is the penalty for sin

> For the life of the flesh *is* in the blood, and I have given it to you upon the altar to make atonement for your souls; for it *is* the blood *that* makes atonement for the soul (Leviticus 17:11).

> For the wages of sin is death, but the gift of God *is* eternal life in Christ Jesus our Lord (Romans 6:23).

So Christ's death on the cross proves the necessity of atonement:

> Then He said to them, 'O foolish ones, and slow of heart to believe in all that the prophets have spoken! Ought not the Christ to have suffered these things and to enter into His glory?' And beginning at Moses and all the Prophets, He expounded to them in all the Scriptures the things concerning Himself (Luke 24:25-27).

> 'Now My soul is troubled, and what shall I say? "Father, save Me from this hour?" But for this purpose I came to this hour … And I, if I am lifted up from the earth, will draw all *peoples* to Myself.' This He said, signifying by what death He would die (John 12:27, 32-33).

7   Seven fruits of Christ's Atonement

i) The Devil is defeated. His power over mankind has been broken. Christ said that when he died on the cross the devil would be cast out (John 12:31). Believers are delivered from the bondage of Satan's kingdom and transferred into Christ's kingdom (Colossians 1:13).

> He who sins is of the devil, for the devil has sinned from the beginning. For this purpose the Son of God was manifested, that He might destroy the works of the devil (1 John 3:8).

ii) Death loses its power. Sin and the law give death a terrible power over mankind (1 Corinthians 15:56). Christ gives every believer the promise of a place with him in heaven when they die. Death therefore holds no terror for the Christian anymore. God's gracious purpose is clear:

> But has now been revealed by the appearing of our Saviour Jesus Christ, *who* has abolished death and brought life and immortality to light through the gospel (2 Timothy 1:10).

iii) The dominion of sin is broken. As the result of the fall mankind came under the dominion of sin (Romans 1:21-32; 3:10-18). Christ through the Holy Spirit not only gives man a new nature but also a new power to live a life of holiness:

> Do not present your members *as* instruments of unrighteousness to sin, but present yourselves to God as being alive from the dead, and your members *as* instruments of righteousness to God. For sin shall not have dominion over you, for you are not under the law but under grace (Romans 6:13-14).

iv) God is propitiated. The wrath of God, revealed from heaven against all ungodliness and unrighteousness of men (Romans 1:18), has been appeased by the vicarious death of the Lamb of God who takes away the sin of the world. That is to say, that because Christ suffered in our place (vicariously) God's righteous anger is propitiated (because Jesus bore it on the cross).

> For Christ has not entered the holy places made with hands, which are copies of the true, but into heaven itself now to appear in the presence of God for us ... but now, once at the end of the ages, He has appeared to put away sin by the sacrifice of Himself (Hebrews 9:24, 26).

v) There has been a change in heaven. The sin of Satan and his defiance of God occurred in heaven before the world was made. His fall from heaven with that of his confederate angels left some stain of sin even in heaven. Christ's sacrifice and his appearing in heaven with his own blood as High Priest purified this stain:

> Therefore *it was* necessary that the copies of the things in the heavens should be purified with these, but the heavenly things themselves with better sacrifices than these (Hebrews 9:23).

vi) The new covenant in Christ's blood is put into effect. At the Last Supper Christ said the cup of wine that he gave to his disciples symbolized 'the new covenant in My blood' (Luke 22:20). This blood was about to be shed on the cross. In order for a covenant in the Old Testament to be ratified, blood had to be shed (Exodus 24:5-8). The same is true for the New Testament (Hebrews 9:14-24).

> How much more shall the blood of Christ, who through the eternal Spirit offered Himself without spot to God, purge your conscience from dead works to serve the living God? And for this reason He is the Mediator of the new covenant, by means of death, for the redemption of transgressions under the first covenant, that those who are called may receive the promise of the eternal inheritance (Hebrews 9:14-15).

vii) What are the blessings of the New Covenant? God gives the believer the following covenant blessings through the Holy Spirit: holiness, sonship, assurance and forgiveness. These were foretold by Jeremiah (31:31-34) and are confirmed in every detail in Hebrews 8:7-13.

- **Holiness**

  I will put My laws in their mind and write them on their hearts (Hebrews 8:10).

- **Sonship**

  I will be their God, and they shall be My people (verse 10).

- **Assurance**

  All shall know Me, from the least of them to the greatest (verse 11).

- **Forgiveness**

  Their sins and their lawless deeds I will remember no more (verse 12).

  ... You are in Christ Jesus, who became for us wisdom, from God – and righteousness and sanctification and redemption (1 Corinthians 1:30).

Questions

1. What is the meaning of propitiation, reconciliation and ransom?

2. What are the negative and positive elements in justification?

CHAPTER EIGHT

JUSTIFICATION BY FAITH

1 Its meaning in the New Testament

2 The two elements in justification – negative and positive

    a) The negative element – the remission of sins
    b) The positive element – the imputation of Christ's righteousness

3 The differences between justification and sanctification

    Four comparisons

4 The relationship of faith to justification

5 Justification and good works – does James agree with Paul?

6 Lessons from the past

Justification by faith is a judicial declaration by God that the penitent sinner, through faith-union with Christ, is righteous and free from the guilt of sin through the perfect obedience and death of Christ on his or her behalf.

> Now to him who works, the wages are not counted as grace but as debt. But to him who does not work but believes on Him who justifies the ungodly, his faith is accounted for righteousness (Romans 4:4-5).

> Therefore, having been justified by faith, we have peace with God through our Lord Jesus Christ, through whom also we have access by faith into this grace in which we stand, and rejoice in hope of the glory of God (Romans 5:1-2).

In the Old Testament and in the New, God is often portrayed as 'the Judge of the whole earth' (Genesis 18:25). A judge either acquits the innocent or condemns the guilty. God's dealings with men are often portrayed in this legal sense – we are answerable to him as our Judge for our behaviour in this world. In the Old Testament God's Law is especially seen as the foundation of his relationship with his people; righteousness means obedience to his law, conforming to its norms. It is therefore quite valid in biblical terms to say that there is a judicial aspect to our relationship with God and that 'justifying' is the prerogative of God, the eternal judge.

1 Its meaning in the New Testament

The Greek verb *dikaioō* means to pronounce righteous, to acquit. Paul uses it in a legal sense: if a person accused in a law court of a crime is found to be innocent the judge pronounces him 'not guilty'. For example:

Knowing that a man is not justified by the works of the law but by faith in Jesus Christ, even we have believed in Christ Jesus, that we might be justified by faith in Christ and not by the works of the law; for by the works of the law no flesh shall be justified (Galatians 2:16).

Therefore let it be known to you, brethren, that through this Man is preached to you the forgiveness of sins; and by Him everyone who believes is justified from all things from which you could not be justified by the law of Moses (Acts 13:38-39).

For all have sinned and fall short of the glory of God, being justified freely by His grace through the redemption that is in Christ Jesus, whom God set forth *to be* a propitiation by His blood, through faith, to demonstrate His righteousness, because in His forbearance God had passed over the sins previously committed, to demonstrate at the present time His righteousness, that He might be just and the justifier of the one who has faith in Jesus ...Therefore we conclude that a man is justified by faith apart from the deeds of the law (Romans 3:23-26, 28).

See also Romans 4:5-8; 5:1,9; 8:30-34; 1 Corinthians 6:11; Philippians 3:9.

Paul is saying that we are declared by God to be righteous not on the basis of anything we have done (law keeping or good deeds), but simply and solely on the basis of faith in Christ Jesus. How does faith in him put us right with God? How can God justify the ungodly? (Romans 4:5) The answer is that justification is a purely judicial act of God which only affects the moral status of a man before God. God does not say that the unholy person is now suddenly holy; he simply declares that through Christ's sacrificial death on the sinner's behalf, the demands of justice have been satisfied. Our relationship to the law and its just demands have been satisfied on the basis of Christ's fulfilling the law for us, and his death in our place.

> Who Himself bore our sins in His own body on the tree, that we, having died to sins, might live for righteousness – by whose stripes you were healed (1 Peter 2:24).

> For He made Him who knew no sin *to be* sin for us, that we might become the righteousness of God in Him (2 Corinthians 5:21).

Our own moral character is not the ground of the declaration that we are justified, and is not affected by it. Justification is objective and only changes our moral relationship to God and to his law; it does not change us ourselves. The moral change occurs through God's work of sanctification through the gift of the Holy Spirit who inwardly renews us. Sanctification is, however, indissolubly linked to justification and can never be separated from it. This will be discussed later in the chapter.

2 The two elements in justification – negative and positive

a) The negative element – the remission of sins. We have forgiveness, the cancelling of our sins, on the ground of the atoning work of Christ. This element in justification, the blotting out of our sins, is emphasised in the Old Testament:

> By His knowledge My righteous Servant shall justify many, for He shall bear their iniquities (Isaiah 53:11).

> Blessed *is he whose* transgression is forgiven, whose sin is covered. Blessed *is* the man to whom the LORD does not impute iniquity, and in whose spirit *there is* no guile (Psalm 32:1-2).

> I, *even* I, *am* He who blots out your transgressions for My own sake; and I will not remember your sins (Isaiah 43:25).

See also Isaiah 44:22; Jeremiah 31:34.

Remission of sins is also emphasised in the New Testament. Justification secures for us the forgiveness of all our sins, past, present and future, and the removal of all guilt and every penalty.

> Knowing that a man is not justified by the works of the law but by faith in Jesus Christ, even we have believed in Jesus Christ, that we might be justified by faith in Christ and not by the works of the law; for by the works of the law no flesh shall be justified (Galatians 2:16).

See also Romans 4:5-8; 5:18-19.

b) The positive element – the imputation of Christ's righteousness. Christ died not only to obtain forgiveness of sins but also to impute, to put to our account, his own positive, spotless righteousness. There is therefore a two-way transaction which takes place when we believe: our sins are imputed to Christ, the sin-bearer and in the same moment his righteousness is imputed to us – both take place together and constitute God's method of justification. This has to be seen as something purely objective. Our sins do not make Christ morally a sinner; neither does his righteousness make us morally perfect. Our sins were the judicial ground for his suffering, and his righteousness the judicial ground for our justification and acceptance with God. This is how God can be seen to be just and the justifier of him that believes in Jesus (Romans 3:26). The negative aspect (forgiveness of sins) and the positive aspect (his imputed righteousness) secure our just standing before God.

> But now the righteousness of God apart from the law is revealed, being witnessed by the Law and the Prophets, even the righteousness of God *which is* through faith in Jesus Christ to all and on all who believe (Romans 3:21-22).

> But to him who does not work but believes on Him who justifies the ungodly, his faith is counted for righteousness, just as David also describes the blessedness of the man to whom God imputes righteousness apart from works (Romans 4:5-6).

> For He made Him who knew no sin *to be* sin for us, that we might become the righteousness of God in Him (2 Corinthians 5:21).

Other aspects of the positive aspects of justification are, 'an inheritance among those who are sanctified' (Acts 26:18), 'peace with God' (Romans 5:1), 'access by faith' into God's presence and the 'hope of the glory of God' (Romans 5:2). 'You are in Christ Jesus, who became for us wisdom from God – and righteousness and sanctification and redemption' (1 Corinthians 1:30).

3 The differences between justification and sanctification

We have seen that justification is God's declaration of acquittal; he pronounces the believer free from all guilt because Christ has died in his place. What does sanctification mean? In the Old Testament the sacred vessels of the Temple were set apart exclusively for the purpose of sacrifices and offerings. They were not only set apart for God they were also used by God. There is therefore a twofold aspect to sanctification, one static and the other dynamic. We are set apart for God, and we are indwelt by God. By the indwelling of his Spirit and the gift of a new nature we become progressively holy.

Four comparisons

i) In justification the righteousness of Christ is imputed to us.
    In sanctification the righteousness of Christ is imparted to
    us.

ii) Justification removes the guilt of sin.
    Sanctification removes the pollution of our natures by sin.

iii) Justification is objective – it takes place outside us.
    Sanctification is subjective – it takes place within us.

iv) Justification is once for all – never needing to be repeated.
    Sanctification is a process – we grow in grace and in know-
    ledge of God.

4 The relationship of faith to justification

We have seen that justification is something that God does for
us. In many places in the New Testament Paul vigorously and
consistently opposes the idea that justification is by works:

> For if Abraham was justified by works, he has *something
> of which* to boast, but not before God. For what does
> the Scripture say? *'Abraham believed God and it was
> accounted to him for righteousness.'* Now to him who
> works, the wages are not counted as grace but as debt.
> But to him who does not work but believes on Him who
> justifies the ungodly, his faith is accounted for righteous-
> ness (Romans 4:2-5).

See also Romans 3:20-28; Galatians 2:16-21; 3:11; Ephesians
2:8-10.

If, therefore, justification is entirely God's action what is the
value of faith? Can we say that we are saved because of our
faith? If this were true it would contradict what Paul is saying

about the impossibility of saving ourselves by our own works. Justification is not based upon our faith but upon the righteousness and work of Christ. It is not our faith but Christ who saves us. What then is the role of faith in our salvation? Faith is the channel through which God's salvation is mediated to us. It is the God-given ability to believe and receive the salvation offered to us in the gospel. Faith is the empty hand stretched out to receive God's free gift of salvation:

> For by grace you have been saved through faith, and that not of yourselves; it is the gift of God, not of works, lest anyone should boast (Ephesians 2:8-9).

What is meant by Abraham's faith being imputed to him for righteousness?

> For what does the Scripture say? 'Abraham believed God, and it was accounted to him for righteousness' (Romans 4:3).

Abraham was justified by God in exactly the same way as we are today. God appeared to Abraham and made a covenant of grace with him through which blessing would come to the whole world. (Genesis 12:1-3) God revealed to him something of the coming Messiah who would be a direct descendant of Isaac, the child of promise, given by God to Abraham and Sarah. In the way God tested Abraham, to sacrifice Isaac his only son on Mount Moriah, God was giving him a foreview of Calvary and the redemption of the world by Christ. We know that Abraham did have some understanding of the way of salvation from the words of Christ: 'Abraham rejoiced to see My day, he saw it and was glad.' (John 8:56) Therefore when it says, 'Abraham believed God', it means that Abraham was given to understand that God's way of salvation is not by works but by faith and trust in the living God. God therefore counted righteousness (right-standing before God) to Abraham on the basis of faith in God. This is the way of salvation in Christ.

5 Justification and good works – does James agree with Paul?

James asks the question:

> What *does it* profit, my brethren, if someone says he has faith but does not have works? Can faith save him? If a brother or sister is naked and destitute of daily food, and one of you says to them, 'Depart in peace, be warmed and filled,' but you do not give them the things which are needed for the body, what does it profit? Thus also faith by itself, if it does not have works, is dead (James 2:14-17).

He goes on to say that when Abraham was tested by God to sacrifice his only son Isaac, his faith was justified by his works because he obeyed God:

> Do you see that faith was working together with his works, and by works faith was made perfect? (James 2:22)

Surely there is a contradiction between James and Paul? However, when we examine the two passages concerned, James 2 and Romans 3 and 4, we can see that Paul and James are really talking about 'faith' and 'works' in quite different ways. They are clearly addressing different kinds of errors in the churches to whom they were writing.

James is writing to Jewish believers who had a type of 'faith', which professed to believe in God and in Christ, but it produced no fruit, no good works. Their 'faith' was dead, like the 'faith' of devils, who believe in God but remain devils still.

Paul, on the other hand, is speaking to those Jews who thought they could earn salvation by their own works. He says the law was not given to help us earn salvation.

By the law *is* the knowledge of sin (Romans 3:20)

Obedience to the law and the doing of good deeds was never meant to replace faith in the mercy and forgiveness of God. Salvation is not by man's efforts to keep the law, but only through faith and by the grace of God.

James uses the word, 'faith', to mean a dead and empty intellectual belief; he uses the word 'works' to mean the evidence of a living and obedient and active faith. Paul on the other hand uses the word faith' to mean a pure and active trust in God and in God's promise of salvation; he uses the word 'works' to mean man's method of trying to merit salvation by keeping the law.

James is criticising a dead faith that produces no good works. Paul is proclaiming a living faith in Christ that produces good works, but does not trust in them in order to be saved.

6 Lessons from the past

The rediscovery of the doctrine of justification by faith was the main reason for the Protestant Reformation in the sixteenth century. The Reformation was a reaction against the false doctrines and corrupt practices that had developed over a considerable period of time in the Roman Catholic Church. That Church taught that a person could be saved by his own works through the sacraments of the Church. Faith was necessary but so were acts of obedience. You saved yourself by your own efforts and by believing in Christ. It was a mixture of faith and works.

Roman Catholicism still teaches that all sin committed before baptism is pardoned by baptism, through which we actually receive spiritual life. Sin committed after baptism is pardoned by confession to the priest, doing penance and suffering in purgatory.

The Reformers disagreed with the Roman Catholic view on four grounds:

i) Baptism does not impart new spiritual life; it does not enable a person to justify himself. We are justified by faith in Christ, not by faith in baptism.

ii) Spiritual life is not received in baptism and therefore cannot be the reason for God accepting the sinner.

(iii) The sinner is not justified by holy actions or by the sacraments but by Christ's work on the cross.

(iv) Justification is by faith in Christ's atoning death on the cross. The cross of Christ is a perfect work of God's grace; penances and purgatory are not needed to complete it.

The Roman Catholic Council of Trent (6) (vii) says:

> Justification itself which is not merely remission of sins but also the sanctification and renewal of the inward man through the voluntary reception of Grace and of the gifts whereby man of unjust becomes just and of an enemy a friend …The instrumental cause is Baptism which is the sacrament of faith without which no man was ever justified.

Here we see how Roman Catholicism confuses justification and sanctification, saying that we are justified by becoming just. The focus is no longer on the righteousness of Christ, but on our own righteousness, received through baptism and evidenced by the renewal of the inward man. The great scholar Erasmus tried to reconcile the opposing views at a meeting of Protestant and Roman Catholic theologians. Surprisingly the latter agreed that justification is by faith, 'on account of the merits of Jesus Christ only'. However it was then discovered that the two parties had a completely different idea as to the meaning of 'faith'! The Protestants said it meant a simple act of complete reliance upon Christ who is the only hope of righteousness for sinners. The Roman Catholics understood faith as working through the influence of the Holy Spirit in believers, producing righteousness in them and making them acceptable to God.

Roman Catholic theologians maintained that faith is a mental acceptance of the teachings of the Church, whereas Luther said it was a response of the heart in simple reliance upon Christ for salvation. Here then are the two opposing views. Rome says justification is, 'to be made righteous', but Paul (and Luther after him) say it is, 'to be declared righteous' because of Christ's death for our sins. The former put their emphasis on man's work while the latter put their emphasis on Christ's work. After almost 500 years the gap between these views is still as wide as ever.

Questions

1 How does the death of Christ on the cross affect the moral status of a believer before God?

2 What are the negative and positive elements in justification?

3 What are the differences between justification and sanctification?

CHAPTER NINE

REGENERATION

1 The words used in the New Testament

Five different words

2 What is regeneration?

a) Negatively: what it is not – four points
b) Positively: what it is – four points

3 The necessity of regeneration – we must be born again

4 Who is the author of regeneration?

a) Is baptism the cause of regeneration?
b) Four objections made against the view that baptism by a Priest regenerates the soul

5 The signs that regeneration has taken place in our souls

Eight signs of the reality of regeneration

What does the Bible mean when it says that in order to be saved we must be 'born again'?

> Jesus ... said to him [Nicodemus], 'Most assuredly, I say to you, unless one is born again, he cannot see the kingdom of God' (John 3:3).

1   The words used in the New Testament

Regeneration is an act of God, whereby he plants the seed of new life within us, so that the governing disposition of the soul is made holy. There is a difference between storing seeds in a barn and planting them in the field, where they spring to life out of the soil as plants. Regeneration is the seed of spiritual life that God sows in our souls springing to life. Conversion, on the other hand, is a change of direction and is the consequence of regeneration. It happens consciously in man, causing him to turn from sin and from self to God. Conversion is the result of regeneration. The following are the biblical terms used to describe the change that takes place in our souls when we are born again by the Holy Spirit.

Five different words

i) **To beget, to be born,** *gennaō*. This is the most frequently used word in the New Testament for the new birth.

> [Jesus said] ...'Most assuredly, I say to you unless one is born again, he cannot see the kingdom of God ...That which is born of the flesh is flesh, and that which is born of the Spirit is spirit. Do not marvel that I said to you, "You must be born again." The wind blows where it wishes, and you hear the sound of it, but cannot tell where it comes from and where it goes. So is everyone who is born of the Spirit' (John 3:3, 6-8).

> If you know that He is righteous, you know that everyone
> who practises righteousness is born of Him (1 John 2:29).

See also 1 Peter 1:3,23 (*anagennaō* in both cases); 1 John 3:9;
4:7; 5:1, 4,18.

ii) *paliggenesia* is used only twice in the New Testament
(Matthew 19:28; Titus 3:5). It means rebirth, regeneration.
In the first text it refers to the renewal of the world at the
end of the age; in the second to the rebirth of a redeemed
person.

> Not by works of righteousness which we have done, but
> according to His mercy He saved us, through the washing
> of regeneration and renewing of the Holy Spirit (Titus 3:5).

iii) **To give birth to,** *apokueō*

> Of His own will He brought us forth by the word of truth,
> that we might be a kind of first-fruits of His creatures
> (James 1:18).

iv) **That which is created,** *ktisis*

> Therefore, if anyone *is* in Christ, *he* is a new creation; old
> things have passed away; behold, all things have become
> new (2 Corinthians 5:17).

> For in Christ Jesus neither circumcision nor uncircum-
> cision avails anything, but a new creation (Galatians 6:15).

See Ephesians 2:10; 4:24. In both verses the verb to create
(*ktizō*) is used.

v) **To make alive,** *zōopoieō*

> For as the Father raises the dead and gives life to *them*,
> even so the Son gives life to whom He will (John 5:21).

Even when we were dead in trespasses [God] made us alive together with Christ (by grace you have been saved) (Ephesians 2:5). See also Colossians 2:13.

2 What is regeneration?

a) Negatively: what it is not — four points:

i)   Regeneration is not something emotional or physical; no new faculties are added to the soul.
ii)   Our fundamental human nature does not change. A quiet introspective person does not become a noisy extrovert.
iii) Regeneration does not make us perfect and incapable of sin.
iv) Regeneration is not just an act of our will producing moral reformation.

b) Positively: what it is — four points:

Regeneration is the planting within us by God of a new principle of spiritual life; holiness now becomes the governing disposition of our souls. What is a disposition? It is something that governs the way we behave because of what we believe. Two twins may have almost identical faculties, abilities and powers but their behaviour and the quality of their lives may be completely different. Why? One has a good disposition and the other evil. One is controlled by good motives and the other by evil. What happens in regeneration is that God so operates upon us by the Holy Spirit that there is a fundamental change in our dispositions; this determines how we use our faculties. For example, look at Saul of Tarsus, a man of intellect and ability persecuting the church with zeal and determination. Then look at him as the great apostle Paul preaching Christ to every creature with humility and love. What has changed? His faculties and powers are just the same, but now he has a new disposition that controls and gives a new direction to his great abilities. We can therefore note four important characteristics of true regeneration;

i) **Regeneration affects the whole man** – mind, heart and will. All our powers are now under new management.

ii) **Regeneration is instantaneous.** It has no intermediate states and is not gradual. Our consciousness and awareness of it, however, may not happen all at once.

iii) **It takes place in the unconscious.** Its origin is a mystery and Jesus said we cannot fully understand it.

> Do not marvel that I said to you,' You must be born again.' The wind blows where it wishes, and you hear the sound of it, but cannot tell where it comes from and where it goes. So is everyone who is born of the Spirit (John 3:7-8).

iv) **It is effected by God.** Just as we had no part in our physical birth so neither have we in our spiritual. According to John 3:8 our new birth is entirely the work of God the Holy Spirit upon us. The new birth is the result of a   supernatural intervention in our lives:

> Who were born, not of blood, nor of the will of the flesh, nor of the will of man, but of God (John 1:13).

3 The necessity of regeneration – we must be born again

As we saw in Chapter Four, 'The Fall of Man', man's spiritual predicament according to the Bible is one of deadness and darkness. He is dead spiritually, a rebel against God and in bondage both to sin and to Satan. There is only one remedy for such a dreadful condition, a totally new life-giving power such as raised Christ from the dead. Man's problem is not lack of information and advice; the world is full of moral teachings telling us how we should live. Man lacks the power that springs from possessing a living relationship with God. Jesus made this perfectly plain to a religious leader of the Jews called Nicodemus. He told him that what he needed was not more information; he needed a new nature:

> Most assuredly, I say to you, unless one is born again, he cannot see the kingdom of God (John 3:3).

Paul says the same thing:

> Therefore, if anyone *is* in Christ *he is* a new creation; old things have passed away; behold, all things have become new (2 Corinthians 5:17).

> For in Christ Jesus neither circumcision nor uncircumcision (religious ceremonies) avails anything, but a new creation (Galatians 6:15).

> For by grace you have been saved through faith, and that not of yourselves; *it is* the gift of God, not of works, lest anyone should boast. For we are His workmanship, created in Christ Jesus for good works, which God prepared beforehand that we should walk in them (Ephesians 2:8-10).

God's purpose in saving us is not only to adopt us into his family but also to transform us into the very image and likeness of his Son. In the plan of God, Christ is to be the firstborn among many brethren:

> For whom He foreknew, He also predestined *to be* conformed to the image of His Son, that He might be the firstborn among many brethren (Romans 8:29).

> But we all, with unveiled face, beholding as in a mirror the glory of the Lord, are being transformed into the same image from glory to glory, just as by the Spirit of the Lord (2 Corinthians 3:18).

Just as earthly children resemble their parents physically so do the children of God spiritually. In order for us to be transformed into Christ's image we need to be born of the Holy Spirit and indwelt by him. It is through the Spirit that we come to share the family likeness:

> ... not by works of righteousness which we have done, but according to His mercy He saved us, through the washing of regeneration and renewing of the Holy Spirit (Titus 3:5).

4 Who is the author of regeneration?

Because of its radical nature regeneration is clearly not the work of man but the work of the Holy Spirit. Regeneration is nothing less than the bringing of new, spiritual life to the dead. The Holy Spirit works directly on the heart of man and changes his spiritual condition. In this inward and spiritual work there is no human co-operation at all. The scriptures already quoted prove that conclusively (John 1:13; 3:3-8; 5:21; Ephesians 2:8-10; Titus 3:5)

Is hearing the word of God a means of regeneration as suggested by James 1:18 and 1 Peter 1:23? It is more likely that these verses are referring to the conscious element in our salvation, when we actually hear the word of the gospel and believe it, rather than to the unconscious and mysterious operation when God puts eternal life into our souls. Just as in the physical realm the moment of conception is distinct and separate in time from the actual moment of birth, so it would appear to be in the spiritual realm as well. The same would apply to the parable of the sower. The word of God can only be effective if the soil into which it falls is good, i.e. it has been prepared by God to receive the seed. There is a preparatory work that God does before we come to Christ. God the Father inclines our unwilling hearts so that we want to come to Christ:

No one can come to Me unless the Father who sent Me
draws him; and I will raise him up at the last day (John
6:44).

a) Is baptism the cause of regeneration? This is the teaching
of the Roman Catholic Church and of the Russian Orthodox Church as well. Both churches teach that all who are
baptised by a priest are born again and immediately
become true Christians.

In 1994 the Pope authorised the publication of *The
Catechism of the Catholic Church,* the most modern and
comprehensive (700 pages) explanation of Roman Catholic
doctrine that had taken nearly thirty years to complete. The
following paragraphs from the Catechism have been selected
to show what the Roman Catholic Church teaches on the
importance of baptism as it affects the doctrine of regeneration.

• **1113** The whole liturgical life of the (Roman Catholic)
Church revolves around the Mass and the seven sacraments
– Baptism, Confirmation, Mass, Penance, Anointing the sick,
Holy Orders and Marriage.

• **1120** The ordained Priesthood guarantees that it really is
Christ who acts in the sacraments through the Holy Spirit for
the Church.

• **1128** This is the meaning of the Church's affirmation that
the sacraments act 'ex opere operato' by virtue of the saving
work of Christ accomplished once for all. ('Ex opere operato'
means that the sacraments work effectively and automatically
on whoever receives them).

• **1213** Holy Baptism is the basis of the whole Christian life,
the gateway to life in the Spirit and the door which gives
access to the other sacraments. Through baptism we are
freed from sin and reborn as sons of God; we become members of Christ, are incorporated into the Church and made

sharers in her mission. Baptism is the sacrament of regeneration through water in the word.

* **1227** The baptized have 'put on Christ'. Through the Holy Spirit, baptism is a bath that purifies, justifies and sanctifies.

* **1250** The baptism of infants. Born with a fallen human nature and tainted by original sin, children also have need of the new birth in baptism to be freed from the powers of darkness and brought into the realm of the freedom of the children of God to which all men are called. The sheer freedom of the grace of salvation is particularly manifest in infant baptism. The Church and the parents would deny a child the priceless grace of becoming a child of God were they not to give baptism shortly after birth.

* **1265** Baptism not only purifies from all sins but also makes the convert a new creature, an adopted son of God, who has become a 'partaker of the Divine Nature', a member of Christ and co-heir with him and a temple of the Holy Spirit.

The reader is left in no doubt that Roman Catholicism teaches that souls are born again, regenerated by the Holy Spirit, when they are baptised by a priest.

b) The following four objections are made against the view that the very act of baptism by a priest actually regenerates a soul.

i) The apostle Paul in all his writings says that salvation is to be received by repentance and faith. How can a person be saved? Paul says:

> The word is near you, even in your mouth and in your heart (that is, the word of faith which we preach): that if you confess with your mouth the Lord Jesus and believe

in your heart that God has raised Him from the dead, you
will be saved (Romans 10:8-9).

Towards the end of his life Paul summarised the basic
message of the gospel as:

Testifying to Jews, and also to Greeks, repentance
toward God and faith toward our Lord Jesus Christ (Acts
20:21).

But if it was baptism that actually saved and regenerated
people how could Paul say:

For Christ did not send me to baptize, but to preach the
gospel, not with wisdom of words, lest the cross of Christ
should be made of no effect (1 Corinthians 1:17).

If baptism is essential to salvation, as the Roman Catholic Church believes, how could Paul say it was not what
Christ had sent him to do? What is it that saves men? Paul
says it is the preaching of the cross of Christ, not the rite of
baptism. This was the reason why Paul gave priority to
preaching rather than to baptism.

ii) The Roman Catholic Church believes that John 3:5 refers to
baptism. But we need to understand that water baptism does
not compel the Holy Spirit to regenerate a person. If we look
at the context surrounding the verse we read that Jesus said:

Do not marvel that I said to you, 'You must be born again.'
The wind blows where it wishes, and you hear the sound of
it, but cannot tell where it comes from and where it goes.
So is everyone who is born of the Spirit (John 3:7-8).

Can we predict what the wind will do and which direction
it will take? Can we control the wind and make it obey our
commands? As we cannot control the wind, neither can

we control the Holy Spirit. Even though we use the sacrament of baptism we cannot control God the Holy Spirit and order him to regenerate whom we will. John said:

> But as many as received Him, to them He gave the right to become children of God, *even* to those who believe in His name: who were born, not of blood, nor of the will of the flesh, nor of the will of man, but of God (John 1:12-13).

It is God who sovereignly gives spiritual life to whom he will, not man, not the Church and not the priest. And notice that this right is given to those that believe in his name. The idea that a baby who can exercise neither repentance nor faith can automatically be regenerated by water baptism is quite foreign to the New Testament. No action of the Church can give a soul regeneration – that is the prerogative of God alone. The Church can ask God to bless its ministrations but it can never command him to do so.

iii) What then of the test of practical experience? Of the hundreds of thousands of baptized babies how many in adult life actually join the Church, follow Christ and show in their lives the fruits of holiness and the indwelling of the Holy Spirit? Only a tiny minority. The vast majority of baptized infants never become true believers or followers of Christ when they grow up. Experience shows that those who join the Church as adults on profession of faith are far more likely to prove true followers of Christ than those who are baptized as infants. Baptism does not in fact regenerate the soul. This is the work of the Holy Spirit alone who by working faith and repentance in our hearts brings us to spiritual rebirth.

iv) Some Christian denominations claim that since male children during the Old Testament era were circumcised it is right for all children of Christian families in New Testament times to be baptized. But baptism in the New

Testament, unlike circumcision in the Old Testament is always the consequence of repentance and faith, never the other way round. Peter says on the day of Pentecost to those who believed his message:

> Repent, and let every one of you be baptized in the name of Jesus Christ for the remission of sins; and you shall receive the gift of the Holy Spirit (Acts 2:38).

The same order is followed in every example of baptism in the Book of Acts, of which there are no fewer than nine – Acts 8:12,36; 9:18; 10:47; 16:15-39; 18:8; 19:5 and 22:16. In Old Testament times circumcision only admitted one to the outward benefits of the old covenant; it was no guarantee of salvation. Paul shows this clearly in Romans 2:25-29:

> For circumcision is indeed profitable if you keep the law; but if you are a breaker of the law, your circumcision has become uncircumcision ... For he is not a Jew who *is one* outwardly, nor *is* that circumcision which *is* outward in the flesh; but *he is* a Jew who *is one* inwardly, and circumcision *is that* of the heart, in the Spirit, *and* not in the letter; whose praise *is* not from men but from God.

If the outward sign of circumcision did not regenerate people in the Old Testament why should baptism in the New? Peter supports this view of baptism when he says:

> [Baptism now saves us] ... (not the removal of the filth of the flesh, but the answer of a good conscience toward God), through the resurrection of Jesus Christ (1 Peter 3:21).

Peter says that the water used to wash our bodies in baptism has no magical power to save us. The person being baptized must have the ingredients of faith and holiness for baptism to be of any value. There is no automatic guarantee of regeneration in the rite itself just as there was not in circumcision.

5 The signs that regeneration has taken place in our souls.

How may we know that we are regenerate, that we have experienced the new birth? If we say that we are true Christians and have received new life from God, how can we be sure that we are not deluding ourselves? The following are signs of the reality of regeneration.

i) **Faith** We believe that Jesus Christ is the Son of God

> Whoever believes that Jesus is the Christ is born of God (1 John 5:1).

> These things I have written to you who believe in the name of the Son of God, that you may know that you have eternal life ... (1 John 5:13). See also 1 John 4:15; 5:5.

ii) **Righteousness** We keep God's commandments

> Jesus answered and said to him, 'If anyone loves Me, he will keep My word ...' (John 14:23).

> Now by this we know that we know Him, if we keep His commandments (1 John 2:3). See also 1 John 1:6-7; 5:2-3.

iii) **The Spirit** We have received the Holy Spirit and are conscious of his presence.

The Holy Spirit is like the wind; we cannot see it but we can see its effects. The Holy Spirit makes us conscious of the fact that God is our Father and we are his children:

> For you did not receive the spirit of bondage again to fear, but you received the Spirit of adoption by whom we cry out, 'Abba, Father.' The Spirit Himself bears witness with our spirit that we are children of God (Romans 8:15-16).

> And by this we know that He abides in us, by the Spirit whom He has given us (1 John 3:24).

See also Galatians 4:6; 1 John 2:20, 27; 4:13.

iv) **Love** We love our Christian brothers and sisters.

> We know that we have passed from death to life, because we love the brethren. He who does not love *his* brother abides in death (1 John 3:14).

> Whoever believes that Jesus is the Christ is born of God, and everyone who loves Him who begot also loves him who is begotten of Him (1 John 5:1)

See also 1 John 2:9-11.

v) **The fight** We are conscious of the conflict of two natures within us. This is more than a struggle between good and evil; its a struggle between the Holy Spirit and Satan. There is a war going on within us as the Holy Spirit tries to make the Christian grow in holiness and the devil tempts him to sin. Paul recognises this:

> I say then: Walk in the Spirit, and you shall not fulfil the lust of the flesh. For the flesh lusts against the Spirit, and the Spirit against the flesh; and these are contrary to one another, so that you do not do the things that you wish (Galatians 5:16-17).

vi) **Hatred of sin** We hate our own sins. A feature of modern life today is the hatred that exists between nations, races, political parties and even football teams! We are quick to point out other people's faults and get very angry with their sins. This is often because of self-righteousness and blindness to our own sins and failures. The true Christian has seen himself as a guilty, hell-deserving sinner, so he has stopped pointing the finger at other people. He knows and acknowledges his own sins and weaknesses and he agrees whole-heartedly with Paul when he says:

> But I see another law in my members, warring against the law of my mind, and bringing me into captivity to the law of sin which is in my members. O wretched man that I am! Who will deliver me from this body of death? (Romans 7:23-24).

Paul agrees also with David when he says:

> Have mercy upon me, O God, according to Your lovingkindness; according to the multitude of Your tender mercies, blot out my transgressions. Wash me thoroughly from my iniquity, and cleanse me from my sin. For I acknowledge my transgressions, and my sin *is* ever before me. Against You, You only, have I sinned and done *this* evil in Your sight ... (Psalm 51:1-4).

vii) **God-centredness** We desire to know and love God more and more. Formerly we had been preoccupied with pleasing ourselves and satisfying the desires of the flesh and of the mind – we were completely self-centred. One of the first signs of the new birth is that all that begins to change and our thinking becomes God-centred.

> But what things were gain to me, these I have counted loss for Christ. But indeed I also count all things loss for the excellence of the knowledge of Christ Jesus my Lord, for whom I have suffered the loss of all things, and count them as rubbish, that I may gain Christ ... that I may know Him and the power of His resurrection, and the fellowship of His sufferings, being conformed to His death (Philippians 3:7-10).

As the deer pants for the water brooks, so pants my soul
for You, O God. My soul thirsts for God, for the living
God. When shall I come and appear before God? (Psalm
42:1-2).

viii) **Spiritual hunger** We hunger and thirst for righteousness. When we are born again we receive a new nature and
the indwelling of God the Holy Spirit. This radically alters
our desires. We want not only to be free from sin, but to be
like God, and to be with God. It has been said that the nine
beatitudes (Matthew 5:3-12) are the characteristics of the new
man in Christ. The fourth beatitude says:

Blessed *are* those who hunger and thirst for righteousness,
for they shall be filled (Matthew 5:6).

Conclusion If we know by experience something of the
reality of each of these eight biblical tests then we know that,
by grace, we have been born of God's Spirit and are indeed
heirs of God and joint-heirs with Christ.

Questions

1 How does regeneration differ from conversion?

2 Who is the author of regeneration in a person's soul?
Why do we call regeneration a mystery?

3 What are the signs that a person has been born again?

CHAPTER TEN

THE PERSON AND WORK OF THE HOLY SPIRIT

1 Another helper

2 He is a person, not a force

   a) He has personal qualities
   b) He has a personal ministry
   c) He has a personal effect on us
   d) He has a personal relationship with us

3 He is God, the third person of the Trinity

   a) He is equal to the Father and the Son
   b) He has divine qualities
   c) He is referred to as God

4 His relationship to other members of the Trinity

5 His work in the Old Testament

6 His work in the New Testament

7 The gifts of the Spirit

   a) 20th century developments
   b) The traditional Protestant view
   c) Spiritual gifts – general conclusions
   d) Spiritual gifts – guidance and warnings

The Bible says that the work of the Holy Spirit is essential and that nothing of spiritual worth can be done apart from him. Without his work:

Christ would not have risen from the dead – no resurrection
No one could be born again   – no Christians
No one could witness effectively   – no evangelism
The apostles would forget Christ's teaching – no Bible
There would be no spiritual gifts   – no power
There would be no fruits of the Spirit   – no life

(Romans 8:11; John 3:8; John 15:26,27; John 14:26; 1 Corinthians 12:7; Galatians 5:22-23).

1 Another helper

Before Jesus went to Calvary he met with his disciples for the last time in an upper room where he also instituted the meal that we call the Last Supper. He spoke to them about many things (John 13-16). He told them very plainly that he was about to leave them to return to his Father in heaven (John 13:1) where he was going to prepare a place for them (John 14:2). He promised not to abandon them like orphans (John 14:18) but that he would give them another Helper, the Spirit of truth, whom God the Father would send to take his place (John 14:16-18). The disciples were filled with alarm and foreboding at this awful news. How could they possibly carry on the work of Jesus without him? But Jesus was quite firm and surprised them still more by saying it was to their advantage that he went away (John 16:7); only then would the Helper (the Holy Spirit) come to them. This mysterious Person would do wonderful things through them that would convince the world of the truth of Jesus life and ministry (John 16:8-11). He would also teach them things, which at present they could neither understand nor receive:

> When He, the Spirit of truth, has come, He will guide you into all truth; for He will not speak on His own *authority*, but whatever He hears He will speak; and He will tell you things to come. He will glorify Me, for He will take of what is Mine and declare *it* to you (John 16:13-14)

Let us look at what the Bible tells us about the Helper, the Spirit of Truth, who would take Jesus' place after his return to heaven.

2 He is a person, not a force

a) He has personal qualities:

i) He has knowledge

> But God has revealed *them* to us through His Spirit. For the Spirit searches all things, yes, the deep things of God. For what man knows the things of a man except the spirit of the man which is in him? Even so no one knows the things of God except the Spirit of God (1 Corinthians 2:10-11).

ii) He has a mind

> Now He who searches the hearts knows what the mind of the Spirit is, because He makes intercession for the saints according to *the will of* God (Romans 8:27).

iii) He has a will

> But one and the same Spirit works all these things, distributing to each one individually as He wills. (1 Corinthians 12:11).

iv) He can be grieved

> And do not grieve the Holy Spirit of God, by whom you were sealed for the day of redemption (Ephesians 4:30).

v) He can be lied to

But Peter said, 'Ananias, why has Satan filled your heart to lie to the Holy Spirit and keep back *part* of the price of the land for yourself?' (Acts 5:3).

vi) He can be insulted

Of how much worse punishment, do you suppose, will he be thought worthy who has trampled the Son of God underfoot, counted the blood of the covenant by which he was sanctified a common thing, and insulted the Spirit of grace? (Hebrews 10:29).

vii) He intercedes for us

Likewise the Spirit also helps in our weaknesses. For we do not know what we should pray for as we ought, but the Spirit Himself makes intercession for us with groanings which cannot be uttered (Romans 8:26).

viii) He teaches us and guides us

However, when He, the Spirit of truth, has come, He will guide you into all truth; for He will not speak on His own *authority*, but whatever He hears He will speak; and He will tell you things to come (John 16:13).

ix) He leads us

For as many as are led by the Spirit of God, these are the sons of God (Romans 8:14).

x) He restrains us

Now when they had gone through Phrygia and the region of Galatia, they were forbidden by the Holy Spirit to preach the word in Asia (Acts 16:6).

xi) **He speaks to us**

He who has an ear, let him hear what the Spirit says to the churches (Revelation 2:7).

xii) **He searches our hearts**

But God has revealed *them* to us through His Spirit. For the Spirit searches all things, yes, the deep things of God (1 Corinthians 2:10).

xiii) **He gives spiritual gifts**

But one and the same Spirit works all these things, distributing to each one individually as He wills (1 Corinthians 12:11).

xiv) **He shows us what he wants us to do**

And as they ministered to the Lord and fasted, the Holy Spirit said, 'Now separate to Me Barnabas and Saul for the work to which I have called them' (Acts 13:2).

b) He has a personal ministry. Jesus told his followers that he was sending someone to look after them who would be like a parent to them. This helper would always be with them (John 14:16), to teach them (John 14:26) guide them (John 16:13) and reveal the things of Christ to them (John 16:14). In John Chapters 13-16 Jesus refers thirteen times to the helper as 'he', so the disciples realised that it was someone who was coming to help them, not something. Peter also says that the Holy Spirit cares personally for the well being of believers (Acts 15:28).

c) He has a personal effect on us. When someone becomes a believer it is through the power of the Holy Spirit that he is made a new person (2 Corinthians 5:17). New qualities begin to appear in his life; these are called 'the fruit of the Spirit'. They are the direct result of God the Holy Spirit dwelling in the heart of the newborn person producing 'love, joy, peace, longsuffering, kindness, goodness, faithfulness, gentleness, self control' (Galatians 5:22-23). We all know what happens when children at school get into bad company – bad language and bad behaviour begin to appear. The personal influence of the Holy Spirit in our hearts replicates his own holy character within us. He makes us like himself (2 Corinthians 3:18).

d) He has a personal relationship with us. We know that both the Father and the Son are persons and that they have a deep personal interest in, and concern for, us. The Bible says that the same is also true of the Holy Spirit, because he has a personal relationship with every believer. This is as true for the Holy Spirit as for the other persons of the Trinity:

> The grace of the Lord Jesus Christ, and the love of God, and the communion of the Holy Spirit *be* with you all. Amen (2 Corinthians 13:14)

3 He is God, the third person of the Trinity

a) He is equal to the Father and the Son. Just before Jesus was taken up into heaven he gave his final commands to his disciples. He speaks of the Holy Spirit being equal to the Father and to the Son and therefore divine:

> Go therefore and make disciples of all the nations, baptizing them in the name of the Father and of the Son and of the Holy Spirit (Matthew 28:19).

b) He has divine qualities.

i) He is eternal

How much more shall the blood of Christ, who through the eternal Spirit offered Himself without spot to God, purge your conscience from dead works to serve the living God? (Hebrews 9:14).

ii) He is omnipresent

Where can I go from your Spirit? Or where can I flee from Your presence? If I ascend into heaven, You are there; if I make my bed in hell, behold, You *are there* (Psalm 139:7-8).

iii) He is omnipotent

And the angel answered and said unto her, '*The* Holy Spirit will come upon you, and the power of the Highest will overshadow you; therefore, also, that Holy One who is to be born will be called the Son of God' (Luke 1:35).

iv) He is omniscient

For what man knows the things of a man except the spirit of the man which is in him? Even so no one knows the things of God except the Spirit of God (1 Corinthians 2:11).

c) He is referred to as God in the Acts of the Apostles. When Peter spoke to Ananias and Sapphira about the offerings that they said they had made, he said:

Why has Satan filled your heart to lie to the Holy Spirit? …You have not lied to men but to God (Acts 5:3-4).

4 His relationship to other members of the Trinity

Each member of the Trinity works in perfect unity and co-operation with the other two. Whatever they do they do harmoniously together. This is beautifully illustrated in Romans 8: 26-27 where the Holy Spirit and the Father both work co-operatively together to help us in our prayers. The Father searches our hearts, while the Spirit speaks (intercedes) to the Father about the needs we have and the petitions we make. The Father, the Son and the Holy Spirit each have their own distinctive part to fulfil in accomplishing our salvation.

i) The Father *planned* salvation by sending his Son.

> And we have seen and testify that the Father has sent the Son as Saviour of the world (1 John 4:14; see also Galatians 4:4).

ii) The Son *accomplished* salvation by dying on the cross.

> I have glorified You on the earth. I have finished the work which You have given Me to do (John 17:4).

iii) The Holy Spirit *applies* salvation to all who truly believe.

> Now we have received, not the spirit of the world, but the Spirit who is from God, that we might know the things that are freely given to us by God (1 Corinthians 2:12).

> The Spirit Himself bears witness with our spirit that we are children of God (Romans 8:16).

iv) The Holy Spirit *proceeds* from the Father and the Son. For the purposes of man's salvation the Holy Spirit subordinates himself to them both:

> But when the Helper comes, whom I shall send to you from the Father, the Spirit of truth who proceeds from the Father, He will testify of Me (John 15:26).

> Nevertheless I tell you the truth. It is to your advantage that I go away; for if I do not go away, the Helper will not come to you; but if I depart, I will send Him to you (John 16:7).

v) • The Father is the fullness of the Godhead, invisible.
   • The Son is the fullness of the Godhead, visible.
   • The Spirit is the fullness of the Godhead active in salvation.

5 His work in the Old Testament

Before Pentecost his work was limited to certain tasks and was not widespread. However, a day would come when he would be poured out on all flesh (Joel 2:28), but this could not happen until New Testament times. Although he was in true believers, as David says (Psalm 51:11), we mostly read of him coming upon men to accomplish things that God wanted them to do.

He came upon leaders, judges and kings.

i) *Leaders*: Moses, Joshua, and seventy elders

> Then I will come down and talk with you there. I will take of the Spirit that *is* upon you and will put *the same* upon them; and they shall bear the burden of the people with you, that you may not bear *it* yourself alone (Numbers 11:17).

ii) *Judges*: Othniel, Gideon, Jephthah and Samuel

> The Spirit of the LORD came upon him [Othniel], and he judged Israel (Judges 3:10).

> But the Spirit of the LORD came upon Gideon; then he blew the trumpet, and the Abiezrites gathered behind him (Judges 6:34). See also Judges 11: 29; 13:25.

iii) *King David*

Then Samuel took the horn of oil and anointed him in the midst of his brothers; and the Spirit of the LORD came upon David from that day forward (1 Samuel 16:13).

He was given to skilled craftsmen working on the Tabernacle.

I have filled him [Bezaleel] with the Spirit of God, in wisdom, in understanding, in knowledge, and in all *manner of* workmanship (Exodus 31:3).

He came upon the prophets of Israel and Judah.

Yet for many years you had patience with them, and testified against them by Your Spirit in Your prophets. Yet they would not listen (Nehemiah 9:30).

For prophecy never came by the will of man, but holy men of God spoke *as they were* moved by the Holy Spirit (2 Peter 1:21; see also 1 Peter 1:10-11).

He was active in the creation of the world.

In the beginning God created the heavens and the earth. The earth was without form, and void; and darkness *was* on the face of the deep. And the Spirit of God was hovering upon the face of the waters (Genesis 1:1-2).

6 His work in the New Testament

Jesus had promised his disciples that when he left them the Holy Spirit, the Helper, would come as his replacement and dwell among them as soon as he had gone back into heaven. The Helper would glorify the absent Christ in the following ways:

- He will teach them the true meaning of what Christ had taught and cause them to remember all that Christ said (John 14:26).
- He will help them to proclaim Christ (John 15:27).
- He will guide them into all truth (John 16:13).
- He will reveal to them things to come (John 16:13).
- He will be with them forever and be in them (John 14:16-17).
- He will give them power to witness boldly and effectively (Acts 1:8).

The Holy Spirit is sometimes called the 'hidden' member of the Trinity because he never speaks about himself but only of Christ. His role is to teach men and women about Jesus Christ, to focus their minds on him and his great salvation:

> He will not speak on his own *authority*, but whatever He hear He will speak; and He will tell you things to come. He will glorify Me, for He will take of what is Mine and declare *it* to you (John 16:13-14).

The Holy Spirit's 'floodlight' ministry to glorify Jesus. Sometimes we see historic buildings or great cathedrals beautifully illuminated at night by the use of floodlights. For the purposes of salvation the relationship of the Holy Spirit to Jesus Christ is similar to that of floodlights. Jesus said of the Spirit, 'He will glorify Me.' Just as the bright beams of the floodlights cut through the surrounding darkness to reveal the glories of a beautiful building, so the Holy Spirit wants to reveal to us the glories of Christ. If the floodlights could speak they would say, 'Don't look at us, look at the building!' There is a dangerous tendency today among some Christians to be so preoccupied with the manifestations and gifts of the Holy Spirit that they lose sight of the centrality that should always be given to 'Jesus Christ and Him cruci-fied'. We need to remember that pre-eminence is always given to Christ both by the Holy Spirit and by the Scrip-tures themselves. The church at Corinth had fallen into this modern error, so when Paul visited them in order to regulate their life he had to say, 'I determined not to know anything among you except Jesus Christ and Him crucified.' (1 Corinthians 2:2). The Holy Spirit is given us to glorify Christ, 'that in all things He may have the pre-eminence' (Colossians 1:18).

The missionary plan of the Holy Spirit. In Matthew chapter 24 Jesus tells his disciples about the major events which will happen to Jerusalem and to the world before his Second Coming. Concerning the preaching of the gospel he says, 'This gospel of the kingdom will be preached in all the world for a witness to all the nations, and the end will come' (v 14).

By the time of his Second Coming there will be believers in every part of the world whom his angels will rescue from the impending judgement, 'And He will send His angels with a great sound of a trumpet, and they will gather together His elect from the four winds, from one end of heaven to the other' (v 31).

From these verses and from other parts of the Bible we learn two things about the missionary plan of the Holy Spirit:

i) Before the end of the world the gospel will have been preached to every nation.
ii) In every part of the world there will be those who have believed the gospel and are saved.

In view of these facts, what is the Holy Spirit's plan? It is simply to ensure that by the end of this present age he has achieved these two things:

i) The gospel has been sent to every nation.
ii) God's elect have been gathered out of all the nations.

The unfolding of the Holy Spirit's missionary plans in the book of Acts. The Holy Spirit came upon the 120 disciples in the upper room with great power and in dramatic fashion – a rushing mighty wind and tongues of fire: 'And they were all filled with the Holy Spirit and began to speak with other tongues, as the Spirit gave them utterance' (Acts 2:4).

This wonderful manifestation of divine power could not be contained in a small room, but spilled over into Jerusalem in a spontaneous overflow of gospel proclamation in as many languages as there were foreigners dwelling in the city at that time. The result was truly amazing. In a few minutes 3,000 people were converted, the Church had been born and a new age, the age of the Holy Spirit, had dawned! The Holy Spirit is the Spirit of mission!

After establishing the new church in Jerusalem the Spirit sent Philip northwards to preach the gospel to the Samaritans. Many believed the message and were themselves filled with the Holy Spirit (Acts 8:17). Next the Spirit sent Philip southwards towards Gaza where he met an Ethiopian court official on his way home: 'Then the Spirit said, 'Go near and overtake this chariot'... Then Philip opened his mouth and beginning at this Scripture, preached Jesus to him.' (Acts 8:27-39) The Ethiopian believed, was baptized, and returned to preach the gospel in Ethiopia – this was all part of the Spirit's plan to spread the gospel to Ethiopia.

As the result of a sudden outbreak of persecution in Jerusalem the church was scattered, and the believers went everywhere preaching the gospel. In Cyprus, Phoenicia and Syrian Antioch their testimony was blessed and many believed and were saved. Barnabas and Paul spent a year at Antioch helping the new church which had been formed there. Then the Spirit told the church to send these two men westwards on a missionary journey to Cyprus and then on to Asia Minor (modern Turkey).

... the Holy Spirit said, 'Now separate to Me Barnabas and Saul for the work to which I have called them' ... So being sent out by the Holy Spirit, they went down to Seleucia and from there they sailed to Cyprus (Acts 13:2,4).

This journey was successful and several churches were established in these new areas. The remaining chapters of the Book of Acts show the Holy Spirit guiding Paul and his helpers from place to place until the gospel was established even in Europe. Sometimes the missionaries' thinking did not accord with God's will. So we read that they were 'forbidden by the Holy Spirit to speak the word in Asia' (i.e. Asia Minor). Then they tried to go to Bithynia 'but the Spirit did not permit them' (Acts 16:6-7). The Holy Spirit was firmly in control of all true missionary endeavour in the time of the early Church and it has been so ever since. God the Father and God the Son have commissioned the Holy Spirit to be responsible for spreading the good news to all nations until that day when Jesus will come again.

The Spirit's work in the believer. We have already seen that the Holy Spirit has been given the great responsibility of putting into effect the salvation achieved by Christ on Calvary's cross. By his mighty power the Holy Spirit caused 3000 souls to repent and believe when the first sermon of the Church was preached at Pentecost. He is the dynamic behind all true missionary work, and is instrumental in bringing the gospel both to nations and also to individuals. Even in large evangelistic crusades where many thousands are present the response to the message has to be a personal one, every one must repent and believe for themselves; so the Holy Spirit is active in the salvation of every single sinner who is ever converted. Jesus tried to explain the necessity of the new birth to Nicodemus, and emphasized that this was solely the work of the Holy Spirit:

> Do not marvel that I said to you, 'You must be born again.'
> The wind blows where it wishes, and you hear the sound of
> it, but cannot tell where it comes from and where it goes.
> So is everyone who is born of the Spirit (John 3:7-8).

But how does the Holy Spirit bring about this radical spiritual transformation in a person's soul whereby they pass from death to life? And is that the end of the story; does he leave them to live the Christian life all on their own? By no means! The Holy Spirit is responsible for the conception, birth and development of every Christian soul. Paul says, I am '... confident of this very thing, that He who has begun a good work in you will complete it until the day of Christ'. (Philippians 1:6). This reminds us of the promise Jesus made to his disciples about the Helper he would send to them; he would be with them forever, 'I will not leave you orphans; I will come to you.' (John 14:18). The Holy Spirit is with us from the cradle to the grave; he who began our salvation will also complete it; whom he saves he also sanctifies.

The Bible clearly teaches that God's work in our salvation has several parts or stages to it. For example Paul says:

> We know that all things work together for good to those
> who love God, to those who are the called according to
> *His* purpose. For whom he foreknew, He also predestined
> *to be* conformed to the image of His Son, that He might
> be the firstborn among many brethren. Moreover whom
> He predestined, these He also called; whom He called,
> these He also justified; and whom He justified, these He
> also glorified (Romans 8:28-30).

In these verses Paul lists five of these stages:
- Foreknowledge
- Predestination
- Calling
- Justification
- Glorification

Is this a complete list? It would appear that it is not intended to be, because Paul is speaking particularly about the certainty of the Christian's hope of future glory. He therefore leaves a large gap between justification and its goal, glorification. For example Paul fully believed that a man must be born again (see Ephesians 2:1-5), yet he makes no mention of it in his list. Likewise he fully believed in repentance (see Acts 20:21) but he does not mention it either. As we read the New Testament we discover a number of important doctrines that must be added to Paul's list in order to complete the full scope of God's work in salvation. These are:

- Foreknowledge
- Predestination
- Calling
- Justification
- Regeneration and conversion
- Adoption
- Repentance and faith
- Assurance
- Sanctification
- Perseverance
- Glorification

Christian theologians differ as to what the precise order should be, but the chronological order is not so important as the reality of the doctrines themselves, because several of these subjects occur simultaneously. What we can say is that because all of them take place in every believer, and are mentioned in the Bible, they deserve to be understood and appreciated by us all.

7 The gifts of the Spirit

a) Twentieth century developments

i) **Pentecostalism.** From 1900 to 1960 only the Pentecostal churches believed that all the spiritual gifts listed in the New Testament are still available (Romans 12:4-8; 1 Corinthians 12:4-11; 28-31; Ephesians 4:8-13; 1 Peter 4:10-11). The four basic beliefs of these churches are:

• **Spirit baptism.** A post-conversion experience called 'the baptism in the Holy Spirit' in which a person receives the full measure of the Spirit; this is evidenced by speaking in tongues. He is now empowered for witness and service.

• **Spiritual gifts.** As a direct result of this experience the person receives one or more of the spiritual gifts.

• **Miraculous healing.** Some sections of the worldwide Pentecostal movement regard illness as Satanic in its origin and its effects. To be ill is therefore a sign of the dominion of evil; some even say that God cannot use illness to correct, chasten or humble his children because all sickness is the work of the devil. Pentecostals quote the verse, 'Jesus Christ is the same yesterday, today, and forever' (Hebrews 13: 8) as proving that he can heal all sickness today just as he did two thousand years ago.

• **The holiness experience.** One of Pentecostalism's mottos is, 'Jesus Christ, Healer and Sanctifier'. Sanctification is not regarded as a process, as historic Protestantism has taught, but a crisis-experience of great emotional impact and significance.

ii) **The Charismatic Movement.** Since 1960 the popularity of tongues, spiritual gifts, healing and prophecy has spread

rapidly into all Protestant denominations and even mar-
ginally into Roman Catholicism. This is now known as
'The Charismatic Movement', so called because the word
'charisma' is the Greek word for a spiritual gift. Its basic
beliefs are:

A Spirit baptism evidenced by:

• **Speaking in tongues**
• **The exercise of spiritual gifts**
• **Congregational 'worship in the Spirit'.** The style of
worship is uninhibited, strongly emotional and unstructured.
Singing, praying and prophesying with arm-waving and
even dancing may continue uninterrupted for long periods
of time to the accompaniment of modern beat-music. The
sole object of this is to praise and worship the Father, the
Son and the Holy Spirit with as much feeling as possible.
Anyone can contribute and use their spiritual gifts; the
atmosphere is relaxed and happy, humorous and friendly.
Complete informality replaces reverence and reserve so that
everybody feels free to join in.
• **The belief that the Charismatic movement is God's strat-
egy of renewal.** Many charismatics believe that these four
elements of Charismatic renewal are God's way of reviving
his Church today. To deny this is to quench and grieve the
Holy Spirit.

iii) **Restorationism .** One offshoot of the Charismatic movement is known as 'Restorationism'. Restorationists believe
the same things as Charismatics but go a step further.
They have a radical view about themselves as separate and
distinct from all other Christian denominations. They believe
that through them alone God is restoring to his Church, in
these days, new apostles and prophets through whom he will
work to restore his kingdom pending the Second Coming
of Christ. Restorationism sees itself as the one true Church,

the answer to all denominations which are doomed to die away. The key to understanding Restorationism is its view of eschatology and its part in God's plan for the last days. In addition to the five characteristics of Charismatic renewal Restorationists believe the following:

- A worldwide end-time revival is near.
- Apostles and prophets are now restored to the Church.
- Missionary teams obedient to the apostles will evangelise the whole world.
- Strict obedience to the apostles is required from all members in every area of life including marriage, work and home.
- The end of all denominations is near.

These three groupings, Pentecostal, Charismatic and Restorationist, believe that all the spiritual gifts mentioned in the New Testament are current and therefore are God's will for his Church today.

b) The traditional Protestant view. Since the Reformation, Protestant denominations have believed that the gifts of the Spirit for carrying on the life of the Church and its ministry are still given, but that the supernatural or miraculous gifts ceased when the last of the apostles died. Calvinistic theologians pointed out that miracles are always connected with times of revelation. In the Old Testament miracles were associated with those who were given the task of revealing God's will – prophets like Moses, Elijah and Elisha. In the New Testament, pre-eminently, Jesus did many 'signs' that proved his claim to be the Messiah. 'If I do not do the works of My Father, do not believe Me' (John 10:37). His chosen apostles also worked miracles because they were agents of revelation, i.e. those who revealed God's will. Paul says of his ministry:

> The signs of an apostle were accomplished among you
> with all perseverance, in signs and wonders and mighty
> deeds (2 Corinthians 12:12).

The writer of the Letter to the Hebrews says of the apostles:

> God also bearing witness both with signs and wonders,
> with various miracles, and gifts of the Holy Spirit, accord-
> ing to His own will (Hebrews 2:4).

In other words, miracles were given by God to show that
the apostles were truly sent by him. Miracles were given,
not to excite interest, but to prove that these men were
indeed true servants of God. Since the New Testament
revelation has been completed, there is no further need for
any fresh miracles to authenticate it. Paul describes the ministry of the apostles and prophets as laying the foundation
of the Church (Ephesians 2:20); once a foundation is laid and
the building erected there is no longer any need for more
foundations. Since God has no new truths to reveal there is
no need for miracles to authenticate them. Those who still
seek for signs and wonders are really wanting further proof
from God that his word is true; for them the Bible on its own
is not enough. The Roman Catholic Church is an example
of this. It claims that the Pope is in a direct line of descent
from the apostle Peter and therefore that its apostolate is a
continuing one. The Pope claims that fresh revelations are
still given to the Church; e.g., the Immaculate Conception, the
Assumption of Mary, the infallibility of the Pope etc. Roman
Catholicism teaches that the Bible is not sufficient; an infallible apostolic Church to interpret the Bible is also needed.
Especially in the Middle Ages it also claimed to produce
various types of wonders and miracles. The Roman Catholic
attitude to the Bible, until the late twentieth century, is
highly significant: it always withheld the Scriptures from the
people on the grounds that the Church, its priests and its
sacraments were sufficient for salvation. False apostles then

as now always want complete obedience to their own teachings. They discourage any independent interest in the Bible,
fearing that this will threaten their own claims to absolute
authority.

c) Spiritual gifts — general conclusions. Our own view is
that none of the aforementioned views is completely correct
or without fault.

Firstly, there is no clear teaching in the New Testament
that certain spiritual gifts i.e., the super-natural ones, were
not given to ordinary church members (1 Corinthians 12:4-
11) but were the special preserve of apostles.

Secondly, there is no mention that the gifts were exclusively for the apostolic period and therefore were of a temporary nature. The gifts are given for the whole Church period
by the Holy Spirit. For example the prophecy of Joel, which
Peter quotes in his sermon on the day of Pentecost (Acts 2:17-
21), refers to an era called 'the last days', the new era of the
Holy Spirit and the Church, not just to the Day of Pentecost.
It also mentions a general outpouring of the Spirit upon all
God's servants, not simply the apostles themselves.

Thirdly, the fact that God used signs and wonders to confirm his word (Hebrews 2:4) in apostolic times, does not mean
that God cannot do so again according to his own sovereign
will. Evidence of this is not lacking in the history of Christian
missions throughout the past eighteen hundred years; what
he has done in the past he is able to do today.

Fourthly, the rapid decline in supernatural activity after
the first century AD may well be due to heretical teachings
and the institutionalisation of the Church, rather than to the
cessation of supernatural gifts.

Fifthly, apostles and prophets have not been restored to
the modern Church.
Ephesians 2:19-20 shows that the foundation that they laid
is the New Testament which they wrote in the first century

and upon which the Church is now built. Once the apostles and prophets had fulfilled their unique commission their role ceased, so there are no more apostles and prophets today.

The word 'apostle' (sent one) is used in two main senses:
i) Those immediately commissioned by Christ as his special witnesses; the Twelve, Paul and James the brother of Christ.
ii) Those who, though not immediately commissioned by Christ, preached the gospel in close association with the apostles as their delegates and co-workers: Barnabas (Acts 14:4); Titus (2 Corinthians 8:23); Timothy and Silvanus (1 Thessalonians 2:6); Epaphroditus (Philippians 2:25), who did pioneer missionary work and planted churches. The special qualifications of the first type of apostle were that they were:

- Chosen and commissioned personally by Christ (Mark 3:13-19).
- Eyewitnesses of his resurrection (Acts 1:21-26).
- Given power to work miracles (Matthew 10:1; 2 Corinthians 12:12).
- Given universal authority (Matthew 28:18-20; Acts 26:16-18).
- Inspired to write Scripture (John 14:26; 2 Peter 3:15-16).

Today some Charismatic churches contend that the apostles and prophets mentioned in Ephesians 4:11 are still necessary for the spread of the gospel. They believe that the apostles described in the secondary sense are still functioning in the Church today as pioneer missionary workers and church-planters. By calling their leaders 'apostles' people can easily be confused into thinking that these 'apostles' have a status and an authority equal to that of Peter or Paul! We believe that this is quite misleading and therefore it is completely wrong to call anyone today an apostle. The prophet in the New Testament was subservient to the apostles and Paul wrote to the Corinthians laying down rules regulating their role in the Church (1 Corinthians 14:29-33). They were occasional organs of the Holy Spirit, sometimes predicting future events (Acts 11:28; 21:11-19), but mostly preaching to and exhorting believers (1 Corinthians 14:3). Unlike the infallible prophets of the Old Testament period, these spoke only to personal and local situations and their messages could be tested by other prophets (1 Corinthians 14:29). Their role therefore was less exalted than that of their Old Testament forbears.

d) Spiritual gifts — guidance and warnings

Modern misunderstandings of prophecy, tongues and healing.

Prophecy. We have already given the reasons why we believe New Testament apostles and prophets were unique and were given by God to lay the foundations of his Church (Ephesians 2:20; 3:5); as such these two offices passed away with the New Testament age. In Charismatic churches today some people think they are inspired by God in almost the same way as Old Testament prophets. Consequently they preface what they say in meetings with the words, 'The Lord says ... ' or 'Hear, O my children ... ' This is meant to give the impression that God is actually speaking through them! The prophet in New Testament times did not speak infallible Scripture, his words had to be tested by others (1 Corinthians 14:29). In this respect he was inferior to the Old Testament prophets whose words were directly inspired and are recorded in the Bible as infallible scripture. Paul says that all such words that are given as 'prophecies' must be tested and not treated as infallible words of God (1 Thessalonians 5:20-21).

Tongues. Paul says, '... he who speaks in a tongue does not speak to men but to God, for no one understands *him*;

however, in the spirit he speaks mysteries '(1 Corinthians 14:2). But in Acts 2:11 when the apostles were publicly praising God they did so in foreign languages that they did not understand. We know that they were ordinary languages because the people in the crowd from foreign countries were all able to understand what they were saying! It would appear that these were human languages that could be understood, whereas the tongues mentioned in Paul's letter to the Corinthians were altogether different and were in a language that no one understood! The rules that Paul lays down for tongues being used in public meetings (1 Corinthians 14) are frequently ignored today:

- Not everyone has the gift of tongues (1 Corinthians 12:30), yet some people teach we should all speak in tongues.
- If no interpreter is present the person with the gift of tongues should be silent (14:28).
- No more than three utterances with tongues is allowed in a church service (14:27), therefore whole congregations singing in tongues is prohibited.

No gift of the Spirit is easier to counterfeit than tongues. Why? Because no one knows what is being said! In many churches today tongues are not being used to praise God, as in the Bible, but when interpreted, to give instructions to the church. This is wrong.

It is important to remember that in 1 Corinthians 14:21, 22 Paul says that tongues were a fulfilment of God's prophecy to the Jews (Isaiah 28:11,12) that a time would come when he would no longer speak to them in Hebrew but in other languages. Why? Because God's word would be taken from the Jews and sent to the Gentile nations. Tongues on the Day of Pentecost and subsequently were a sign of this, a transition from the old to the new covenant era. Tongues was therefore a revelatory sign of the apostolic era and disappeared completely thereafter, as the great Patristic theologians Chrysostom and Augustine specifically said that they had by their times.

Present day tongue speakers claim they are enjoying communicating with God in a mystical non-rational way and quote the verse 'my spirit prays, but my understanding is unfruitful' (1 Corinthians 14:14), and they claim that this edifies them (verse 4). The great biblical test that Jesus gave to check all claims of true spirituality was 'You will know them (i.e. false prophets) by their fruits' (Matthew 7:16). Do their words agree with his Word and do their lives conform to his teaching? Sadly, many tongue-speakers today are talking more about tongues than about Christ, and selfishly seek ecstatic emotional experiences only for their own self-gratification, not for the good of others or of the church. It is extremely dangerous to try to by-pass the mind in order to enjoy mystical feelings. Like drug addicts such people become more and more dependent on feelings and become depressed whenever they cannot find the satisfaction they crave. Much tongue speaking today is taught by evangelists who tell people to sing sounds not words, and that this will progress to true, though non-rational, praise. It is a learnt psychological phenomenon but has no resemblance to the tongues in 1 Corinthians 14.

Healing. Some churches today teach that physical healing is part of the atonement. This is because Matthew 8:16-17 quotes from Isaiah 53:4 in relation to Jesus' healing ministry. Now Isaiah 53 is the most famous chapter in the Old Testament prophesying about Christ's work of atonement and the spiritual healing he gives us. Does this mean therefore that physical healing is also in the atonement? When Peter quotes from Isaiah 53 he makes it clear that the healing being referred to is our sin not our sicknesses (1 Peter 2:24). This prophecy about Christ predicts his suffering for sinners on the cross as well as his earthly ministry to the sick and suffering of his own day. The New Testament everywhere promises full forgiveness of sins through Christ but, very significantly, it does not also promise complete healing and perfect health as well. Concerning the biblical teaching on physical healing and health we need to remember the following points:

i) With the rest of humanity Christians also inherit from the Fall of Adam, a body that Paul calls 'the body of this death', which is subject to age, decay, disease and death. Christians are exempt from none of these things; we all know pain and illness, the decay of old age and eventually death.

ii) Illness is not always due to sin or a lack of faith in God's power to heal. Consider the following examples from Scripture:

* Job was not bereaved or sick because of sin but because God allowed Satan to test his faith in God (Job 1:6-12).
* Paul had a 'thorn in his flesh' (his body) to keep him humble (2 Corinthians 12:7), probably an eye disease (Galatians 4:13-15).
* David was afflicted that he might be obedient to God's Law (Ps 119:67). See also Ps 107:17-19.
* A blind man whom Jesus healed was not blind because of sin, but to be an example of Jesus' healing power (John 9:3).

iii) Illness is sometimes a punishment for sin and healing can only come through repentance and the 'prayer of faith' (James 5:15).

* The disobedient Christians in Corinth (1 Corinthians 5:5; 11:29-30) and Thyatira (Revelation 2:22) were punished with sickness.
* The man healed at the pool of Bethesda (John 5:14) was warned by Jesus not to sin anymore or else something worse would happen.

iv)   Illness can come through over-work and not because of any sin. Epaphroditus is an example (Philippians 2:27-30).

v) When God made the world he made it 'very good'. There are herbs and fruit and minerals in it which have healing properties and can be used as good medicine for healing our illnesses. Using medicine prayerfully is not a lack of faith.

vi) As children of our Father in heaven we can always ask for God to lay his healing hand upon us but we can never demand it! God sometimes has good and sanctifying reasons for allowing us to be ill. Jesus, our perfect pattern and example, prayed ... 'O My Father… not as I will, but as You will' (Matthew 26:39). We should always do the same.

vii) One day, when the Lord Jesus returns, there will be 'new heavens and a new earth' (2 Peter 3:13). In that new world there will be no sickness, pain, or death (Revelation 21:4). But now we as believers live in a world that groans under the curse of God, and in this world we 'groan within ourselves, eagerly waiting for the adoption, the redemption of our body' (Romans 8:22-23).

Not everything described in the Bible is also commanded .
Not everything that is described in the Bible is commanded by God to be done by us today. Nowhere does the New Testament say that all Christians must speak in tongues, nor that because some people spoke in tongues when the Spirit fell upon them in the Book of Acts, everyone who is filled with the Spirit today must also speak in tongues. Paul says that tongues is a separate spiritual gift that is not given to all (1 Corinthians 12:30; 14:29-30). Apart from Pentecost, the three examples where tongues followed the gift of the Holy Spirit in the Book of Acts were clearly exceptional events, witnessing to the fact that God was adding three new classes of people into his Church; the Samaritans (Acts 8), the

Gentiles (Acts 10) and the followers of John the Baptist (Acts 19). The fact that Christians in Acts 4 practised the sharing of private property (to meet a need at that particular time) is not a command for all Christians to do the same in all ages and circumstances. If God wanted us to follow their example and abolish all private property, he would surely have given specific commands for us to do so.

The danger of pride. Spiritual gifts were not given to make Christians famous or admired like a film star! Nor were they given to make us individualists but rather to promote the unity, growth and edification of the church: 'But the manifestation of the Spirit is given to each one for the profit of all' (1 Corinthians 12:7). The Corinthian Christians had misused their spiritual gifts and instead of helping the church they had become a source of pride, arrogance and division. They can do so again today. The answer is not to suppress spiritual gifts but for the elder of a church to see that they are used correctly for mutual edification and love.

Test the spirits. No person exercising a spiritual gift should resist or object to being tested and checked by other Christians. The prophets at Corinth were specially told to submit their utterances to the judgement of others (1 Corinthians 14:29). Paul told the churches to test all prophetic utterances in case Satan deceived them (1 Thessalonians 5:21). John told us to test the spirits because many false spirits are in the world (1 John 4:1). Spiritual pride can deceive us into thinking that because we have a spiritual gift we are not answerable to the church but only to God. This is completely wrong.

The Word of God is our only infallible guide. Everything that we do must be judged by the Scriptures. The Word of God is our only authority: all our spiritual feelings, our dreams, visions, words of prophecy, etc. must be tested by the Bible:

> Whoever transgresses and does not abide in the
> doctrine of Christ does not have God. He who abides in
> the doctrine of Christ has both the Father and the Son
> (2 John 9)

> He who rejects Me, and does not receive My words, has
> that which judges him – the word I have spoken will judge
> him in the last day (John 12:48).

The Holy Spirit decides what gifts to give. The Holy Spirit is God. He is the One who determines to whom he will give his gifts, when and where. He is not obliged to give all His gifts to the Church in every period of history. Because there are approximately twenty-seven gifts listed in the New Testament this does not mean that we need all of them in every local church! The Holy Spirit alone knows to whom to give his gifts and for what purpose. He knows which ones are needed most at any particular time and place. He is the Spirit of wisdom and works infallibly according to his own will:

> But one and the same Spirit works all these things,
> distributing to each one individually as He wills
> (1 Corinthians 12:11).

Submission to the Spirit. We are not encouraged to seek those gifts which are most spectacular, but those which are most useful to the church (1 Corinthians 14:1-5). We may, and indeed should, seek to help the church by receiving and using a spiritual gift – we may ask but we can never demand. What we receive is the Holy Spirit's prerogative; he knows best and we must accept his will both for ourselves and for the church. Our desire must always be to serve Christ in a spirit of humility, thankfulness and love. If our motives are right we will not go astray in seeking spiritual gifts.

Is there a baptism in the Spirit? Pentecostal and Charismatic Christians believe that there is a two-stage work
of the Spirit in the believer, the second stage being called
'baptism in the Holy Spirit'. This teaching is based on the fact
that the disciples, who already believed in Jesus (John 17:8,12),
and had some measure of the Holy Spirit (John 20:22), were
baptised in the Spirit on the day of Pentecost. This was in
fulfilment of the prophecy that Jesus would baptise with the
Holy Spirit and with fire (Luke 3:16; Acts 1:4-5). They also
say that what happened to the first Gentile convert, Cornelius, was an example of a believer being baptised with the
Spirit (Acts 11:16). But nowhere else in the New Testament
is a two-stage work of the Spirit mentioned. The idea that
there is something lacking or defective in the work of the
Spirit at conversion, that requires a further work to enable
us to witness effectively, has no support in Scripture. What
we can say is that the disciples were the only believers who
could ever experience a two-stage work of the Spirit simply
because they were the only ones who believed in Jesus before
Pentecost! Cornelius, although a good man and a worshipper
of God, had not received or believed the gospel so he cannot
be regarded as a reliable model to prove that every believer
must have a two-stage experience of the Spirit. Paul clearly
teaches the very opposite!

> For by one Spirit we were all baptised into one body –
> whether Jews or Greeks, whether slaves or free – and have
> all been made to drink into one Spirit (1 Corinthians 12:13).

Yet Pentecostalism bases its teaching on a post-conversion
work of the Spirit entirely on these four examples. The
Christian is told to walk in the Spirit, be led by the Spirit,
bring forth the fruits of the Spirit (Galatians 5:16-23) and be
constantly filled with the Spirit (Ephesians 5:18). There is
no teaching in any of the epistles where we are told to be
baptised in the Spirit. There is only one baptism with the
Spirit but there can be many fillings.

The new gospel of health and wealth. During the past forty years a new heretical movement has grown rapidly in the United States of America from roots in the Pentecostal churches. Due to its astonishing success and the financial support of millions of easily deceived people it has spread throughout the world into almost every country. It was the first Christian organisation to use satellite TV in 1982 and by using the latest marketing techniques its fast-talking, good looking, amusing evangelists claiming exciting new revelations from God, have persuaded hundreds of thousands of Americans to donate billions of dollars to them in the belief that the more they give the more God is going to bless them with health and material prosperity. This movement is known variously as, The Word-Faith movement, Health and Wealth, Positive Confession or Prosperity Gospel. Its leaders during these forty years have been Kenneth Hagin, Kenneth Copeland, Benny Hinn, Frederick Price, Robert Tilton, Jerry Savelle, Morris Cerullo and Paul Crouch. But a new generation of younger evangelists are taking their place. All of them are now extremely wealthy with big houses, the most expensive cars and the latest fashionable clothes, and their individual organisations are worth billions of dollars. How do they do it? Here is a true example that happened to Pastor John MacArthur of California.

Through the post he and thousands of other innocent people received from a 'Word-Faith' preacher a packet containing a letter and a bar of 'prayer-blessed' soap! The letter said that just as Jesus had helped a man wash blindness from his eyes so if you use this soap you can receive healing or a money-miracle. The letter then gave these instructions, 'After you wash the poverty from your hands, take out a cheque or some money $100, or $50 or $20 and while holding it in your clean hands say, "In Jesus' Name I dedicate this gift to God's work," then expect a miracle of money in return.' (The money, of course, must be sent to the Word-Faith preacher!) The letter ended with these words, 'I see someone sending me an offering of $25 and God is showing me a large cheque coming to them shortly. It's large and it looks like $1000! I know this sounds strange but you know me well enough to know I have to obey God when he speaks. I will wait for your answer.' Many thousands of people respond and send gifts of money.

What does this Word-Faith movement believe? It believes that all sin, sickness, natural disasters, troubles, starvations and poverty come from Satan. God is good and wants all Christians to be released from Satan's control and all these evil things and to enjoy a life of blessing, health and prosperity. Through faith all these things are possible in Jesus' name because God wants us to enjoy health and riches – all we need to do is to believe and to command health and wealth to come into our lives by speaking 'words of faith' whenever we need it! The 'Word-Faith' movement believes that God is powerless to intervene until we speak these magic words of faith. They say this is because God gave Adam the legal right to rule the Earth for six thousand years and now He can do nothing without us! Faith is seen, not as an attitude of sincere belief in God's Word and personal trust in him, but as a force that is released into the world by man's co-operation!

Word-Faith evangelists actually believe and teach that when a person is born again they become 'little gods'. Kenneth Copeland says, 'Peter says in the Bible that we have become partakers of the Divine Nature. That nature is life eternal in absolute perfection. And that was imparted, injected into your spirit-man just the same as you imparted into your child the nature of your humanity. Your child was not born a whale, it was born a human being! Is that not true? You don't have a human in you – you are one! You don't have a god in you – you are one!'

This amazingly heretical teaching deceives people into believing that they are no longer weak human beings but can behave as God and command health and wealth to obey them! Sadly, some very ill people have believed this and refused medical treatment, commanding their disease to disappear, but then they have died. The Word-Faith evangelists have blamed the sufferers, saying it was their own fault for not having enough faith!

Their sermons often relate personal revelations, visions and conversations with God telling them what he wants them to teach. Charles Capps says:

'In 1973, the Word of the Lord came unto me saying, "If men would believe Me, long prayers are not necessary. Just speaking the Word will bring you what you desire. My creative power is given to Man in Word-form. I have ceased for a time from my work and have given Man the Book of my creative power, that power is still in My Word. But for it to be effective men must speak it and that creative power will come forth performing what is spoken in faith"'.

So man has now become as God with magic powers to do whatever he wants! And how do we know this is true? Is it in the Bible that all power is given to man? No, but Charles Capps had need of a special revelation to tell him so! But Jesus said something very different to his disciples about who has the power:

> ... All authority has been given to Me in heaven and on earth. Go therefore and make disciples of all the nations ... and lo, I am with you always, *even* to the end of the age (Matthew 28:18-20).

And Paul, when he was physically afflicted by Satan's attacks, prayed to God three times to remove his thorn in the flesh but God said to him:

> My grace is sufficient for you, for My strength is made perfect in weakness (2 Corinthians 12:9).

So Paul said:

> Therefore most gladly I will rather boast in my infirmities,
> that the power of Christ may rest upon me ... for when I
> am weak, then I am strong (2 Corinthians 12: 9-10).

The notable apostle Paul had to learn to rely, not on his own
powers or on his own words of faith, but on the power of
God which is made perfect in his weakness! He wasn't a
'little god' ruling the world and commanding everything to
happen by his own 'words of faith'. He found his weakness
and affliction made him live depending daily on the grace
of God alone.

The dangers of wealth. When a rich young ruler wanted
to follow Jesus he told him to sell all he had. But he loved
his wealth more than following Jesus and went away sad:

> ... How hard it is for those who have riches to enter the
> kingdom of God!. . . It is easier for a camel to go through
> the eye of a needle, than for a rich man to enter the king-
> dom of God (Mark 10:23,25).

In his parable of the sower Jesus said that the good seed of
the word of God can be destroyed by riches:

> Now he who received seed among the thorns is he who
> hears the word, and the cares of this world and the
> deceitfulness of riches choke the word, and he becomes
> unfruitful (Matthew 13:22).

Jesus is our example in all things. He was so poor that he
had no home and no possessions. When he died he was not
wealthy; he left only a cloak and a pair of sandals! The same
was true of Paul as he tells us about his life as an apostle
(2 Corinthians 6:4-10; 11:23-30). And he tells Timothy:

And having food and clothing, with these we shall be content. But those who desire to be rich fall into temptation and a snare, and *into* many foolish and harmful lusts which drown men in destruction and perdition. For the love of money is a root of all *kinds of* evil: for which some have strayed from the faith in their greediness, and pierced themselves through with many sorrows. (1 Timothy 6:8-10).

The cross is a symbol of death, not a symbol of health and wealth! Jesus was crucified on a cross and he calls everyone who would be his disciple to take up that cross for themselves and be ready to lay down their lives for him:

... If anyone desires to come after Me, let him deny himself, and take up his cross, and follow Me. For whoever desires to save his life will lose it, and whoever loses his life for My sake will find it. For what is a man profited if he gains the whole world, and loses his own soul? Or what will a man give in exchange for his soul? (Matthew 16:24-26).

So the Word-Faith evangelists have perverted the gospel of Christ and preached instead a gospel of personal greed and uncompromising materialism. The worship of God is transformed into the American dream – the worship of money and personal luxury! By avoiding all New Testament references to Christian discipleship involving suffering, hardship, persecution, poverty and death, Word-Faith evangelists go round the world deceiving thousands of poor and simple people to give away their money, in the belief that God will give them back far more than they have given to the evangelists. The health and wealth teaching is an evil perversion of Christ's gospel and must be resisted and exposed as one of Satan's modern deceptions.

Those who propagate it in fact insult millions of poor Christians, particularly in underdeveloped countries, by implying that they are lacking in faith, whereas James says precisely the opposite – they are rich in faith (2:5).

Questions

1 How do we know from the Bible that the Holy Spirit is not a force but a person?

2 How do we know from the Bible that the Holy Spirit is God?

3 What is the ministry of the Holy Spirit in the church since Pentecost?

4 Should we expect to see all the gifts of the Holy Spirit functioning in the church today?

CHAPTER ELEVEN

REPENTANCE AND FAITH

1 What is repentance?

2 What leads to repentance?

3 What is involved when a person repents?

4 What does repentance lead to?

    a) A changed view of God
    b) A changed view of ourselves

5 The difference between remorse and repentance

6 Faith

    a) What is faith?
    b) How does faith come into being?
    c) What does faith achieve?

In a parable that Jesus told (Luke 15) the prodigal son rebelled against his father, left home, and lived a life of sin and depravity in a far country. When he came to himself and realised all the wrong that he had done, he did four things:

i)   He admitted his sin.
ii) He confessed it to God.
iii) He asked for forgiveness.
iv) He turned from his evil ways.

True repentance is therefore a sorrow for sin that leads to a changed life.

> For godly sorrow produces repentance *leading* to sal-
> vation, not to be regretted; but the sorrow of the world
> produces death (2 Corinthians 7:10).

1 What is repentance?

It is a turning from sin and sinful ways to God and his service. The Greek noun 'metanoia' means to think again, to change one's mind. In both the Old and New Testaments repentance always involves a change of heart leading to a change of conduct.

In order to explain what true repentance is Jesus told a parable about a man who had two sons (Matthew 21:28-32). The father told his son to go to work in his vineyard. At first he refused to go but later he regretted his refusal, changed his mind, and went to work in the vineyard. The second son at first agreed to go but later decided not to. The first son not only changed his mind, he also regretted saying no to his father and this led to a change of conduct. Repentance therefore involves a change of mind, regret for what we have done, and a corresponding change of conduct.

In chapters two and three of the book of Revelation, Jesus gives us some models of repentance. The risen Christ speaks to each of his seven churches, telling five of them that there are specific sins of which they need to repent. For example, he says to the church at Ephesus:

> Nevertheless I have *this* against you, that you have left your first love. Remember therefore from where you have fallen; repent and do the first works, or else I will come to you quickly and remove your lampstand from its place – unless you repent (Revelation 2:4-5).

2 What leads to repentance?

Only the grace of God! It is the Holy Spirit who begins the work of salvation in the heart of every believer. He takes the initiative by convicting us of our sins, thus enabling us to see ourselves as sinners. This leads us to repentance, turning from our sins to God.

> And when He has come, He will convict the world of sin, and of righteousness, and of judgement (John 16:8).

> And I will pour on the house of David and on the inhabitants of Jerusalem the Spirit of grace and supplication; then they will look on Me whom they pierced; they will mourn for Him as one mourns for *his* only *son*, and grieve for Him as one grieves for a firstborn (Zechariah 12:10).

> When they heard these things they became silent; and they glorified God, saying, 'Then God has also granted to the Gentiles repentance to life' (Acts 11:18).

In addition to the work of the Holy Spirit, God also uses his Word, either read or preached. The preaching of the gospel is his usual means of leading men and women to repentance.

We see it in the preaching of Jonah to the Ninevites:

> And Jonah began to enter the city on the first day's walk.
> Then he cried out and said, 'Yet forty days, and Nineveh
> shall be overthrown!' So the people of Nineveh believed
> God, proclaimed a fast, and put on sackcloth, from the
> greatest to the least of them (Jonah 3:4-5).

In the New Testament we see the same thing through Peter's preaching on the day of Pentecost (Acts 2:37-39), also in Paul's preaching to various towns on his missionary journeys (for example, 1 Thessalonians 1:5).

3 What is involved when a person repents?

The whole personality is involved – the mind, the heart and the will. When, for the first time a man or woman recognizes their own sinfulness it affects their whole life, their minds, their emotions and their wills. In mass-evangelism too much stress is often placed on the will. People are urged to come forward to the front, to make a decision and sign a decision-card. But truth must come first of all to the mind. Unless a person understands their sinfulness, and feels the need of forgiveness, no action that they can take will save them.

- The mind must be informed:

  > ... for by the law *is* the knowledge of sin (Romans 3:20).

- The heart must be moved:

  > For godly sorrow produces repentance *leading* to salva-
  > tion, not to be regretted; but the sorrow of the world pro-
  > duces death (2 Corinthians 7:10; see also Luke 18:13).

- The will must respond:

> Then Zaccheus stood and said to the Lord, 'Look, Lord, I
> give half of my goods to the poor; and if I have taken any-
> thing from anyone by false accusation, I restore fourfold'
> (Luke 19:8; see also Isaiah 55:7).

4 What does repentance lead to?

a) A changed view of God. The unconverted man has a very
distorted understanding of the glorious character of God and
his holiness. God says to the wicked:

> You sit *and* speak against your brother; you slander your
> own mother's son. These *things* you have done, and I
> kept silent; you thought that I was altogether like you; *but*
> I will reprove you, and set *them* in order before your eyes
> (Psalm 50:20-21).

When Isaiah had a vision of God in the temple he saw him
in all his glory and holiness (Isaiah 6:1-7). He saw him as he
really is. This led to his repentance and a dramatic change
in his understanding of the holiness and righteousness of
Almighty God. The same was true of Job who, when he saw
God, repented of his unbelief, self-righteousness and rebellion:

> I have heard of You by the hearing of the ear, but now my
> eye sees You. Therefore I abhor *myself*, and repent in
> dust and ashes (Job 42:5-6).

b) A changed view of ourselves. Once we were proud and
self-righteous, made excuses for ourselves, refused to admit
our sinfulness and denied that we were worse than anyone
else. But when God opened our eyes to our true condition
we immediately ceased to justify ourselves and our past
way of life. This was also true of King David. He did not
consider that murder and adultery was reprehensible in a

king. But when the prophet Nathan showed him that in the sight of God these are terrible sins, he immediately repented and said:

> Have mercy upon me, O God, according to Your loving-kindness; according to the multitude of Your tender mercies, blot out my transgressions (Psalm 51:1).

5 The difference between remorse and repentance

Remorse is only regret for the consequences of our sin and for its unpleasant effects in punishment and suffering. We feel sorry for ourselves and for the humiliation of being found out and exposed to public contempt.

Repentance is a sorrow for sin as sin against God, a desire to be cleansed and forgiven, and a determination to confess it and forsake it at all costs.

6 Faith

During the Russian Revolution communists chided those who believed in God by saying, 'Faith is believing in something you know is not true!' Secular humanists in the West have also derided faith in similar fashion as being 'Pie in the sky when you die!' However the Christian faith is not based on fanciful and ethereal speculations about the invisible spiritual world and a mystical after-life. It is based on historical events and historical characters. We say that true faith is composed of three things – knowledge, belief and trust. Christian faith is therefore a proclamation about Jesus Christ as an historical person and what he came into the world to accomplish:

- It is a message to be understood.
- It is a message to be believed.
- It is a person to be trusted.

Faith is therefore a message that is addressed firstly to our minds, secondly to our hearts and thirdly to our wills, and in that order. The message is called by Paul, 'the word of God', which is preached to men in order that they might believe. A person hears the message, understands it, believes it is true and commits himself to it:

> So then faith *comes* by hearing and hearing by the word of God (Romans 10:17)

At the Reformation the Reformers opposed the Roman Catholic view that faith is only a mental assent to the doctrines of Christianity. Between the individual person and Christ the Catholic Church had intruded a number of mediators – the priest, the saints, the Virgin Mary, and the Church. The Reformers said this was totally wrong; 'There is only one mediator between God and man, Jesus Christ, therefore put your trust directly in Him!' (see 1 Timothy 2:5) They stressed the importance of every soul having a personal encounter with the living Christ, leading to trust and confidence in him as their personal Saviour.

In the New Testament the word 'faith' is very prominent. The noun pistis and the verb pisteuô both occur more than 240 times while the adjective pistos is found 67 times. This stress on faith is to be seen against the background of the saving work of God in Christ. Central to the New Testament is the message that God sent his Son to be the Saviour of the world. Christ accomplished man's salvation by dying an atoning death on his behalf on Calvary's cross. Faith is the response of belief in the claims of Christ, coupled with a complete trust in him for salvation.

When the Philippian jailer asked, 'What must I do to be saved?' (Acts 16:31) Paul and Silas reply without hesitation, 'Believe on the Lord Jesus Christ, and you will be saved', i.e. put your faith in Christ.

A chronically sick woman, in a dense crowd surrounding Jesus, succeeded in touching him. Because she believed in his ability to heal her, he said to her. 'Daughter, be of good cheer; your faith has made you well' (Luke 8:48).

When the disciples were in a boat with Jesus that was caught in a sudden storm, they awoke him because they thought their boat was about to sink. He reproved them for not trusting in him with the words, 'How is it that you have no faith?' (Mark 4:40). Jesus expected them to believe that all would be well because he was with them.

Faith in Christ is therefore essential for salvation, for answers to our prayers, for healing and for having confidence in God.

> But without faith *it is* impossible to please *Him*, for he who comes to God must believe that He is, and *that* He is a rewarder of those who diligently seek Him (Hebrews 11:6).

a) What is faith?

Negatively – it is not a natural human quality that we are born with, like courage or kindness. It is not the ability to take calculated risks. Sometimes we read of mountaineers having faith in their equipment or astronauts in the scientists who design their rockets. Saving faith is radically different: it is not a natural quality – it is supernatural!

Positively – spiritual faith is something that God works in us at regeneration, and which leads to a fundamental change in our natural dispositions (see Chapter Nine, paragraph 1[v]). Faith is the gift of God:

> For by grace you have been saved through faith, and that not of yourselves; *it is* the gift of God (Ephesians 2:8).

Faith is the ability given to us by God that enables us to believe in the truths of his revelation and to put our trust in him.

b) How does faith come into being? God's normal method of granting faith is, firstly, to inform the mind. Sometimes he has to disturb the pattern of our lives to awaken us to a sense of our need. He brings the truth to us either by the written or spoken word. When Christ gave his farewell commission to the apostles he told them to tell the whole world about him:

> Go therefore and make disciples of all the nations, baptizing them in the name of the Father and of the Son and of the Holy Spirit, teaching them to observe all things that I have commanded you ... (Matthew 28:19-20).

> Faith *comes* by hearing, and hearing by the word of God. (Romans 10:17)

The apostles engaged in public preaching and private teaching following the method that Christ himself had taught them. Those who heard the message would respond, either in faith or in unbelief. Paul says that God's written word, the Scriptures, can also make us wise unto salvation (2 Timothy 3:15).

c) What does faith achieve? One of the most important chapters in the Bible on the subject of faith is Hebrews eleven. The author's definition of faith refers not so much to what faith is but what it does:

> Now faith is the substance of things hoped for, the evidence of things not seen (Hebrews 11:1).

Faith is the God-given ability that enables us to see things that are still in the future as already present, and unseen things as now visible. The author then surveys the most notable men and women of faith throughout the Old Testament. He shows that what they were and what they achieved was by their faith.

By faith Abel ... by faith Enoch ... by faith Noah ... by faith Abraham ... by faith Sarah ... by faith Isaac ... by faith Jacob ... by faith Joseph ... by faith Moses ... by faith Rahab, Gideon, Barak, Samson, Jephthah, David, Samuel and the prophets ... subdued kingdoms, worked righteousness, obtained promises, stopped the mouths of lions, quenched the violence of fire, escaped the edge of the sword, out of weakness were made strong, became valiant in battle, turned to flight the armies of the aliens (vv.4-34).

Faith enabled all these men and women not just to talk about God but also to do things! They knew what they believed, but more importantly, they knew whom they believed. Without faith it is impossible to please God. He who comes to God must believe that he is and that he is a rewarder of those who diligently seek him (Hebrews 11:6). Here are some of the things that the Bible says about faith:

- We are justified by faith (Romans 5:1)
- We live by faith (Romans 1:17)
- We walk by faith (2 Corinthians 5:7)
- We stand by faith (2 Corinthians 1:24)
- We have access to God by faith (Romans 5:2)
- Christ dwells in our hearts through faith (Ephesians 3:17)
- We overcome through faith (Hebrews 11:33-34)
- We pray in faith (James 1:6)
- We resist the devil firm in faith (1 Peter 5:9)
- We please God by faith (Hebrews 11:6)

Although faith is the gift of God it is also God's will that our faith should become strong and that it should increase. When the disciples thought that their boat was about to sink in a sudden storm, Jesus reproved them, saying, 'Where is your faith?' (Matthew 8:26). He expected their faith to have overcome their fears, but their faith was too small. How can our faith grow? Here are some of the ways that the Bible recommends:

- By trusting God's word as Abraham did (Romans 4:19-20).
- By praying for a stronger faith (Luke 17:5).
- By hearing and reading God's Word (Romans 10:17)
- By obeying God's Word (James 1:22-25).
- By exercising faith at all times (1 Thessalonians 1:3-8).
- By making love the motive for our deeds of faith (Galatians 5:6).

Questions

1   Why is repentance essential to salvation?

2   What means does God use to bring a person to repentance?

3   What are the three essential elements of true faith?

4   What means has God provided to help our faith to grow?

CHAPTER TWELVE

ADOPTION

1 The meaning of adoption

    a) The meaning of the word 'son' in Scripture
    b) New Testament references to adoption

2 The error of universalism

3 Is our sonship the same as Christ's?

4 What are the proofs of adoption?

    Five evidences

5 What are the results of adoption?

    Eight results

But when the fulness of the time had come, God sent forth
His Son, born of a woman, born under the law, to redeem
those who were under the law, that we might receive the
adoption as sons (Galatians 4:4-5)

Surely adoption is the summit of all our privileges for by
it God has made us nearer to Himself than the angels.
They are the friends of Christ but we are His children.
(Thomas Watson)

1 The meaning of adoption

Many years ago, when Christians were being severely
persecuted in Korea, an angry mob attacked the home of a
Christian preacher. The preacher's son was murdered and
subsequently a young man was arrested by the police and put
on trial. To everyone's amazement the father of the murdered
boy forgave the murderer, withdrew the charges and took
him into his own home. He adopted the boy as his own son
and brought him up in his own family. The murderer who
had been his enemy became his adopted son. This is what
God does for us. We who were his enemies become, through
Christ, his adopted sons and daughters, and receive the Spirit
of adoption (Romans 8:15)!

The word adoption in the Greek, *huiothesia*, means 'placing
a son' as from one family into another. It is the loving and
legal action of God whereby he bestows on us the status of
sons. This includes our justification and regeneration but
our adoption gives us something still more wonderful: God
becomes our Father, and we become his sons and partakers
of the privileges of his children.

a) The meaning of the word 'son' in Scripture

- In the singular the 'Son of God' refers to Christ as the unique Son of God (See Chapter Five, para. 4a).

- In the plural, the sons of God refers to the angels (Job 1:6).

- In Psalm 82:6 it is used of human magistrates who in their office exercise a power over men similar to that of God.

- 'Sons' as the subjects of divine adoption – for example,
  i) Israel in the Old Testament (Romans 9:4; see Exodus 4:22).
  ii) The Christian in the New Testament (Galatians 4:5)

b) New Testament references to adoption

Who are Israelites, to whom *pertain* the adoption, the glory, the covenants, the giving of the law, the service *of God*, and the promises (Romans 9:4).

For you did not receive the spirit of bondage again to fear, but you received the Spirit of adoption by whom we cry out, 'Abba Father' (Romans 8:15).

And not only *they*, but we also who have the firstfruits of the Spirit, even we ourselves groan within ourselves, eagerly waiting for the adoption, the redemption of our body (Romans 8:23).

Having predestined us to adoption as sons by Jesus Christ to Himself, according to the good pleasure of His will (Ephesians 1:5).

2 The error of universalism

The idea of the universal fatherhood of God and brotherhood of man is widespread today even in the professing Christian Church. Many believe that all religions are but different ways to God and that therefore Christ is not the only way. Paul in his sermon to the Greek philosophers in Athens conceded that all men are in a sense God's children, but this is only in their relationship to him as their Creator (Acts 17:25-29). In a general sense he is the Father of all, but in a particular sense, so far as redemption is concerned, he is not:

> For to this *end* we both labour and suffer reproach, because we trust in the living God, who is *the* Saviour of all men, especially of those who believe (1 Timothy 4:10).

Indeed Paul makes it very clear that by nature we were all the children of wrath (Ephesians 2:3). According to Christ the Pharisees were of their father the devil (John 8:44). The ample references to hell in the New Testament are further proof that not all men are saved: and therefore 'Universalism' (the belief that all will be saved) is an erroneous doctrine.

3 Is our sonship the same as Christ's?

We become sons of God only by adoption – there is a basic change in our status. The Bible tells us that formerly we were children of wrath, in the kingdom of darkness, dead to God and slaves to sin. But Christ did not *become* the Son of God, for he is God's Son eternally. When he had risen from the dead he said to Mary Magdalene:

> ... I am ascending to My Father and your Father, and *to* My God and your God (John 20:17).

We should note that he did *not* say to *our* Father or to *our* God. He wants his disciples to see that there is a distinction between the relationship that he has to God and that which they have to God. In the same way he says to them, 'When you pray ...' he does not include himself as being in the same relationship to God as ourselves. The sonship of adoption that we enjoy is not on the same level as the sonship of Christ, the second Person of the Trinity.

4 What are the proofs of adoption?

Many people claim to be Christians because they are members of a particular denomination. But they have no experience of conversion and show no evidence of the fruit of the Spirit in their lives. Those who have professed faith in Christ, and follow him in the path of Christian discipleship, will have the following evidences in their lives that God has adopted them into his heavenly family:

i) They have faith in Christ as Saviour and Lord

> For you are all sons of God through faith in Christ Jesus (Galatians 3:26).

ii) They have experienced the Spirit of adoption in their hearts

> For you did not receive the spirit of bondage again to fear, but you received the Spirit of adoption by whom we cry out, 'Abba, Father' (Romans 8:15). See also Galatians 4:4-5.

iii) They have experienced the inward testimony of the Spirit with their spirits.

> The Spirit Himself bears witness with our spirit that we are children of God (Romans 8:16).

iv) They experience the leading and guidance of the Spirit in their lives.

> For as many as are led by the Spirit of God, these are sons of God (Romans 8:14). See also Galatians 5:16-18.

v) They love righteousness and strive to be holy

> In this the children of God and the children of the devil are manifest: Whoever does not practice righteousness is not of God, nor is he who does not love his brother (1 John 3:10).

5 What are the results of adoption?

As newly adopted members of God's family we have the honour and privilege to be called children of God. We have him as our heavenly Father, Jesus as our Lord and Saviour and the Holy Spirit as our helper who also lives in us. This means that we become the special objects of his loving care and protection. All the members of the Trinity each play a vital role not only in the salvation of each child of God but also in their preservation.

i) We receive the gift of the Holy Spirit. This is the greatest spiritual gift that any human being can receive; God the Holy Spirit is given to live in each child of God to guide, comfort, teach and to transform them into God's image. It is through the work of the Holy Spirit that we become children of God (John 3:5; Titus 3:5). The apostle Peter preached the first sermon of the Christian church on the day of Pentecost in which he confirmed the promise of God to give the Holy Spirit to all who would repent and believe:

> Then Peter said to them, 'Repent, and let every one of you be baptised in the name of Jesus Christ for the

remission of sins; and you shall receive the gift of the Holy Spirit' (Acts 2:38).

See also John 14:16-18; Acts 5:32; 10:44; 19:6.

ii) We lose the spirit of bondage

This phrase occurs in Romans 8:15 and refers to the conviction of sin and the fear of God that the Holy Spirit works in our hearts to bring us to repentance (John 16:8). The Holy Spirit shows us the fact that we have sinned against God and this brings with it a sense of guilt, condemnation and uncleanness. We feel we are helpless to improve ourselves or to make ourselves right with God. Those who heard Peter's sermon on the day of Pentecost cried out under conviction of sin, 'Men and brethren, what shall we do?' (Acts 2:37). Similarly the Philippian jailer cried out, 'Sirs, what must I do to be saved?' (Acts 16:30). We must experience this spirit of bondage to sin, which makes us afraid because it makes us realise that we have sinned against God. Only then can we repent and receive the light and liberty of God's salvation:

> For you did not receive the Spirit of bondage again to fear, but you received the Spirit of adoption by whom we cry out, 'Abba, Father' (Romans 8:15).

iii) A new spiritual freedom

The apostle Paul says that when sinners are born again and repent of their sins God has worked a miracle, delivering us 'from the power of darkness' and translating us 'into the kingdom of the Son of His love' (Colossians 1:13). We are therefore freed from our bondage to sin and to Satan (Romans 6:14; Luke 11:20-22) and we experience the liberty of those who have been released from a lifetime in the prison of sin and shame.

> Jesus answered them, 'Most assuredly, I say to you, whoever commits sin is a slave of sin. And a slave does not abide in the house forever, *but* a son abides forever. Therefore if the Son makes you free, you shall be free indeed' (John 8:34-36).

> Now the Lord is the Spirit; and where the Spirit of the Lord *is*, there *is* liberty (2 Corinthians 3:17).

iv) A new spiritual family relationship with God

The new-born believer is brought into a very warm and intimate relationship with God as his Father. But some earthly fathers are often severe and not very loving or sympathetic toward their children. The Bible, however, tells us that this Father/child relationship between God and ourselves is so loving and tender that instinctively we call our heavenly Father 'Abba' (an expression of deep intimacy). Through the witness of his Spirit within us we know he loves and cares for us:

> And because you are sons, God has sent forth the Spirit of His Son into your hearts, crying out, 'Abba, Father!' (Galatians 4:6).

But not only so, for we are also told that now we have the Lord Jesus Christ as our brother! When Christ became man he took on himself our humanity and in so doing called himself our brother:

> For both He who sanctifies and those who are being sanctified *are* all of one, for which reason He is not ashamed to call them brethren ... Inasmuch then as the children have partaken of flesh and blood, He Himself likewise shared in the same, that through death He might destroy him who had the power of death, that is, the devil... Therefore, in all things He had to be made like *His*

brethren, that He might be a merciful and faithful High priest in things *pertaining* to God, to make propitiation for the sins of the people (Hebrews 2:11,14,17).

For whom He foreknew, He also predestined *to be* conformed to the image of His Son, that He might be the first-born among many brethren (Romans 8:29).

Jesus said to her, 'Do not cling to Me, for I have not yet ascended to My Father; but go to My brethren and say to them, "I am ascending to My Father and your Father and to My God and your God"' (John 20:17).

v) A new people

When Jesus came into the world his purpose was to open the door of salvation not only to the Jews but also to the Gentiles. When Simeon saw Jesus as a baby with his parents he said, 'My eyes have seen Your salvation which You have prepared before the face of all peoples, a light to bring revelation to the Gentiles, and the glory of Your people Israel' (Luke 2:30-32). It was a special privilege given to the apostle Peter to make the first gentile convert when he preached the gospel to the Roman soldier Cornelius. Referring to this momentous event James said,

Simon [Peter] has declared how God at the first visited the Gentiles to take out of them a people for His name (Acts 15:14).

Since that time God has been taking out of all the nations of the world a people for his name – a redeemed people, called the people of God:

Even us whom He called, not of the Jews only, but also of the Gentiles? As He says also in Hosea: '*I will call them My people, who were not My people, and her beloved,*

*who was not beloved. And it shall come to pass in the
place where it was said to them, 'You are not My people,'
there they will be called sons of the living God* (Romans
9:24-26).

The believer in Christ is therefore a member of God's new
kingdom, a redeemed humanity who one day will inhabit
the new heaven and earth which God will create after the
judgement and destruction of this present evil world:

But you *are* a chosen generation, a royal priesthood, a
holy nation, His own special people, that you may proclaim
the praises of Him who called you out of darkness into
His marvellous light; who once *were* not a people but *are*
now the people of God, who had not obtained mercy but
now have obtained mercy (1 Peter 2:9-10).

vi)   A new security

What a wonderful blessing it is to be cared for by our Father
in heaven! Peter says we should take all our problems and
anxieties to him: 'Casting all your care upon Him because he
cares for you' (1 Peter 5:7). When by faith in Christ we become
members of God's kingdom it means we belong to God; he
is both our King and our Father. Before our conversion we
were like orphans in the world who, once they leave their
orphanage, have to look after themselves or perish. But once
we become members of God's family all this changes because
we are cared for and protected by God.

Therefore do not worry, saying, 'What shall we eat?' or
'What shall we drink?' or 'What shall we wear?' For after
all these things the Gentiles seek. For your heavenly
Father knows that you need all these things. But seek first
the kingdom of God and His righteousness, and all these
things shall be added to you (Matthew 6:31-33).

Let your conduct be without covetousness, *and be* content with such things as you have. For He Himself has said, '*I will never leave you nor forsake you.*' So we may boldly say: '*The* LORD *is my helper; I will not fear. What can man do to me?*' (Hebrews 13:5-6).

vii) A new discipline

In our modern world today we see the breakdown of family life. Young people are neglected or forsaken by their parents and left to look after themselves. Too often they fall into evil ways and don't know right from wrong. Good parents, on the other hand, are very attentive to their children and teach them how to behave and to recognise right from wrong. This means they have to discipline and correct them. Our heavenly Father is the wisest and kindest of fathers and he too corrects us when we sin and do wrong. How we behave is very important to him! This was true of God's relationship with the Jews in the Old Testament – he was a father to them:

In spite of this they still sinned, and did not believe in His wondrous works. Therefore their days He consumed in futility, and their years in fear ... But He, *being* full of compassion, forgave *their* iniquity, and did not destroy *them.* Yes, many a time He turned His anger away, and did not stir up all His wrath (Psalm 78:32, 33, 38).

And you have forgotten the exhortation which speaks to you as to sons: '*My son, do not despise the chastening of the* LORD, *nor be discouraged when you are rebuked by Him; for whom the* LORD *loves He chastens, and scourges every son whom He receives*' (Hebrews 12:5-6).

(viii) A new inheritance

When parents die they usually leave all their earthly possessions to their children who then inherit their wealth. The children are the heirs of their parents. It is an amazing fact that God has made the same principle apply to those who have become his children by faith in Christ! We are called his heirs and have been given the right to inherit the riches of his eternal kingdom!

> The Spirit Himself bears witness with our spirit that we are children of God, and if children, then heirs – heirs of God and joint heirs with Christ, if indeed we suffer with *Him*, that we may also be glorified together (Romans 8:16-17).

> Blessed be the God and Father of our Lord Jesus Christ, who according to His abundant mercy has begotten us again to a living hope through the resurrection of Jesus Christ from the dead, to an inheritance incorruptible and undefiled and that does not fade away, reserved in heaven for you (1 Peter 1:3-4).

> Giving thanks to the Father who has qualified us to be partakers of the inheritance of the saints in light (Colossians 1:12).

Believers rejoice because they know that they can never be deprived of their inheritance, nor will it ever lose its value. It is theirs for all eternity!

Questions

1 In what sense is everyone a child of God and in what sense are they not?

2 How may we know that we are children of God by adoption, and what signs should we look for?

CHAPTER THIRTEEN

SANCTIFICATION

1 Sanctification is a two-fold activity

   a) God's part in sanctification
   b) Man's part in sanctification

2 The meaning of the word

3 How does sanctification take place?

   a) Through our being set apart from the world by God
   b) Through our being made holy by God and used by him
   c) By the Holy Spirit's activity in us
   d) By virtue of our union with Christ
   e) By feeding our souls on God's Word
   f) By actively co-operating with the Holy Spirit
   g) Sanctification does not happen suddenly but progressively

4 The old man and the new man

5 The Ten Commandments

   a) God's Law is eternal
   b) God's Law is spiritual, searching the heart
   c) Sunday

1   Sanctification is a twofold activity

a) God's part in sanctification

God made man in the beginning in his own image, but sin has now defiled that image. Sanctification is that work of God the Holy Spirit whereby he is progressively making us holy and restoring that image from one degree of glory to another (2 Corinthians 3:18).

b) Man's part in sanctification

Paul likens his spiritual life to running a race and fighting a battle (2 Timothy 4:7). Sanctification is therefore both a race to be finished and a fight to be won; holiness is never achieved without endurance, determination and effort. This is because the world, the flesh and the devil constantly trouble us.

Holy living means dying to self, taking up the cross, and following Jesus – you do it all and the Holy Spirit does it all! It is a combined effort, though without the energising power of the Holy Spirit it would not take place at all.

2   The meaning of the word

In the Old Testament the verb qadesh means to separate or to set apart from other things. The priests (see Exodus 28:41) and the various vessels and furnishings (see 1 Kings 8:4) used in worship in the tabernacle and the temple were regarded as set apart for God for holy service. Because the holy vessels, for example, were set apart they could not be used for ordinary purposes. They were not only set apart from the world but also they were set apart for God and his purposes. There is therefore a passive and an active aspect to sanctification.

The Greek verb in the New Testament *hagiazō* (noun, *hagiasmos*) means separation from the sinful practices of the world and consecration to the service of God. Whereas in justification God removes the guilt of sin, in sanctification God progressively removes the stain or the pollution of sin.

Sanctification is that gracious operation of the Holy Spirit by which he delivers us from sin's polluting influence, progressively renews our entire nature in God's image and enables us to live lives pleasing to God. This is a work in which the believer must fully co-operate. The measure to which he grows in holiness will be the measure to which he is obedient to the Spirit in thought, word and deed.

3 How does sanctification take place?

a) Through our being set apart from the world by God.

Then Moses took the anointing oil, and anointed the tabernacle and all that *was* in it, and sanctified them. He sprinkled some of it on the altar seven times, anointed the altar and all its utensils, and the laver and its base, to sanctify them. And he poured some of the anointing oil on Aaron's head and anointed him, to sanctify him (Leviticus 8:10-12).

And such were some of you. But you were washed, but you were sanctified, but you were justified in the name of the Lord Jesus and by the Spirit of our God (1 Corinthians 6:11).

Elect according to the foreknowledge of God the Father, in sanctification of the Spirit, for obedience and sprinkling of the blood of Jesus Christ (1 Peter 1:2).

See also John 10:36, 17:19; Acts 26:18; Ephesians 5:25-26, Hebrews 10:10-14.

b) Through our being made holy by God and used by him

Sanctify them by Your truth. Your word is truth (John 17:17).

Now may the God of peace Himself sanctify you completely; and may your whole spirit, soul, and body be preserved blameless at the coming of our Lord Jesus Christ (1 Thessalonians 5:23).

But in a great house there are not only vessels of gold and silver, but also of wood and clay, some for honour and some for dishonour. Therefore if anyone cleanses himself from the latter, he will be a vessel for honour, sanctified and useful for the Master, prepared for every good work (2 Timothy 2:20-21).

c) By the Holy Spirit's activity in us

Although God the Father (Hebrews 13:20-21), and God the Son (Titus 2:14) are active in our sanctification, it is especially the work of the Holy Spirit whose task is to apply the work of God's salvation to us. Christ said that the Spirit would come to help believers, 'He will glorify Me, for He shall take of what is Mine and declare it to you' (John 16:14).

But we are bound to give thanks to God always for you, brethren beloved by the Lord, because God from the beginning chose you to salvation through sanctification by the Spirit and belief in the truth (2 Thessalonians 2:13).

Not by works of righteousness which we have done, but according to His mercy He saved us, through the washing of regeneration and renewing of the Holy Spirit (Titus 3:5).

> Therefore, my beloved, as you have always obeyed, not as in my presence only, but now much more in my absence, work out your own salvation with fear and trembling; for it is God who works in you both to will and to do for *His* good pleasure (Philippians 2:12-13).

See also Romans 15:16; 1 Peter 1:2 and 2 Corinthians 3:18.

d) By virtue of our union with Christ. The believer is not left alone to look after himself when he is born again and recreated in God's likeness. He is adopted into God's family, indwelt by the Holy Spirit and mystically united with Christ in his death and in his resurrection:

> Therefore we were buried with Him through baptism into death, that just as Christ was raised from the dead by the glory of the Father, even so we also should walk in newness of life. For if we have been united together in the likeness of His death, certainly we also shall be *in the likeness* of *His* resurrection (Romans 6:4-5).

There is also a corporate aspect to this union. Because the believer is supernaturally united to Christ by the Holy Spirit, he is now also a member of the Church, the body of Christ, with other believers:

> But, speaking the truth in love, may grow up in all things into Him who is the Head – Christ – from whom the whole body, joined and knit together by what every joint supplies, according to the effective working by which every part does its share, causes growth of the body for the edifying of itself in love (Ephesians 4:15-16).

Christ not only died on the cross for us, but now in heaven he ever lives to make intercession for us. Through him believers receive all the benefits of salvation because they are united to him by faith. His resurrection power is spiritually communicated to us and sustains us day by day.

But of Him you are in Christ Jesus, who became for us wisdom from God – and righteousness and sanctification and redemption (1 Corinthians 1:30).

e) By feeding our souls on God's Word. In his High Priestly prayer Christ prayed to his Father for his disciples, 'Sanctify them by Your truth. Your word is truth' (John 17:17). Christ, who came to bear witness to the truth, was about to leave his disciples, so he prayed that the Father would keep them through the sanctifying influence of his own word. God's word was the means through which God had communicated his will to Israel in the Old Testament through the law and the prophets. This word was their most treasured possession, as it is for the believers today:

Your word *is* a lamp to my feet and a light to my path (Psalm 119:105).

The law of the LORD *is* perfect, converting the soul; the testimony of the LORD *is* sure, making wise the simple; the statutes of the LORD *are* right, rejoicing the heart; the commandment of the LORD *is* pure, enlightening the eyes (Psalm 19:7-8).

How can a young man cleanse his way? By taking heed according to Your word ... Your word I have hidden in my heart, that I might not sin against You (Psalm 119:9-11).

In Old Testament times and still today the Bible is the only way we can know God's holy will. It is given to us so that we can obey him and grow in holiness and conformity to the truth. It was these Old Testament scriptures that Paul commended to Timothy:

All Scripture *is* given by inspiration of God, and is profitable for doctrine, for reproof, for correction, for instruction in righteousness, that the man of God may be

complete, thoroughly equipped for every good work
(2 Timothy 3:16-17).

The New Testament amplifies and illuminates the teaching
of the Old Testament. The words of Christ and his apostles
give even clearer light and instruction as to how we can
please God:

> If you keep My commandments, you will abide in My love,
> just as I have kept my Father's commandments and abide
> in His love (John 15:10).

f) By actively co-operating with the Holy Spirit.
Although we are totally dependent upon the grace of God,
and while recognising that fundamentally sanctification is his
work in us, the Scriptures are full of commands to the believer
to co-operate with the Spirit and to be actively obedient to
his word. The following verses are examples of God's clear
command to us to be active in our sanctification:

Work out your own salvation with fear and trembling
– Philippians 2:12
Let us *cleanse* ourselves from all filthiness of the flesh and spirit
– 2 Corinthians 7:1
Reckon yourselves to be dead indeed to sin
– Romans 6:11
Present yourselves to God   – Romans 6:13
Be holy, for I am holy   – 1 Peter 1:16
Watch, stand fast in the faith   – 1 Corinthians 16:13
Fight the good fight of faith   – 1 Timothy 6:12
Flee… youthful lusts; but *pursue* righteousness
– 2 Timothy 2:22
Make straight paths for your feet   – Hebrews 12:13
Do not be conformed to this world, but *be transformed*
– Romans 12:2
Keep yourselves from idols   – 1 John 5:21
Keep yourselves in the love of God – Jude 21

Submit to God. *Resist* the devil   – James 4:7
If anyone *cleanses himself*   – 2 Timothy 2:21

g) Sanctification does not happen suddenly but progressively. The Christian life is described in the New Testament as involving growth. Christ said that he is the vine and we are the branches; he wants us to be fruitful. Paul also talks of the believer bringing forth the fruit of the Spirit (Galatians 5:22-25). Trees first bring forth leaves, then blossom and finally fruit; this is a living process which takes time. New believers are also called 'babes in Christ', children who need to grow to maturity. John in his first letter (1 John 2:13) refers also to 'young men' and 'fathers', showing that the spiritual life has a natural progression, even as our physical life has. There is no sudden jump from youth to old age; God is at work in us to make us grow. Peter tells us to 'grow in grace and in the knowledge of our Lord and Saviour Jesus Christ' (2 Peter 3:18). In the parable of the sower, the good seed (the believer), gradually grows up and brings forth fruit with patience:

> But the ones *that* fell on the good ground are those who, having heard the word with a noble and good heart, keep *it* and bear fruit with patience (Luke 8:15).

The Christian is exhorted continually to present his body and his mind as holy instruments for God to use in his service. This command is to be obeyed every day; we need to grow in holiness throughout our lives:

> Therefore having these promises, beloved, let us cleanse ourselves from all filthiness of the flesh and spirit, perfecting holiness in the fear of God (2 Corinthians 7:1).

> I beseech you therefore, brethren, by the mercies of God, that you present your bodies a living sacrifice, holy, acceptable to God, *which is* your reasonable service (Romans 12:1).

4 The old man and the new man

Every Christian has, at one time or another, been perplexed by the apparent contradiction between what the New Testament says about his being a new man in Christ, and the reality of the power and prevalence of sin in his life. For example, Paul says that we are dead to sin and our old man has been crucified with Christ:

> What shall we say then? Shall we continue in sin that grace may abound? Certainly not! How shall we who died to sin live any longer in it? ... Knowing this, that our old man was crucified with *Him*, that the body of sin might be done away with, that we should no longer be slaves of sin (Romans 6:1-2, 6).

How can Paul say that our old man is dead, when we all know that our sinful nature, far from being dead, shows itself every day to be very much alive? What is our 'old man'?

Some have taught that the old man is that which belongs to our pre-Christian life. The new man is our new life in Christ; the believer is therefore both an old man and a new man. When he does well he is behaving according to the new man, when he sins he is acting according to the old man. This is definitely not what Paul is teaching. We are not at one and the same time an old man and a new man. This interpretation confuses our sinful flesh, 'the body of sin', with the old man. What then is the 'old man'? It is the person I was 'in Adam' before I believed and became a new man 'in Christ'. It is the person I was, dominated by the flesh and by sin. The old man is the unregenerate man; the new man is the regenerate man, created in Christ Jesus unto good works. We cannot at one and the same time be an unregenerate man and a new man. We are never called upon to crucify the old man. Why not? Because he has already been crucified with Christ in virtue of our union with him

(Romans 6:6). But we are called upon to crucify the flesh with its affections and lusts (Galatians 5:24). The old man, the person I was in my unregenerate days has gone, but the sinful flesh remains. This is what Paul calls 'the body of sin', our physical bodies of which sin has taken possession. The body itself is not sinful, but Satan tempts us to use it in a worldly and instinctual way, instead of using it as God has prescribed in his Word. When the New Testament refers to 'the flesh' it is speaking about the 'body of sin'. The flesh does not mean our physical bodies. Paul tells us elsewhere that, as Christians, we are to look after our physical bodies and to present them to God for His service (Romans 12:1). It means the sinful activities which the body can be used for, through Satan's temptations. Paul says, 'if we through the Spirit do put to death these sinful deeds we shall live' (Romans 8:13). The body itself is not sinful, but it can be used in sinful ways and must be controlled by our new mind and Christian values.

In Romans 6:6 Paul says that, 'our old man was crucified with ...' Christ so that the body of sin might be destroyed, that henceforth we should not serve sin. The effect of Christ's objective death for us on the cross was not only to pay sin's penalty, but also to break its power over us. So Paul can conclude, 'sin shall not have dominion over you, for you are not under law but under grace' (Romans 6:14). We not only receive forgiveness but we also experience liberation in Christ from the dominion of sin over our lives. So Paul does not only say, 'O wretched man that I am! Who shall deliver me from this body of death?' but also, 'I thank God – through Jesus Christ our Lord' (Romans 7:24-25). Now through the indwelling of the Spirit the believer has the power and the desire to subdue sin and temptation. Although his outward man is decaying, yet his inward man (the new man) is being renewed day by day (2 Corinthians 4:16).

In view of this teaching, some have asked why Paul tells the Ephesians to 'put off the old man who is corrupt

according to deceitful lusts ... and put on the new man'
(Ephesians 4:22-24). How can we reconcile this verse with
Romans 6:6, where Paul tells us our old man was crucified
with Christ? We need to understand that our old man, the
unregenerate person I was in Adam, born under the law,
born in sin and a child of wrath, has indeed been crucified
with Christ. This means that 'there is now therefore no condemnation to those who are in Christ Jesus' (Romans 8:1),
for we have been delivered both from sin's bondage and
from sin's curse: 'If anyone is in Christ, he is a new creation; old things have passed away; behold, all things have
become new' (2 Corinthians 5:17). Christ has made us new
creatures and our old unregenerate selves have been crucified
with him. What then is Paul telling us to do in Ephesians
4:22-24? He is simply telling us not to imitate the habits
and life-style of our former unregenerate selves. We have
finished with that way of life. Now we can put on the new
life-style in Christ through the new spiritual power and
desires he has put within us. There is no way we can wear
two suits of clothes at the same time! We must throw away
the old clothes that we wore in our old life. We must put on
the new clothes of the new man, whom God has created in
righteousness and true holiness.

5 The Ten Commandments

Do the Ten Commandments have any place in the New
Testament teaching on sanctification? Some preachers have
taught that the law of God has nothing to say to the Christian
because Christ has died for our sins and we are no longer
justified by the works of the law but by faith:

> Therefore by the deeds of the law no flesh will be justi-
> fied in His sight, for by the law *is* the knowledge of sin...
> Therefore we conclude that a man is justified by faith apart
> from the deeds of the law (Romans 3:20, 28).

Before we can answer this question we must ask another –
what is meant by the law?

In the Old Testament the law of Moses was in three parts:

i) **The civil law** – relating to the national life of Israel
ii) **The ceremonial law** – relating to the tabernacle and temple worship, their sacrifices and offerings
iii) **The moral law** – relating to man's relationship with God.

The civil law has disappeared because Israel as a theocracy
was rejected by God and ceased to be his special nation
(cf. Matthew 21:43). The gospel of Christ is now for every
nation.

The ceremonial law has disappeared because the death of
Christ on the cross abolished all animal sacrifices and the
worship of the temple.

The moral law, as summarised in the Ten Commandments,
has not disappeared but is still God's moral standard for
humanity. It is not given to justify him but to show him what
sin is (Romans 3:20).

Are the Ten Commandments still in force for mankind and
do they have any part to play in Christian teaching on sanctification? The answer to both questions is, yes. Paul says:

> But we know that the law *is* good if one uses it lawfully,
> knowing this: that the law is not made for a righteous person,
> but for *the* lawless and insubordinate, for *the* ungodly and for
> sinners, for *the* unholy and profane, for murderers of fathers
> and murderers of mothers, for man-slayers, for fornicators,

for sodomites, for kidnappers, for liars, for perjurers, and if there is any other thing that is contrary to sound doctrine, according to the glorious gospel of the blessed God which was committed to my trust (1 Timothy 1:8-11).

Paul shows that the moral standards of the law are in full agreement with the truths of the gospel. The law is given to prevent man from sinning; it shows him what is right from what is wrong. The righteous man obeys this law and keeps its commandments. The Christian neither forgets nor disobeys God's law because, in the new covenant, God has put it within his heart (Hebrews 8:10). Our Lord Jesus Christ showed that obedience to God's law was not a thing of the past or something that his followers could ignore. He told them that keeping God's commandments was not just a matter of outward behaviour but of the heart, relating to our inward thoughts, our motives and our desires.

a) God's Law is eternal

Do not think that I came to destroy the Law or the Prophets. I did not come to destroy but to fulfil. For assuredly I say to you, till heaven and earth pass away, one jot or one tittle will by no means pass from the law till all is fulfilled (Matthew 5:17-18).

b) God's Law is spiritual, searching the heart

You have heard that it was said to those of old, '*You shall not murder,*' and whoever murders will be in danger of the judgement. But I say to you that whoever is angry with his brother without a cause shall be in danger of the judgement. And whoever says to his brother, 'Raca!' shall be in danger of the council. But whoever says, 'You fool!' shall be in danger of hell fire ... You have heard that it was said to those of old, '*You shall not commit adultery.*' But I say

to you that whoever looks at a woman to lust for her has
already committed adultery with her in his heart (Matthew
5:21-22, 27-28).

May a Christian kill or commit adultery because he is no
longer under the law? No, of course not! God's law applies
to the whole of mankind. When a lawyer asked Jesus which
was the most important commandment in the law, Jesus
answered by summarising the two sections of the Ten
Commandments, saying:

'You shall love the LORD your God with all your heart,
with all your soul, and with all your mind.' This is the first
and great commandment. And the second is like it: 'You
shall love your neighbour as yourself.' On these two commandments hang all the Law and the Prophets (Matthew
22:37-40).

The Ten Commandments (Exodus 20:1-17) show us firstly
our duty to God (1-4) and secondly our duty to our neighbour (5-10). Jesus said we are to love them both. How? By
paying attention to what God tells us to do in the two parts
of the Ten Commandments. Jesus shows that God's law is
eternally true and will always be relevant to mankind, both
believer and unbeliever. This is because it is the expression
of God's holy will, which never changes:

It is easier for heaven and earth to pass away than for
one tittle of the Law to fail. Whoever divorces his wife and
marries another commits adultery; and whoever marries
her who is divorced from her husband commits adultery
(Luke 16:17-18).

The Ten Commandments as interpreted by Jesus in Matthew
5 show us the way God wants us to think in our hearts and
to behave in our lives. For this reason they provide the moral

foundation for our sanctification, a foundation that never changes. When we understand the spirituality of God's holy law, that it is concerned with loving God and loving our neighbour, then we can see why its high and holy standards are necessary today for our sanctification (James 2:8).

Paul says that by the deeds of the law no one can be justified because all the law can do is to expose our sin (Romans 3:20). The law is a mirror which shows us how God sees us. There is nothing wrong with God's law; the fault lies in us:

> Therefore the law is holy, and the commandment holy and just and good …For we know that the law is spiritual, but I am carnal, sold under sin (Romans 7:12,14).

Through the new birth and the gift of the indwelling Holy Spirit the believer has been given the desire and the power to keep God's law, not to justify himself, but as a rule of life:

> For what the law could not do in that it was weak through the flesh, God *did* by sending His own Son in the likeness of sinful flesh, on account of sin: He condemned sin in the flesh, that the righteous requirement of the law might be fulfilled in us who do not walk according to the flesh but according to the Spirit (Romans 8:3-4).

The Ten Commandments

- God's Commandments are not merely negative, telling us what not to do.
- God's commandments are very positive, telling us what we should do.

Commandments 1-4:   My duty to God.
Commandments 5-10:   My duty to my neighbour.

Jesus confirmed the truth of this division of the Law in Matthew 22:36-40

1 God alone is to be worshipped
(-) Don't worship anyone or any-thing but God.
(+) Love, serve and honour God.

2 All idol worship is forbidden.
(-) Don't make an idol of anything or anyone.
(+) Give God the worship of your heart and soul.

3 God's name is holy and sacred
(-) Never use God's name as a swear word.
(+) Reverence everything that God is and does

4 Remember to keep Sunday holy
(-) Avoid all work and things that keep you and your family away from God.
(+) Give yourself to the worship and praise of God.

5 Honour your parents.
(-) Do not despise, hate or disobey your parents.
(+) Love, care and respect them.

6 Do not kill.
(-) Do not hate in your heart or hurt with your hand.
(+) Protect your neighbour's property and his life.

7 Do not commit adultery.
(-) Avoid all sexual impurity in thought, word and deed.
(+) Be pure in thought, word and deed.

8 Do not steal.
(-) Do not take away your neigh-bour's property or reputation.
(+) Protect your neighbour's prop-erty and reputation.

9 Do not tell lies	(-) Do not lie, slander or deceive your neighbour.
	(+) Defend your neighbour's well-being.
10 Do not envy other people.	(-) Do not desire to have what is not yours.
	(+) Be glad in your neighbour's success and prosperity.

c) **Sunday**. Some Christians have queried the rightness of equating the observance of the fourth commandment with the Christian Sunday. The reasons for believing that Sunday is the Christian Sabbath are as follows:

• The Ten Commandments are a summary of God's moral law and since God's nature does not and cannot change so his moral values do not change.

• When God created man at the beginning in Genesis 1-3 he gave him certain rules. These were: marriage and procreation, subduing nature, work and the Sabbath day. These five commands pre-date the Ten Commandments and remain God's will for man for all time. They are called creation ordinances.

• In the Law of Moses when Israel was a theocracy the death penalty was instituted for the following crimes: idol worship, witchcraft, murder, adultery, rape, homosexuality, sexual sins, disobedience to parents, blasphemy, false teaching and Sabbath breaking. If God hated those sins then why should it be thought that he hates any of them any the less now? However, it would seem that Jesus modified the sanction in the case of adultery (see John 8:11).

• Christ observed the Sabbath day (Luke 4:16) and taught that the Sabbath was made for *man* (Mark 2:27) not just for the Jews. God made the day of rest for the good of *all* his creatures.

• In the New Testament period the early Christians began to assemble together on the first day of the week (Acts 20:7; 1 Corinthians 16:2), the day on which the Lord Jesus rose from the dead and which came to be known as 'the Lord's day' (Revelation 1:10). Sunday then became the Christian Sabbath, a day of rest and a holy day that celebrated Christ's resurrection.

• The observance of all kinds of different religious days was a feature of Judaism. False teachers from among the Jews tried to impose their ceremonials, festivals and traditions on the early Church. It is this that Paul rejects in Romans 14:5 and Colossians 2:16, *not* having a Sabbath day according to God's commandment.

Questions

1 What means has God provided to help us to live a holy life?

2 What are the differences between the 'old man' and the 'new man'?

3 How do the Ten Commandments help us to live a holy life?

CHAPTER FOURTEEN

ASSURANCE

1 The meaning of the word

2 The grounds of assurance

   a) Objective: believing the promises of God:five
      examples
   b) Subjective: evidences of spiritual life in our hearts: seven
      examples
   c) The inward witness of the Holy Spirit: three
      evidences in the life of the believer

3 Is assurance essential to salvation?

Is it possible for believers to know they are children of God and will inherit everlasting life? Yes, it is.

> These things I have written to you who believe in the name of the Son of God, that you may know that you have eternal life (1 John 5:13).

Those who truly believe in Jesus Christ as their Lord and Saviour, love him in sincerity and endeavour to walk before him in all good conscience, can in this life be genuinely and scripturally confident that they are truly saved and rejoice in hope of the glory of God.

This certainty is a true assurance of faith that is founded upon three things.

Firstly, on the divine truth of God's promises of salvation by faith written in the Bible.

Secondly, on the evidences of spiritual life wrought in us by the Holy Spirit.

Thirdly, on the inward witness of the Holy Spirit who witnesses with our spirits that we are children of God.

1 The meaning of the word

Pistis in the New Testament is usually translated 'faith', but in some instances it is translated 'assurance', meaning adequate ground for certainty or belief. For example:

> Because he has appointed a day on which He will judge the world in righteousness by the Man whom He has ordained. He has given assurance of this to all by raising Him from the dead (Acts 17:31; see also 2 Timothy 3:14).

Plērophoria means a state of certainty, entire confidence, full assurance. Paul writes that the gospel came to the Thessalonian believers 'in power, and in the Holy Spirit and in much assurance' (1 Thessalonians 1:5; see also Hebrews 6:11; 10:22).

Assurance has therefore a twofold aspect. Firstly, the *objective* element: we can trust God's word in its testimony that those who believe Christ's salvation and His word of promise shall have everlasting life. Secondly, the *subjective* element: the Holy Spirit produces in us evidences of spiritual life and also witnesses with our spirit that we are children of God. This gives an inward sense of fellowship with God, of forgiveness of sins, of cleansing and peace. If we take these two elements together, the objective and the subjective, we can assure ourselves that we are born of God.

2 The grounds of assurance

a) Objective: believing the promises of God . Our first ground of assurance comes from believing what God says. If God promises to give salvation to those who believe his Word, if he says that we can know for certain that we are saved through trusting in Christ, if he says that we can know our sins have been forgiven, then is it not our duty to believe him and accept his promised salvation?

> For God so loved the world that He gave His only begotten Son, that whoever believes in Him should not perish but have everlasting life (John 3:16).

i) Do we believe this?

> He who believes in the Son has everlasting life; and he who does not believe the Son shall not see life, but the wrath of God abides on him (John 3:36).

ii) Do we believe this?

> Most assuredly, I say to you, he who hears My word and believes in Him who sent Me has everlasting life, and shall not come into judgement, but has passed from death into life (John 5:24).

iii) Do we believe this?

> Most assuredly, I say to you, he who believes in Me has everlasting life (John 6:47).

iv) Do we believe this?

> To Him all the prophets witness that, through His name, whoever believes in Him will receive remission of sins (Acts 10:43).

v) Do we believe this?

> And this is the testimony: that God has given us eternal life, and this life is in His Son. He who has the Son has life; he who does not have the Son of God does not have life. These things I have written to you who believe in the name of the Son of God, that you may know that you have eternal life (1 John 5:11-13).

What could be clearer than this? God promises eternal life here and now to all who truly believe in Christ as Lord and Saviour; those who do so pass at that moment from death to life! The promise is sure to all who have faith and put their trust in him. The matter is therefore quite simple: do we believe in the Son of God and his saving work for us? If we do, in sincerity and in truth, then the Bible says we have everlasting life. This objective Word of God is our sure foundation; it guarantees us a place in heaven, based not on our merit or feelings, but on his promise. This is the first step to obtaining full assurance of faith – believing God's Word.

b) Subjective: evidences of spiritual life in our hearts .

In addition to believing the promises of God's Word addressed to all those who put their trust in Christ for salvation, the Bible mentions other tests that we should apply to ourselves. These tests relate to the manifestation of new life in those who have been regenerated by God's Spirit. When the Holy Spirit comes into a person's life certain results will follow – the life of God will begin to show itself in that person's beliefs, behaviour and appetites. The seed of eternal life planted by the Holy Spirit will begin to grow so that gradually but inexorably the whole personality is transformed from sin to holiness.

i) Holiness – obedience to God's Word. This obedience is progressive because it is something that grows as the result of the new principle of life within the believer and his increasing understanding of God's Word and its application to his thoughts, words and actions. This manifestation of holiness comes from within the person's heart as a result of the inward work of the Holy Spirit. He who once scorned morality and goodness now discovers that it is his greatest desire to be Christ-like, and to please God becomes the main priority of his life.

> Now by this we know that we know Him, if we keep His commandments. He who says, 'I know Him,' and does not keep His commandments, is a liar, and the truth is not in him. But whoever keeps His word, truly the love of God is perfected in him. By this we know that we are in Him. He who says he abides in Him ought himself also to walk just as He walked (1 John 2:3-6).

> Whoever abides in Him does not sin. Whoever sins has neither seen Him nor known Him. Little children, let no one deceive you. He who practises righteousness is righteous, just as He is righteous (1 John 3:6-7).

(ii) Love for the people of God. Those we formerly despised, ridiculed and rejected for going to church and making an effort to follow Christ we now find to be the very people we want to be with. Once we hated Christians but now we love them. This is the direct result of the radical change that the Holy Spirit has worked in our hearts.

> We know that we have passed from death to life, because we love the brethren. He who does not love *his* brother abides in death (1 John 3:14).

A love for holiness (obeying God's Word) is linked to a love for holy people (the people of God). How can we know if our love for the people of God is a fruit of the Spirit and not simply an admiration for religious people who live good moral lives? The apostle John says we can test it by asking ourselves if we also want to be like them and be holy ourselves:

> By this we know that we love the children of God, when we love God and keep His commandments (1 John 5:2).

(iii) Hatred of the materialistic, hedonistic values of this world. What are the values of a materialistic godless, sin-loving society? The apostle John tells us and warns Christians not to love the life of human society living in rebellion against God and his holy standards.

> Do not love the world or the things in the world. If anyone loves the world, the love of the Father is not in him. For all that *is* in the world – the lust of the flesh, the lust of the eyes, and the pride of life – is not of the Father but is of the world. And the world is passing away, and lust of it; but he who does the will of God abides forever (1 John 2:15-17).

When a person is born again by God's Spirit he is soon aware that he no longer loves the words and ways of those he formerly associated with. Sinful behaviour used to amuse him, but now it shocks him. Drunkenness, immorality, cursing, lying, stealing and the lust for money and power, all these things are suddenly hateful to him. This is one of the signs that he is no longer a child of the devil but a child of God.

(iv) The inward witness of the Holy Spirit. No one can become a true believer in Christ without the inward work of the Holy Spirit. He himself said so (John 3:5-8) and so did the apostle Paul:

> But you are not in the flesh but in the Spirit, if indeed the Spirit of God dwells in you. Now if anyone does not have the Spirit of Christ, he is not His (Romans 8:9).

When the Spirit of God comes with His holy and transforming power into a person's life the effects will be seen and known even by the person himself:

> For you did not receive the spirit of bondage again to fear, but you received the Spirit of adoption by whom we cry out, 'Abba, Father.' The Spirit Himself bears witness with our spirit that we are children of God (Romans 8:15-16).

> And by this we know that He abides in us, by the Spirit whom He has given us (1 John 3:24; see also 4:13).

> But you have an anointing from the Holy One, and you know all things (1 John 2:20; see also 2:27).

The 'anointing' refers to the giving of the Holy Spirit, as in Acts 10:38, 'God anointed Jesus of Nazareth with the Holy Spirit and with power...'. Assurance is an inward and experimental knowledge of God produced in us by the Holy Spirit.

(v) Faith in Christ as Saviour and Lord. Before conversion we may have believed theoretically in the existence and in the divinity of Jesus but it made absolutely no difference whatsoever to our lives. Similarly we may have feared God as the vengeful judge, but this did not lead us to trust our souls to him. The Father reveals the person and work of his Son to the seeking soul. Jesus said:

> No one can come to Me unless the Father who sent Me draws him; and I will raise him up at the last day. It is written in the prophets, 'And they shall all be taught by God.' Therefore everyone who has heard and learned from the Father comes to Me (John 6:44-45).

Faith in Christ as Saviour and Lord is therefore one of the signs that we are born of God:

> Whoever believes that Jesus is the Christ is born of God, and everyone who loves Him who begot also loves him who is begotten of Him (1 John 5:1).

> Whoever confesses that Jesus is the Son of God, God abides in him, and he in God (1 John 4:15).

(vi)   Love to others. When a person is born again of God's Spirit not only is his attitude towards God changed but also his attitude toward other people as well. He still has his likes and dislikes, but God has put a new principle of love in his heart which enables him not only to admire but also to obey the word of Christ:

> But I say to you, love your enemies, bless those who curse you, do good to those who hate you, and pray for those who spitefully use you and persecute you, that you may be sons of your Father in heaven; for He makes His sun rise on the evil and on the good, and sends His rain on the just and on the unjust (Matthew 5:44-45).

Whenever a Christian puts this into practice it will be a sign to him that he is indeed a child of God, because before his conversion not only could he not have loved his enemies, he would not even have wanted to do so!

> My little children, let us not love in word or in tongue, but in deed and in truth. And by this we know that we are of the truth, and shall assure our hearts before Him (1 John 3:18-19).

(vii) Fruit of the Spirit. Jesus said that the spiritual relationship between him and the believer is like that which exists between a branch and a tree: the branch draws its life from the main trunk of the tree. There can only be fruit on the branch if it is connected to the tree. Jesus said:

> Abide in Me, and I in you. As the branch cannot bear fruit of itself, unless it abides in the vine, neither can you, unless you abide in Me. I am the vine, you *are* the branches. He who abides in Me, and I in him, bears much fruit; for without Me you can do nothing (John 15:4-5).

The apostle Paul says that through the regenerating work of the Holy Spirit the heavenly influence of the Spirit will manifest itself in the person's life by the presence of his fruit:

> But the fruit of the Spirit is love, joy, peace, longsuffering, kindness, goodness, faithfulness, gentleness, self-control (Galatians 5:22-23).

Jesus confirmed that fruitfulness is a sign of the true Christian when he said:

> By this My Father is glorified, that you bear much fruit; so you will be My disciples (John 15:8).

c) The inward witness of the Holy Spirit.

How can we know that we have the Holy Spirit and that we are not deluding ourselves? How can we be sure that we have his presence with us? Might it not simply be that we have elevated feelings of happiness or some kind of emotional ecstasy? Paul tells us certain things that characterize the work of the Spirit in the life of the believer:

i)   The sealing of the Holy Spirit. What is a seal used for?

* *To authenticate or certify something as genuine.* Pharaoh handed his seal to Joseph as a sign to everyone that he was now his deputy (Genesis 41:42).
* *To indicate ownership.* Jeremiah sealed a deed when he bought a field, as a sign that the transaction was in his name (Jeremiah 32:10).
* *To render secure.* The Jews sealed Jesus' tomb to make it secure (Matthew 27:65-66).

  Now He who establishes us with you in Christ and has anointed us *is* God, who also has sealed us and given us the Spirit in our hearts as a deposit (2 Corinthians 1:21-22).

  In Him you also *trusted*, after you heard the word of truth, the gospel of your salvation; in whom also, having believed, you were sealed with the Holy Spirit of promise, who is the guarantee of our inheritance until the redemption of the purchased possession, to the praise of His glory (Ephesians 1:13-14; see also Ephesians 4:30).

When God seals us with his Holy Spirit he does each of these three things to us at the same time:

Firstly, on receiving the gift of the Holy Spirit we are shown to be genuine children of God.

Secondly, we are marked out as being owned by God and belonging to God, who has redeemed us by the death of his Son.

Thirdly, we are made safe and secure by receiving God's protection against all our enemies.

God is calling out of the world a believing people for his own special possession (Titus 2:14). God seals us with the threefold seal of his Holy Spirit. As we receive the Holy Spirit he brings an inward sense of assurance that we really belong to God. The indwelling presence of the Spirit not only makes us Christians, it is also a proof to us that we are Christians, and that we are heirs of an eternal inheritance.

ii) The pledge of the Spirit. The Greek word *arrabōn* was commonly used in commerce in New Testament times. When a contract was entered into or a deal completed, one paid an *arrabōn*, a 'deposit' or pledge which guaranteed that full payment would follow. In modern Greek *arrabōn* means an engagement ring, a pledge that the full relationship of marriage will follow. In the NewTestament there are three references to this word, two are quoted above (2 Corinthians 1:21-22; Ephesians 1:13-14), see paragraph c, i) in connection with 'sealing', and the third is in 2 Corinthians 5:5:

> Now He who has prepared us for this very thing, *is* God who also has given us the Spirit as a guarantee.

Our experience of the Spirit after conversion is only the deposit, but it is a guarantee that we will have the full payment of eternal life in heaven with God. The Spirit is given as a pledge of all that is to come. In Ephesians 1:14 we are told that the Holy Spirit of promise is the guarantee of our inheritance. How do we know that we shall really have the fullness of our eternal inheritance? By the pledge of the Spirit who is given to us as the first instalment of the riches of the inheritance that awaits us.

iii) The Spirit of adoption. One of the most blessed discoveries that we make after we have been born again, is the awareness that he whom we formerly ran away from in fear, is now our heavenly Father.

> For you did not receive the spirit of bondage again to fear, but you received the Spirit of adoption by whom we cry out, 'Abba, Father.' The Spirit Himself bears witness with our spirit that we are children of God (Romans 8:15-16).

There is a twofold work of the Spirit here:

Firstly, as the result of being born again by God's Spirit, our own spirits are made alive to God and instinctively we cry out, 'Abba, Father'.

Secondly, the Holy Spirit also bears his own witness with our spirits that we are children of God. He directly and inwardly assures us of our sonship in a most intimate and delightful manner, so that we know Him and rejoice in God according to the word in Romans 5:5, '...because the love of God has been poured out in our hearts by the Holy Spirit who was given to us.' This is one of the most wonderful and divine works of the Spirit. It completes his work of assuring the believer that he is a child of God, and that he is a partaker of the eternal inheritance laid up for him in heaven (1 Peter 1:4).

3 Is assurance essential to salvation?

No, it is not essential, but it is attainable and always accompanies a healthy and active faith. Some believers, particularly those who are new to the faith, have a weak faith. For example, Peter had been a follower of Christ for quite some time and definitely believed in Jesus, but his faith was weak. When Christ called him to walk on the water he started out well, but then he doubted and began to sink. Jesus said to him, 'O you of little faith, why did you doubt?' (Matthew 14:31) Similarly Peter denied Jesus just before the crucifixion for the same reason. Paul mentions those whose weak faith caused them to eat only herbs (Romans 14:1-2). We are not to reprove such people, but treat them very gently, because they can easily be hurt by disputes about things they do not yet understand. They *have* faith but it is still only a *weak* faith. In the letter to the Hebrews we read of those who had come to doubt their faith due to their sufferings, so they needed to learn again the first principles of the faith:

> For though by this time you ought to be teachers, you need *someone* to teach you again the first principles of the oracles of God; and you have come to need milk and not solid food (Hebrews 5:12).

The writer then goes on, not only to warn them, but also to encourage them to continue in the faith, and to go forward with perseverance:

> And we desire that each one of you show the same diligence to the full assurance of hope until the end (Hebrews 6:11).

A weak faith still truly believes in Christ, but it has doubts, fears and misgivings. Yet it is a true faith that needs to grow and mature. Full assurance of faith is not only desirable and attainable, but it is God's will for all his children. John writes:

> These things I have written to you who believe in the name of the Son of God, that you may know you have eternal life (1 John 5:13).

Questions

1 How can we know that we are children of God?

2 What part does the Holy Spirit play in assuring believers that they are children of God?

3 Can a true Christian lack assurance?

CHAPTER FIFTEEN

UNION WITH CHRIST

1 The terms used to describe it

   a) To be 'in Christ'
   b) Branches of the vine
   c) He is the head, we are the body
   d) The husband/wife relationship
   e) Christ is the corner-stone
   f) 'In Adam' – 'in Christ'

2 The nature of the believer's union with Christ

   a) Negatively: what it is not: two aspects
   b) Positively: what it is: six aspects

3 How is this union established and enjoyed?

   a) By the Holy Spirit
   b) Through faith

4 The fruitful consequences of this union

   a) Objective : things he has done for us: five consequences
   b) Subjective : things he has done in us: five consequences

For if we have been united together in the likeness of His death, certainly we also shall be *in the likeness* of *His* resurrection (Romans 6:5).

I am the vine, you *are* the branches. He who abides in Me, and I in him, bears much fruit; for without Me you can do nothing (John 15:5).

What does the Bible mean when it says that the believer is spiritually united to Christ? To be united to Christ means being united with him in the whole scope of his redemptive work: crucified with him, dead with him, buried with him, raised with him and reigning with him. Faith is the bond that unites us to Christ.

1 The terms used to describe it

a) To be 'in Christ'. A Christian is described as a person who is *in* Christ (an expression used 153 times by the apostle Paul); he is not only spiritually joined to Christ but, in a mystical sense, he is also united to him as a whole person.

For we are members of His body (Ephesians 5:30).

So we, *being* many, are one body in Christ, and individually members of one another (Romans 12:5).

Therefore, if anyone *is* in Christ, *he is* a new creation; old things have passed away; behold, all things have become new (2 Corinthians 5:17).

b) Branches of the vine. In order to describe the living relationship between himself and the Christian, Jesus gave the illustration of the vine and its branches. He is the living vine and we are his branches:

I am the vine, you *are* the branches. He who abides in Me,
and I in him, bears much fruit; for without Me you can do
nothing (John 15:5).

c) He is the head, we are the body. Surely there can be
no closer relationship than that which exists between the
several parts of the human body and the head:

But, speaking the truth in love, may grow up in all things
into Him who is the head – Christ – from whom the whole
body, joined and knit together by what every joint supplies,
according to the effective working by which every part
does its share, causes growth of the body for the edifying
of itself in love (Ephesians 4:15-16).

d) The husband/wife relationship. There is no more loving
and intimate relationship in our earthly human experience
than that between a man and a woman in the marriage relationship. Paul says that such a union between two believers
points to the union between Christ and his church:

'*For this reason a man shall leave his father and mother
and be joined to his wife, and the two shall become one
flesh.*' This is a great mystery, but I speak concerning
Christ and the church (Ephesians 5:31-32).

See also Revelation 21:2, 9 where the church is the bride of
Christ.

**e) Christ is the corner-stone supporting us in God's
temple.** The Christian is described as being an essential part
of God's building, the church. We each share a place as individual stones in the walls of his holy temple:

... Jesus Christ Himself being the chief corner*stone*, in
whom the whole building, being joined together, grows into
a holy temple in the Lord, in whom you also are being built

together for a habitation of God in the Spirit (Ephesians 2:20-21).

See also 1 Peter 2:4-6; Christ is the corner-stone, we the living stones of a spiritual house.

f) 'In Adam' – 'in Christ'. By our natural birth we were part of the old fallen humanity, but by our spiritual birth we are made part of the new humanity in Christ Jesus:

For as in Adam all die, even so in Christ all shall be made alive (1 Corinthians 15:22). [This includes the resurrection of the body].

See also Romans 5:12-21

2 The nature of the believer's union with Christ

a) Negatively: what it is not

i) Union with Christ is not a merging of our individual human existence with the divine in such a way that we are absorbed into the Infinite, causing the individual soul to lose its unique identity. Christ remains who and what he is and always has been, and we remain the individual souls that we became by creation. When we shall see him in heaven we shall be like him, yet without losing our own identity (1 John 3:2).

ii) It is not merely a union of sympathy or of interest. For example members of a club or a society share common interests and aims but in every other respect may be radically different from one another. The only thing that unites them is their shared interest.

b) Positively: what it is

i) It is a spiritual union. By the power of the Holy Spirit we are born again into God's heavenly family. By the same Spirit Christ now lives in us and unites us to himself by faith. This is a living spiritual relationship that is both everlasting and transforming:

> But he who is joined to the Lord is one spirit *with Him* (1 Corinthians 6:17).

> For by one Spirit we were all baptized into one body – whether Jews or Greeks, whether slaves or free – and have all been made to drink into one Spirit (1 Corinthians 12:13).

ii) It is a mystical union. It is called 'mystical' because it is effected by the Holy Spirit in a mysterious and supernatural way. Marriage is an illustration of this relationship: two people become one without either of them losing their identity:

> *'For this reason a man shall leave his father and mother and be joined to his wife, and the two shall become one flesh.'* This is a great mystery, but I speak concerning Christ and the church (Ephesians 5:31-32).

iii) It is a living union. Our union and relationship with Christ is a living and dynamic thing; it is not something static or theoretical. We actually receive his life-giving power into our souls. He is intimately concerned about us, cares for us, hears our prayers, guides our lives and transforms us into his likeness:

> But we all, with unveiled face, beholding as in a mirror the glory of the Lord, are being transformed into the same image from glory to glory, just as by the Spirit of the Lord (2 Corinthians 3:18).

And of His fulness we have all received, and grace for grace (John 1:16).

A little while longer and the world will see Me no more, but you will see Me. Because I live, you will live also. At that day you will know that I *am* in My Father, and you in Me, and I in you (John 14:19-20).

See also John 17:22-23; Galatians 2:20.

iv) It is an organic union. Christ and his church are one body. The mutual relationship that exists between us is therefore a living one of great intensity. In this relationship he ministers life, gifts, comfort and intelligence to us. We in turn minister to him in praise, prayer and service.

For as we have many members in one body, but all the members do not have the same function, so we, *being* many, are one body in Christ, and individually members of one another (Romans 12:4-5).

See also 1 Corinthians 6:15-19; Ephesians 1:22-23; 4:15-16; 5:29-30.

v) It is a personal union. We are apt to forget that God is a Person, not some kind of mysterious spiritual influence; he always deals with us as persons. The danger of Roman Catholic and Orthodox thinking concerning our individual relationship with God is that they place 'the Church', between the individual soul and God. They say that without, 'the Church', no one can be saved. They believe that the all spiritual blessings are mediated to men only through the church. But the Bible does not say we are saved by the church but only by a personal relationship to the Son, Jesus Christ. Jesus himself said:

> Come to Me, all *you* who labour and are heavy laden,
> and I will give you rest. Take My yoke upon you and learn
> from Me, for I am gentle and lowly in heart, and you will
> find rest for your souls (Matthew 11:28-29).

The Bible does not say that we are dependent upon the church
for spiritual life, but upon the Son who alone is the author
and giver of spiritual life:

> And this is the testimony: that God has given us eternal
> life, and this life is in His Son. He who has the Son has
> life; he who does not have the Son of God does not have
> life (1 John 5:11-12).

vi) It is an indissoluble union. When we are born again into
God's family we come into an eternal and indissoluble life-
giving relationship with him. Nothing can break this powerful
bond, not even our sin. We remain his children because we
are his and he is ours for ever and ever. Sin can rob us of the
joy of our salvation, but not of salvation itself:

> Who shall separate us from the love of Christ? *Shall*
> tribulation, or distress, or persecution, or famine, or
> nakedness, or peril, or sword? As it is written: *'For Your*
> *sake we are killed all day long; we are accounted as sheep*
> *for the slaughter.'* Yet in all these things we are more than
> conquerors through Him who loved us. For I am persuaded
> that neither death nor life, nor angels nor principalities nor
> powers, nor things present nor things to come, nor height
> nor depth, nor any other created thing, shall be able to
> separate us from the love of God which is in Christ Jesus
> Our Lord (Romans 8:35-39).

3 How is this union established and enjoyed?

a) By the Holy Spirit. All spiritual life, which is the life of
heaven, comes to us only through the ministry and power
of the Holy Spirit:

> Most assuredly, I say to *you*, unless one is born of water
> and the Spirit, he cannot enter the kingdom of God. That
> which is born of the flesh is flesh, and that which is born
> of the Spirit is spirit (John 3:5-6).

b) Through faith. We are not passive spectators in this
relationship; we are active participants. Although God has
established this spiritual union we have to be obedient and
prayerful in order to enjoy his presence, life and power. Faith
strengthens our relationship so that our union with him
becomes more and more real to us. That is why faith is
spoken of so highly in the Scriptures:

> I have been crucified with Christ; it is no longer I who live,
> but Christ lives in me; and the *life* which I now live in the
> flesh I live by faith in the Son of God, who loved me and
> gave Himself for me (Galatians 2:20).

See also Romans 5:1-2.

4   The fruitful consequences of this union

a) Objective: things he has done for us.

- We died, were buried, raised and are seated with him in
  glory (Romans 6:4-5; Ephesians 2:6).
- We are sealed with the Holy Spirit of promise (Ephesians
  1:13).
- We are adopted as sons (Ephesians 1:5).
- We are heirs of God and joint heirs with Christ (Romans
  8:17).
- He is made to us wisdom, righteousness, sanctification
  and redemption (1 Corinthians 1:30).

b) Subjective: things he does in us.

- We have fellowship with him (John 17:3; 1 John 1:3-7).
- We are transformed into his likeness (2 Corinthians 3:18).
- We bear spiritual fruit (John 15:4-8).
- We receive spiritual gifts (Ephesians 4:7-12; Romans 12:4-8).
- We suffer reproach for his sake (Philippians 3:10; Colossians 1:24).

Questions

1 Name all the biblical metaphors used to describe our union with Christ

2 Give reasons why the union between Christ and the believer can never be broken

3 What are the results of this union in the life of a believer?

CHAPTER SIXTEEN

ETERNAL SECURITY

1 Definition

2 Biblical evidence for eternal security

Eight evidences

3 The main elements of God's salvation cannot be destroyed

   a) Election
   b) Justification
   c) Redemption
   d) Regeneration
   e) Adoption
   f) Sanctification
   g) Assurance
   h) Glorification

4 Grace is more powerful than sin

5 Objections to eternal security

   a) The parable of the sower
   b) The man with the unclean spirit
   c) The parable of the vine and the branches
   d) Those who have apostatised
   e) Warnings to two churches

Can true believers lose their salvation? What does the Bible teach?

Throughout history Bible-believing Christians have been divided in their opinions on this question. Traditionally many Arminian churches have taught that it is possible for a born again believer to fall from grace, turn away from the Lord and finally be lost. In support of their view they quote the following examples:

• King Saul received the ability to prophesy through the Holy Spirit but in the end, because of his sinfulness, God rejected him, and the Spirit of the Lord departed from him for ever (1 Samuel 16:14).

• Jesus says, in the parable of the unmerciful servant, that the Father will punish those of his servants who remain unmerciful and unforgiving (Matthew 18:25).

• In the parable of the sower two of those who heard the gospel word believed for a time but were finally lost (Matthew 13:20-22).

• In the parable of the vine and the branches Jesus says that some branches which did not stay in the vine will be rejected and burned (John 15:6).

• In Hebrews 6:4-8 the author says its impossible for those who were once enlightened, have tasted of the heavenly gift, and have become partakers of the Holy Spirit, and have tasted the good word of God, and the powers of the age to come, to be renewed again to repentance if they fall away. And later in this book (10:26-29) it is said that the believer who comes to reject the gospel has no forgiveness.

• There are several places in the New Testament where we are warned of the dangers of being deceived and falling away (Matthew 24:4; 2 Peter 1:10; 2:20-21)

While we acknowledge that these passages do appear to teach that a child of God can lose his salvation, we believe that it is possible to reconcile them with those that positively teach the opposite view. In what follows we shall seek to show the biblical reasons that persuade us that the believer in Christ Jesus has eternal security according to his promise:

> My sheep hear My voice, and I know them, and they follow Me. And I give them eternal life, and they shall never perish; neither shall anyone snatch them out of My hand. My Father, who has given *them* to Me, is greater than all; and no one is able to snatch *them* out of My Father's hand (John 10:27-29).

1 Definition

The doctrine that once a person has truly believed in Christ he or she can never be lost is based upon a number of Scriptures. These say that no one can rob Christ of his sheep. They can never perish, for those whom God has given to Christ cannot be lost. God himself will protect and keep them by his mighty power; he who began the work of salvation in us will himself complete it. In other words salvation is not the work of man but the work of God – he begins it, he sustains it, and he completes it.

2 Biblical evidence

a) No one can take Christ's sheep from him

> My sheep hear My voice, and I know them, and they follow Me. And I give them eternal life, and they shall never

perish; neither shall anyone snatch them out of My hand. My Father, who has given *them* to Me, is greater than all; and no one is able to snatch *them* out of My Father's hand (John 10:27-29).

b) Those whom God has given to Christ will not be lost

This is the will of the Father who sent Me, that of all He has given Me I should lose nothing, but should raise it up at the last day (John 6:39).

c) God the Father keeps us from falling away

Now I am no longer in the world, but these are in the world, and I come to You. Holy Father, keep through Your name those whom You have given Me, that they may be one as We *are* (John 17:11)

Now to Him who is able to keep you from stumbling, and to present *you* faultless before the presence of His glory with exceeding joy (Jude 24).

Blessed *be* the God and Father of Our Lord Jesus Christ, who according to His abundant mercy has begotten us again to a living hope through the resurrection of Jesus Christ from the dead, to an inheritance incorruptible and undefiled and that does not fade away, reserved in heaven for you, who are kept by the power of God through faith for salvation ready to be revealed in the last time (1 Peter 1:3-5).

For this reason I also suffer these things; nevertheless I am not ashamed, for I know whom I have believed and am persuaded that He is able to keep what I have committed to Him until that Day ... And the Lord will deliver me from every evil work and preserve *me* for His heavenly kingdom. To Him be glory for ever and ever. Amen! (2 Timothy 1:12; 4:18).

d) God who began salvation in us will also complete it.

Being confident of this very thing, that He who has begun a good work in you will complete *it* until the day of Jesus Christ (Philippians 1:6).

But the Lord is faithful, who will establish you and guard *you* from the evil one (2 Thessalonians 3:3).

e) The true believer is delivered from the final judgement to damnation.

Most assuredly, I say to you, he who hears My word and believes in Him who sent Me has everlasting life, and shall not come into judgement, but has passed from death into life (John 5:24).

f) The seed of eternal life cannot die. Those who are born of God cannot return to the life of sin.

Whoever has been born of God does not sin, for His seed remains in him; and he cannot sin, because he has been born of God (1 John 3:9).

g) God works in us according to a predetermined plan. As we will see in chapter seventeen, the fall of man was foreknown by God. His plan of salvation was ready to be put into operation as soon as Adam sinned (see Genesis 3:15). The death of Christ was also planned by God before man fell into sin:

But with the precious blood of Christ, as of a lamb without blemish and without spot. He indeed was foreordained before the foundation of the world, but was manifest in these last times for you (1 Peter 1:19-20).

This was because the fall of Satan and his confederate angels occurred before the creation of the world. Several verses in the Bible refer to God working according to a predetermined plan:

> But we speak the wisdom of God in a mystery, the hidden *wisdom* which God ordained before the ages for our glory (1 Corinthians 2:7).

> Just as He chose us in Him before the foundation of the world, that we should be holy and without blame before Him in love (Ephesians 1:4).

See also Romans 8:28; 9:11 and 11:25; Galatians 4:4; 2 Timothy 1:9.

God's plan affects the life of each individual believer because, in the deep mystery of his will, each one of us was chosen by him before the world began. What did he choose us for? He chose us to receive the salvation that is in Christ Jesus, a salvation that is complete only when we arrive safely in heaven. God does not rest content with giving us the forgiveness of sins; he is determined to fulfil his plan and to bring us to heaven to join the great company of the redeemed in his kingdom. He does not regard his work as complete until we are with him in eternity; what he begins he always completes:

> Moreover whom He predestined, these He also called; whom He called, these He also justified; and whom He justified, these He also glorified (Romans 8:30).

God's plan of salvation for each individual soul is the foundation of our eternal security.

h) The radical and irreversible nature of the new birth.
When a man is born again through the power of the Holy
Spirit he becomes a new creation. He is delivered out of
Satan's power and into the kingdom of God's dear Son (Colossians 1:13):

> Therefore, if anyone *is* in Christ, *he is* a new creation; old
> things have passed away; behold, all things have become
> new (2 Corinthians 5:17).

Through the new birth we are liberated from the power of
the carnal mind and enabled through the power of the Holy
Spirit to have a new and a spiritual mind:

> For to be carnally minded *is* death, but to be spiritually
> minded *is* life and peace. Because the carnal mind is
> enmity against God; for it is not subject to the law of God,
> nor indeed can be. So then, those who are in the flesh
> cannot please God (Romans 8:6-8).

> But the natural man does not receive the things of the
> Spirit of God, for they are foolishness to him; nor can
> he know *them*, because they are spiritually discerned
> (1 Corinthians 2:14).

The Scriptures speak of a most radical and irreversible change
that takes place in a man's soul when he is truly converted
to God – he becomes alive to God through the Holy Spirit.
There is no middle ground, one is either a carnal man or a
spiritual man. Once we have passed from death to life we
are new men and women in Christ Jesus: we can never again
become carnally minded and dead to God.

Once we have received the mind of Christ we cannot lose
it and return to a carnal mind. This is because the carnal mind
is enmity against God and regards the things of the Spirit as
foolishness. Those who hold that a man can lose his salvation, and revert to being a worldling again, fail to realise the

profound and irreversible nature of the change that takes place in our minds at the new birth:

> Jesus answered and said to him, 'Most assuredly, I say to you, unless one is born again, he cannot see the kingdom of God ... that which is born of the flesh is flesh, and that which is born of the Spirit is spirit' (John 3:3,6).

When a man has been born of the Spirit he becomes a new man and a child of God. It is impossible for him to become spiritually dead again and for God to reject him as an outcast. Jesus said:

> All that the Father gives Me will come to Me, and the one who comes to Me I will by no means cast out (John 6:37).

If believers are given by God to Christ, and he has promised never to reject them, do we not have an unshakable foundation for our faith? God's promises assure us that such confidence in an eternally secure salvation is not misplaced, because they are made by the God who always keeps his promises. He is the God of truth and infinite power, so what he promises he always performs.

3 The main elements of God's salvation cannot be destroyed

The following doctrines describe what God has done for us. They are not temporary measures but are permanent both in their duration and their effects.

a) Election. We have been chosen in Christ before the foundation of the world (Ephesians 1:4).

b) Justification. We have been declared by God free from guilt and righteous in his sight. This is because our sins have been laid on Christ and his righteousness imputed to us; Christ has kept the law and fulfilled all its demands for us. The believer therefore has an eternally new relationship both to God and to the law through Christ's death on the cross (Romans 3:20-24).

c) Redemption. We have been delivered out of our slavery to sin and to Satan by the blood of Christ. He has purchased helpless captives out of the kingdom of darkness and brought them into the freedom of his eternal kingdom (Colossians 1:13).

d) Regeneration. We have been born again through the Holy Spirit and received new spiritual life and a new nature. Christ said that the believer has the seed of eternal life in him, a life that can never die (John 3:16; 1 John 3:9).

e) Adoption. We have been born again into God's family. He is now our Father and we will always be his children (Galatians 4:5).

f) Sanctification. We have been set apart from the world by the Holy Spirit for God and his service. God is transforming us into the image of his Son to be holy in word and deed (2 Corinthians 3:18).

g) Assurance. We are enabled to know that we have salvation. John writes to the believers to confirm their faith. He explains that they can be fully confident that they have eternal life (1 John 3:14 and 5:13). Belief in the doctrine of assurance of salvation is impossible if there is no guarantee that salvation, once obtained, cannot be lost, but is eternally safe and secure.

h) Glorification. We have not only been saved and forgiven but also made heirs of God and joint heirs with Christ. Full salvation ends in heaven; he has not only justified us, he will also glorify us (Romans 8:17, 30).

God's activity in these eight doctrines comprehends our complete deliverance from the power of Satan and sin. We often think of salvation merely in human terms, something that we ask for and that gives us certain blessings. It is very important to see that in reality salvation is God's work from beginning to end:

- He elects us.
- He justifies us.
- He redeems us.
- He regenerates us.
- He adopts us.
- He sanctifies us.
- He assures us.
- He glorifies us.

Eternal security can be justly inferred from the fact that these eight doctrines all describe God's work in our salvation.

4 Grace is more powerful than sin

Paul has said, 'Sin shall not have dominion over you, for you are not under law but under grace' (Romans 6:14). Is Satan stronger than God? Can he plunder God's kingdom and take captive those for whom Christ died? Satan certainly can tempt us and temporarily lead us into sinful behaviour. But he cannot snatch us out of God's hand or rob us of our salvation (John 10:27-28). Although believers can stray away from God, and for a time live a sinful life, this does not mean that God utterly forsakes and disowns them. God's great grace toward his born again children ensures that he never abandons them. The work he began in their lives he will complete (Philippians 1:6).

He takes steps to restore backsliders so that, if we are rebellious or lazy, he will deal with us as a father who disciplines his children. He does not forsake us when we fall into sin but punishes us, as our loving heavenly Father, in order to cure us of our sinful ways.

> 'My son, do not despise the chastening of the LORD, nor be discouraged when you are rebuked by Him; for whom the LORD loves He chastens, and scourges every son whom He receives.' If you endure chastening, God deals with you as with sons; for what son is there whom a father does not chasten? (Hebrews 12:5-7).

He who has chosen us before the foundation of the world, and given his only begotten Son to die for us upon the cross, has determined with set purpose to deliver us completely from Satan's kingdom and power. By giving us his Holy Spirit he empowers us with the ability, not only to see the way to heaven, but actually to arrive there:

> Who shall bring a charge against God's elect? It is God who justifies. Who is he who condemns? It is Christ who died, and furthermore is also risen, who is even at the right hand of God, who also makes intercession for us. Who shall separate us from the love of Christ? Shall tribulation, or distress, or persecution, or famine, or nakedness, or peril, or sword? As it is written: 'For Your sake we are killed all day long; we are accounted as sheep for the slaughter.' Yet in all these things we are more than conquerors through Him who loved us. For I am persuaded that neither death nor life, nor angels nor principalities nor powers, nor things present nor things to come, nor height nor depth, nor any other created thing, shall be able to separate us from the love of God which is in Christ Jesus our Lord (Romans 8:33-39).

5 Objections to eternal security

a) **The parable of the sower** (Matthew 13:3-23). Four types of person are described as hearing the word, but only one of them is finally saved. It is alleged that this parable teaches it is possible, therefore, for a person to believe the gospel but then be lost. But if we examine our Lord's explanation as to the reason why in three cases the seed failed to produce a harvest (verses 18-23), it will be seen in each instance that there was something wrong with the type of soil into which the seed fell. The only one who had spiritual life was the one whose heart is described as, 'good ground'.

There are many who hear the gospel and who show a temporary interest, but then fall away. Why? Because the word never takes root and grows in their hearts. The Bible tells us that there is such a thing as a false or temporary faith. This would apply to people like Judas Iscariot (John 17:12), Hymenaeus (1 Timothy 1:20) and Philetus (2 Timothy 2:17-18). The apostle John in his first letter refers to those who once were in the church but then left because 'they were not of us' (1 John 2:19).

People can be in the church and members of it without ever experiencing the new-birth. The first three categories describe those who never had spiritual life; that is why they fell away, though for a time those in the second and third categories appeared to be true believers.

b) **The man with the unclean spirit** (Luke 11:24-26). Jesus tells us of an unclean spirit that has been removed from a man. After a while he returns again to live in the man's life, taking seven more spirits with him, so his last state is worse than the first. It is alleged that this can only refer to a man who was once a Christian but who then lost his salvation. However, the previous verses provide the answer. The Pharisees had just accused Jesus of casting out devils by using the ruler of devils in order to do so. Jesus therefore in this parable is referring to his opponents who had professed some kind of repentance under John the Baptist's ministry, but now, by calling Christ a collaborator with the devil, were in a worse state spiritually than before. Jesus is not using this example to refer to those who once had faith in him but then fell away.

c) The parable of the vine and the branches (John 15:1-8). Jesus says that every branch in the vine that does not bear fruit will be taken away and burnt. Those who believe that a person can lose their salvation believe that 'every branch' means every believer. But the reason the dead branches were thrown away was because they were without life, they did not bear fruit.

What is the difference between a dead church member and a living one? One is fruitful while the other is not. One has life and the other has not. Jesus had many followers but on one occasion, because of something he said many forsook him (John 6:66). Up till that point they appeared to be his true followers and no different from the apostles themselves. They appeared to be true branches in the vine, but in reality they were lifeless and fruitless. So it is with the Church; there are always some members who are religious without being truly Christian, who look like branches but bear no fruit. Such will be destroyed because they have no life in them. Fruitfulness is the proof that we are true believers; unfruitfulness, that we are not.

d) Those who have apostatised (Hebrews 6:4-10; 10:26-31). A class of temporary believer is here described. They were enlightened, they tasted the heavenly gift, the good word of God, the powers of the world to come and were made partakers of the Holy Spirit. Is this a description of a true Christian? Apparently not, for in the next verse we read:

> But, beloved, we are confident of better things concerning you, yes, things that accompany salvation, though we speak in this manner (Hebrews 6:9).

Evidently the things described in verses 4 to 8 were not things that accompanied salvation. In verse 10 the author says that their practical love to the Lord and to his people were the true signs of salvation. It is tragically possible to receive the enlightenment of the gospel only in one's mind. One may experience some of the blessings of the Holy Spirit and the power of God without being born again. The Bible tells us that Judas, as one of the apostles, preached Christ, healed the sick and cast out devils. Yet he was dominated by Satan and used by him to betray Christ. Nor is he the sole example of those who are active Church workers and yet not real Christians:

> Many will say to Me in that day, 'Lord, Lord, have we not prophesied in Your name, cast out demons in Your name, and done many wonders in Your name?' And then I will declare to them, 'I never knew you; depart from Me, you who practise lawlessness!' (Matthew 7:22-23).

It is a solemn fact that it is possible for a man to be in the church and yet not in Christ, to look like a true branch in the vine yet have no life. Even in the Old Testament there were men like Saul and Balaam, who were clearly influenced by the Holy Spirit, yet remained outside the life and purposes of God.

e) Warnings to two churches (Revelation 3:5,16). Christ speaks very severely to two churches, Sardis and Laodicea. Because of their sinful conduct they are on the point of being judged unless they repent:

To Sardis he says:

> He who overcomes shall be clothed in white garments, and I will not blot out his name from the Book of Life; but I will confess his name before My Father and before His angels.

To Laodicea he says:

> So then, because you are lukewarm, and neither cold nor
> hot, I will spew you out of My mouth.

Does this mean that those whom God chose before the foundation of the world and whose names he placed in the Book of Life can be lost? The Lamb's Book of Life is referred to again in Revelation 13:8; 17:8 and 21:27. Only those whose names are recorded there are preserved from Satan and have a right to a place in heaven. This underlines the fact that it is only by God electing a people for himself that can ensure a bride for the Lamb. Such is the power and cunning of Satan in deceiving the whole world, that if God were to leave man to choose salvation or reject it perhaps no one would ever be saved! God makes no mistakes in those whom he chooses. This statement does not say he will blot out anyone's name but that he will not! The warning could not be more serious. The church in Sardis was in a dreadful condition and about to be closed down. What about the individual believers there who did not repent? They will share the same fate as all believers who live disobedient lives – they will be severely judged, lose their reward, and be deprived of everything except their salvation;

> Each one's work will become manifest; for the Day will
> declare it, because it will be revealed by fire; and the fire
> will test each one's work, of what sort it is ... If anyone's
> work is burned, he will suffer loss; but he himself will be
> saved, yet so as through fire (1 Corinthians 3:13,15).

These severe warnings to both churches, Sardis and Laodicea, show that they were in imminent danger of judgement. We have seen already that within the membership of most churches there are some who are merely religious without being truly Christian. Such people often cause divisions and scandals, and it is very likely that they are in fact the ones being referred to in these two churches. In another church, Thyatira, a woman called Jezebel who claimed to be a prophetess, was the source of the grossest wickedness (2:20). Christ will not tolerate sin in his people and the fire of his judgement falls on all who will not repent. This is the reason why he uses the severest language to warn them of their danger. These solemn warnings, if not heeded, will result in very painful punishments and those who experience them, 'suffer loss'. It is a fearful thing to provoke God to anger and incur his judgement on our sin. These warnings and punishments do not deprive his children of their salvation, though they do deprive them of their reward at the Last Day.

Questions

1 The doctrine of eternal security is based on the fact that our salvation is God's work from first to last. How can we prove this from Scripture?

2 Does eternal security mean that the Christian who has led a lazy and backslidden life will receive the same reward as those Christians who have been fruitful and obedient?

3 How do you explain the threat Christ makes to the churches of Sardis and Laodicea, to blot some of their members out of the Book of Life and to spew others out of his mouth?

CHAPTER SEVENTEEN

ELECTION AND PREDESTINATION

1 Definition of predestination

2 The order of salvation

3 The problem stated

4 Election in the Old Testament

5 Election in the New testament

    a) The Father gives us to Christ
    b) The Father draws us to Christ

6 Why do we need to understand election?

    a) To give us comfort and confidence
    b) To help us give God all the praise and glory
    c) To give us confidence in evangelism

7 Predestination

    a) In the Old Testament
    b) In the New Testament

8 Foreknowledge

9 Calling

    a) The general call
    b) The effectual call

10 Five difficulties

1 Definition of predestination

The word means an act of choice whereby God chooses an individual or group out of a larger company for a purpose or destiny of his own appointment. In the Old Testament this is expressed by the verb *bachar* (to choose,) and in the New Testament by the verb *eklegomai* (to choose, select, see Luke 6:13) and the nouns *eklektos* (chosen, see Romans 8:33) and *eklogē* (election, Romans 9:11).

2 The order of salvation

Theologians see this doctrine as chronologically the first in a series of events, all of which have their origin in God's plan of salvation. This series is called by theologians 'the order of salvation', (Latin, *ordo salutis*).

Election	–	God's choice of people
Calling	–	The effective work of the Holy Spirit
Regeneration	–	The new birth
Conversion	–	Faith and repentance
Justification	–	Right legal standing
Adoption	–	Membership of God's family
Sanctification	–	Holy living
Perseverance	–	Remaining a Christian
Death	–	Absent from the body, present with the Lord
Glorification	–	A new body in a new world

3 The problem stated

Throughout the history of the Christian Church there has been much controversy over the doctrines of election and predestination. This is due to the fact that these doctrines raise profound questions both about the justice and love of God and the nature and freedom of man's will.

Some Christians are opposed to some of the teachings we believe to be biblical, which are expressed in this chapter; particularly the view that election precedes foreknowledge and that man's will is not free because of his bondage both to sin and to Satan. They hold a contrary view for the reasons set out below:

a) The Fall. Although man is a sinner he is not a helpless slave of sin and Satan. He is able to respond to God's grace, having free will to accept or reject God's offer of salvation.

b) Faith. Man has the ability both to desire and to receive saving faith through the grace of the Holy Spirit, who strives to persuade all men to believe the gospel.

c) Foreknowledge. Because God is omniscient he knows precisely all that will happen in the future. Foreknowledge simply means that God foresees the faith of all those who will believe and be saved.

d) Predestination. God then predestinates to salvation all those whom he foreknew would accept his salvation. Predestination and election are the result of God's foreknowledge.

e) Election. God chooses those whom he knows will one day respond to him and his salvation.

f) Christ died for all. Many verses in the New Testament declare that the gospel invitation is made to all men:

Come to Me, all *you* who labour and are heavy laden, and I will give you rest (Matthew 11:28).

Who desires all men to be saved and to come to the knowledge of the truth (1 Timothy 2:4).

> For the grace of God that brings salvation has appeared
> to all men (Titus 2:11).
> ... not willing that any should perish but that all should
> come to repentance (2 Peter 3:9).

Some Christians believe that the expression 'all men' referred to in these verses means the whole world, and therefore everyone is eligible for salvation upon repentance and faith in Christ without further qualification.

4 Election in the Old Testament

God chose Abraham, a pagan living in Ur of the Chaldees, for his own redemptive purpose. From this man God would make a nation, the Israelites, through whom blessing would come to the whole world. The calling of Abraham and the formation of the people of Israel was solely due to God's election:

> Now the LORD had said to Abram: 'Get out of your country,
> from your kindred and from your father's house, to a land
> that I will show you. I will make you a great nation; I will
> bless you and make your name great; and you shall be a
> blessing. I will bless those who bless you, and I will curse
> him who curses you; and in you all the families of the earth
> shall be blessed' (Genesis 12:1-3).

When, some hundreds of years later, Israel had become a nation God rescued them from the captivity in Egypt. Through Moses he told them that this was because they were his elect people, separated from other nations and consecrated by him for his own purpose to be a testimony to the whole world:

> For you are a holy people to the LORD your God; the LORD
> your God has chosen you to be a people for Himself, a
> special treasure above all the peoples on the face of the
> earth. The LORD did not set His love on you nor choose
> you because you were more in number than any other

people, for you were the least of all peoples; but because the LORD loves you, and because He would keep the oath which He swore to your fathers … (Deuteronomy 7:6-8).

The source of Israel's election was God's gracious choice and loving purpose. The object of Israel's election was to receive God's blessing, to be his witness in the world and to be the nation from which Christ would come.

Christ himself is referred to in prophecy as 'God's elect'. This was because he was chosen by God to be the one and only mediator between God and man, the redeemer, who as Prophet, Priest and King would accomplish man's salvation:

Behold! My Servant whom I uphold, My Elect One *in whom* My soul delights! I have put My Spirit upon Him; He will bring forth justice to the Gentiles (Isaiah 42:1; see Matthew 12:17-18).

5 Election in the New Testament

The following are the main passages where the doctrine of election is clearly taught:

And He will send His angels with a great sound of a trumpet, and they will gather together His elect from the four winds, from one end of heaven to the other (Matthew 24.31).

But the Lord said to him (about Paul), 'Go, for he is a chosen vessel of Mine to bear My Name before Gentiles, kings, and the children of Israel' (Acts 9:15).

And not only *this*, but when Rebecca also had conceived by one man, *even* by our father Isaac (for *the children* not yet being born, nor having done any good or evil, that the purpose of God according to election might stand, not of works but of Him who calls), it was said to her, *'The older shall serve the younger'* (Romans 9:10-12).

Even so then, at this present time there is a remnant according to the election of grace. And if by grace, then *it is* no longer of works; otherwise grace is no longer grace... Concerning the gospel *they are* enemies for your sake, but concerning the election *they are* beloved for the sake of the fathers (Romans 11:5-6, 28).

For you see your calling, brethren, that not many wise according to the flesh, not many mighty, not many noble, *are called*. But God has chosen the foolish things of the world to put to shame the wise, and God has chosen the weak things of the world to put to shame the things which are mighty; and the base things of the world and the things which are despised God has chosen, and the things which are not, to bring to nothing the things that are, that no flesh should glory in His presence (1 Corinthians 1:26-29).

But we are bound to give thanks to God always for you, brethren beloved by the Lord, because God from the beginning chose you for salvation through sanctification by the Spirit and belief of the truth (2 Thessalonians 2:13).

Who has saved us and called *us* with a holy calling, not according to our works, but according to His own purpose and grace which was given to us in Christ Jesus before time began (2 Timothy 1:9).

Elect according to the foreknowledge of God the Father, in sanctification of the Spirit, for obedience and sprinkling of the blood of Jesus Christ (1 Peter 1:2).

And those who dwell on the earth will marvel, whose names are not written in the Book of Life from the foundation of the world ... (Revelation 17:8).

In the gospel of John we have a glimpse of both aspects of the mystery of election, the human and the divine. The disciples were confident that when Jesus called them to follow him it was they who had made the final choice whether to be his disciples or not. At the beginning some of them had said, 'We have found the Messiah' (John 1:41, 45), really believing that they had chosen to follow him and not the other way round. But towards the end of his ministry Jesus said to them without any qualification, 'You did not choose Me, but I chose you and appointed you that you should go and bear fruit' (John 15:16).

These verses show us that in the mystery of God's plan of redemption he chose us in Christ even before the world began (Ephesians 1:4). This was not because God knew we should have faith to believe, nor because of anything in us, but solely because of 'His own purpose and grace which was given us in Christ Jesus before time began' (2 Timothy 1:9). In order to begin to understand election we have to go back in time before the creation of the world and accept that God's own purpose and grace began for us when he chose us in Christ in the distant past before we were born. This is indeed a mystery! The words we need to remember are 'His own purpose and grace given us in Christ before time began'. These focus our attention on 'His purpose' and 'His grace'. These are the root of our election, and both emphasise that salvation is absolutely and entirely of God and not of man. We are not saved because of our faith; otherwise salvation would depend upon something in us. Paul says that even our faith is not really ours it is in fact God's gift to us:

> For by grace you have been saved through faith, and that not of yourselves; *it is* the gift of God, not of works, lest anyone should boast. For we are His workmanship, created in Christ Jesus for good works, which God prepared beforehand that we should walk in them (Ephesians 2:8-10).

The Bible teaches us that before we can come to Christ two things need to have happened. The first is that we must be given to Christ by the Father, and the second is that the Father must do an inward work of preparation deep in our hearts, of which we may be totally unaware.

a) The Father gives us to Christ. Christ said that he was the good shepherd (John 10:11, 14) who came to give his life for his sheep. How can a person become one of his sheep? Only if the Father gives him to Christ. Do we realise that we came to Christ because God the Father gave us to him before the foundation of the world?

> All that the Father gives Me will come to Me, and the one who comes to Me I will by no means cast out...This is the will of the Father who sent Me, that of all He has given Me I should lose nothing, but should raise it up at the last day (John 6:37, 39).

> I give them eternal life, and they shall never perish; neither shall anyone snatch them out of My hand. My Father, who has given *them* to Me, is greater than all; and no one is able to snatch *them* out of My Father's hand (John 10:28-29).

See also John 5:21; 17:2; Ephesians 1:4.

b) The Father draws us to Christ, The Bible also says that before we can come to Christ God the Father must draw us to him:

> No one can come to Me unless the Father ... draws him ... (John 6:44).

Only God can induce us to want to come to Christ by making us feel our need of him. Do we realise how much we owe to God the Father in saving us and bringing us to Christ?

It is written in the prophets, *'And they shall all be taught by God.'* Therefore everyone who has heard and learned from the Father comes to Me (John 6:45).

True believers agree that it was solely through God's grace working in their hearts that led them to faith in Christ. This is beautifully illustrated in the story of Lydia:

Now a certain woman named Lydia heard *us*. She was a seller of purple from the city of Thyatira, who worshipped God. The Lord opened her heart to heed the things spoken by Paul (Acts 16:14).

How was it that she gave heed to Paul? Because the Lord worked faith in her heart! Saving faith is itself the gift of God (Ephesians 2:8). We often think of saving faith as an act of the human will, operating on its own, but the Bible says it is the gift of God.

6 Why do we need to understand election?

There are a number of reasons why we should do so.

a) To give us comfort and confidence. In order to give comfort and encouragement to the Christians at Rome Paul tells them that God makes 'all things work together for good to those who love God, to those who are the called according to His purpose' (Romans 8:28). How can Paul be so sure? And on what is he basing his confidence? He continues by explaining in greater detail the meaning of being 'called according to God's purpose':

For whom He foreknew, He also predestined *to be* conformed to the image of His Son, that He might be the firstborn among many brethren. Moreover whom He predestined, these He also called; whom He called, these He also justified; and whom He justified, these He also glorified (Romans 8:29-30).

Paul is saying that God always acts for the good of those whom he predestines and calls to himself. Their salvation, which he began in the distant past when he predestined them, continues to the present when he called them to faith in Christ, and will continue into the distant future when they appear in glory! God is the author of salvation and he works all things for the good of his elect; good in the past, good in the present and good in the future because 'He who has begun a good work in you will complete it until the day of Jesus Christ' (Philippians 1:6) God began our salvation and he will surely complete it.

b) To help us give God all the praise and all the glory for our salvation. When we realise that our salvation is completely and utterly the result of God's undeserved mercy to us, and not in any way due to our own ability or faith, then Paul says we will want to give God all the glory and all the praise! For Paul predestination and praise go together! This is what he says to the Ephesians:

> Having predestined us to adoption as sons by Jesus Christ to Himself, according to the good pleasure of His will, to the praise of the glory of His grace, by which He has made us accepted in the Beloved (Ephesians 1:5-6).

Paul says the same thing to the Thessalonian Christians:

> But we are bound to give thanks to God always for you, brethren beloved by the Lord, because God from the beginning chose you for salvation through sanctification by the Spirit and belief in the truth (2 Thessalonians 2:13).

To whom does Paul give thanks and for what reason? He gives thanks to God because he knows that their salvation was solely due to the fact that God had chosen them! When we truly understand how the doctrine of election glorifies and magnifies the grace of God we will begin, like Paul, to thank him and praise him for choosing such helpless and unworthy sinners as ourselves. Truly our salvation is all of God's grace!

c) To give us confidence in evangelism. Paul had no difficulty whatsoever in reconciling the doctrine of election with God's command to preach the gospel; for him there was no contradiction between two things:

> Paul, a servant of God and an apostle of Jesus Christ, according to the faith of God's elect and the acknowledgement of the truth which is according to godliness, in hope of eternal life which God, who cannot lie, promised before time began, but has in due time manifested His word through preaching, which was committed to me according to the commandment of God our Saviour (Titus 1:1-3).

Paul knows without a doubt that God has chosen some people to be saved and that the God-appointed means for their salvation is the preaching of the gospel. Election, for Paul, is a guarantee that there will be success in his evangelism, even though there will also be suffering to be endured because of the opposition of Satan:

> For which I suffer trouble as an evildoer, *even* to the point of chains; but the word of God is not chained. Therefore I endure all things for the sake of the elect, that they also may obtain the salvation which is in Christ Jesus with eternal glory (2 Timothy 2:9-10).

Paul gladly endured the suffering that came upon him as a preacher of the gospel – why? 'For the sake of the elect that they also might obtain salvation in Christ Jesus.' His confidence was built on the fact that it was the purpose of God for the elect to obtain salvation through the preaching of the gospel. This helped him to endure much opposition in obeying God's command that he should bring the gospel to the Gentiles.

7 Predestination

In Greek *proorizō* (verb) means to determine something before it happens, to foreordain (see Romans 8:29). Linked in meaning is *proginōskō*, to choose beforehand (see also Romans 8:29). Whereas election refers to God's choice of particular persons, predestination refers to God's foreordination of world events as well as the choice of persons. The Scriptures teach that in eternity past God, in full foreknowledge of the plans and actions of Satan and of evil men, foreordained all the events of world history without either being the author of sin or violating the will of his creatures. His great plan of redemption perfectly anticipates the reactions and plans of every evil force active in the world. He is able to do this because he has perfect foreknowledge of everything that will happen, both good and bad. This enables him to make his plans accordingly.

a) In the Old Testament. Although the word predestination is not used in the Old Testament many verses speak of human history as being under the control of almighty God. He is portrayed not as a helpless spectator but as one who plans and purposes future events for his glory and the good of his creatures. Here are some of them:

> The LORD brings the counsel of the nations to nothing; He makes the plans of the peoples of no effect. The counsel of the LORD stands forever, the plans of His heart to all generations (Psalm 33:10-11).

> This *is* the purpose that is purposed against the whole earth, and this *is* the hand that is stretched out over all the nations. For the LORD of hosts has purposed, and who will annul it? His hand *is* stretched out, and who will turn it back? (Isaiah 14:26-27).

Remember the former things of old, for I *am* God, and *there is* no other; *I am* God, and *there is* none like Me, declaring the end from the beginning, and from ancient times *things* that are not *yet* done, saying, 'My counsel shall stand, and I will do all My pleasure,' calling a bird of prey from the east, the man who executes My counsel, from a far country. Indeed I have spoken *it*; I will also bring it to pass. I have purposed *it*; I will also do it (Isaiah 46:9-11).

... For His dominion *is* an everlasting dominion, and His Kingdom *is* from generation to generation. All the inhabitants of the earth *are* reputed as nothing; He does according to His will in the army of heaven and *among* the inhabitants of the earth. No one can restrain His hand or say to Him, 'What have You done?' (Daniel 4:34-35).
The LORD has made all for Himself, Yes, even the wicked for the day of doom (Proverbs 16:4).

A man's heart plans his way, but the LORD directs his steps (Proverbs 16:9).

The lot is cast into the lap, but its every decision is from the LORD (Proverbs 16:33).

The king's heart is in the hand of the LORD, *like* the rivers of water; He turns it wherever He wishes (Proverbs 21:1).

Then He said to Abram: 'Know certainly that your descendants will be strangers in a land *that is* not theirs, and will serve them, and they will afflict them four hundred years ... But in the fourth generation they shall return here, for the iniquity of the Amorites is not yet complete' (Genesis 15:13,16).

In the first announcement of the gospel in Genesis 3:15, God declares that the Seed of the woman will crush the seed of the serpent:

And I will put enmity between you and the woman, and
between your seed and her Seed; He shall bruise your
head, and you shall bruise His heel.

The Fall did not take God by surprise, because his own plans
were ready and waiting to be put into operation to save
the world and defeat Satan through Christ (the Seed of the
woman) at Calvary.

The choice and call of Abraham (Genesis 12:1-3) is but the
first step in God's plan to establish the nation of Israel, God's
chosen people, through whom, in the fullness of time, would
come the Messiah, God's own Son. Through him the purpose
of God's salvation for the whole world would find its fulfilment. Thus in the call of Abraham and in the formation of the
people of Israel we discover the beginning of the redemptive
purpose of God. This unfolds and develops throughout the
pages of the Old Testament.

Prophecy. All Biblical prophecy is founded on the basis
that it is God who plans the future! Messianic prophecies in
the Law of Moses, in the Prophets, and in the Psalms, find
their fulfilment in Christ, but all find their origination in the
purpose of God planned before the dawn of history. In the
prophet Daniel a climax is reached, with the vision of God
over-ruling the rise and fall of world empires in order to
set up the everlasting kingdom of the Son of Man. Such a
global eschatology as this could not be contemplated without
the presupposition that Almighty God is the absolute Lord
of history foreseeing and foreordaining its whole course
(Daniel 2:28-45). Isaiah more than any other book in the Old
Testament expands the theme of the omnipotent God whose
plans are the determining factor in human history. He says
that nothing can prevent what God has purposed to do (Isaiah
14:24-27; 44:24-28 to 45:25), and that he has planned present
and future events 'long ago'. Biblical prophecy therefore
provides concrete evidence that God not only predicts future
events – he plans them!

b) In the New Testament. The main examples of the occurrence of the word 'predestinate' are the following:

> For whom He foreknew, He also predestined *to be* conformed to the image of His Son, that He might be the firstborn among many brethren. Moreover whom He predestined, these He also called; whom He called, these He also justified; and whom He justified, these He also glorified (Romans 8:29-30).

> Having predestined us to adoption as sons by Jesus Christ to Himself, according to the good pleasure of His will, to the praise of the glory of His grace, by which He has made us accepted in the Beloved (Ephesians 1:5-6).

> In whom also we have obtained an inheritance, being predestined according to the purpose of Him who works all things according to the counsel of His will (Ephesians 1:11).

Further evidence that God foreordains events is found in the Gospels and other New Testament documents. Their writers all attribute the coming and the ministry of Christ to the foreordained plan of God, foretold in biblical prophecy and now fulfilled in him. For example:

> And she will bring forth a Son, and you shall call His name JESUS, for He will save His people from their sins. Now all this was done that it might be fulfilled which was spoken by the Lord through the prophet, saying: *'Behold, a virgin shall be with child, and bear a Son, and they shall call His name Immanuel,'* which is translated, 'God with us' (Matthew 1:21-23).

The New Testament takes for granted that God is the sovereign Lord and controller of events, the ruler of history. In the Acts of the Apostles the death and resurrection of Christ is seen as the supreme example of God's foreordination. God knew that his Son would be rejected and crucified by the Jews (and the Romans) and made his plans accordingly even using (by foreknowledge only) the hands of wicked men:

> Him, being delivered by the determined purpose and fore-knowledge of God, you have taken by lawless hands, have crucified, and put to death (Acts 2:23).

> For truly against Your holy Servant Jesus, whom You anointed, both Herod and Pontius Pilate, with the Gentiles and the people of Israel, were gathered together to do whatever Your hand and Your purpose determined before to be done (Acts 4:27-28).

The Church. One of the clearest examples of God's foreordination is his plan (see Ephesians 2:11 to 3:11) to bring the Gentiles into his church as one body with the Jews. Paul says that this eternal plan (Ephesians 3:11) that had been hidden from previous ages has now been revealed to the apostles (Ephesians 3:5-6). The Gentiles who had formerly been strangers and foreigners, are now to be members of God's family with the Jews; together they will form a holy temple in the Lord. God has had this plan from all eternity but only now has he unveiled it and put it into operation. The Holy Spirit, witnessing to the world about the salvation that is in Christ, brings the church into being:

> How that by revelation He made known to me the mystery... which in other ages was not made known to the sons of men ... that the Gentiles should be fellow heirs, of the same body, and partakers of His promise in Christ through the gospel (Ephesians 3:3-6).

Objection to predestination. Some have suggested that there is really no problem here at all: Romans 8:28 is simply saying that God foreknew all those who would accept his salvation – God makes no choice in the matter, it is man who chooses and God simply confirms his choice. On this understanding foreknowledge is just a part of God's omniscience – he knows exactly what will happen in the future. But there are serious difficulties with this interpretation:

Answer:

i) It makes the word predestinate quite meaningless. To predestine means *to actively foreordain future events*. If predestination simply means that God knows who will accept his salvation in the future, he has no need to actively foreordain anyone because they will believe anyway! On this understanding God has no active role in predestination and the word completely loses its true meaning – actively to foreordain future events.

ii) Romans 8:28-30 clearly emphasises that it is God's action which is essential at each stage of our salvation: *he* foreknew, *he* predestined, *he* called, *he* justified and *he* glorified. God is the initiator of each step, and not simply a passive spectator wondering what will happen next.

iii) The Bible does not use the word 'foreknowledge' merely to mean to know what will happen in the future. It is not used as a synonym for omniscience.

8 Foreknowledge

In Scripture, the word 'knowledge' (Hebrew: *yada*), with reference to the God/man relationship, means more than a mere intellectual awareness that someone exists. It means to know someone personally by entering into a personal relationship with them. For example, God says to Israel:

> You only have I known of all the families of the earth;
> therefore I will punish you for all your iniquities (Amos 3:2).

Does this verse mean that God did not know that anyone was living in his world apart from Israel? Of course not! It simply means that at this time, of all the nations in the world, he only had a *covenant relationship* with Israel.

Similarly in the New Testament Jesus says that he never knew those who claimed to belong to him, even though they had prophesied in his name, cast out demons and worked miracles in his name:

> And then I will declare to them, 'I never knew you; depart from Me, you who practise lawlessness!' (Matthew 7:23).

This cannot mean that Jesus, who shares God's omniscience, was unaware of the physical existence of these false believers; it means that these people never had any personal relationship with him, so He never recognized them as his own.

The Greek words for foreknowledge, *proginōskō, prognōsis*, mean 'to know before, foreknowledge'. The Septuagint (the Greek translation of the Old Testament) uses these words to mean, to know in terms of a loving relationship. We see an amazing example of this in the call of Jeremiah to be a prophet:

> Then the word of the LORD came to me, saying: 'Before I formed you in the womb I knew you; Before you were born I sanctified you; I ordained you a prophet to the nations' (Jeremiah 1:4-5).

God is not merely telling Jeremiah that he knew what would happen in the future and that one day he would decide to be a prophet. He is telling him that he knew him before he was born!

The Greek words mentioned in the previous paragraph are used only seven times in the New Testament and always imply foreordination and purpose, not simply an awareness of what will happen in the future. Here are four examples:

i)

> Him, being delivered by the determined counsel and
> foreknowledge of God, you have taken by lawless hands,
> have crucified, and put to death (Acts 2:23).

Peter says the cross had been planned long ago by God; it
was no accident. God's foreknowledge actually foresaw the
murderous hatred of the Jews and used it to bring his Son to
the cross. God overrules their evil deeds to fulfil his mighty
plan. See also Acts 4:27-28.

ii)

> God has not cast away His people whom he foreknew
> (Romans 11:2).

Paul says that although God was in covenant relation with
Israel in Old Testament times, he has foreordained his purpose of grace to restore them in the future so that they will
believe and be saved.

iii)

> Elect according to foreknowledge of God the Father
> (1 Peter 1:2).

We were chosen before the foundation of the world according
to God's foreknowledge, i.e. his foreordained plan.

iv)

> He indeed was foreordained before the foundation of
> the world, but was manifest in these last times for you
> (1 Peter 1:20).

Before the world began God planned to redeem the world
through Christ's death. He was the Lamb slain from the foundation of the world (Revelation 13:8). This is what foreknowledge means – God's purpose and plan for the future.

The way the New Testament uses this word suggests that God's foreknowledge means a knowledge that selects a person as an object of love. God has loving purposes with respect to those he foreknew. 'Whom He foreknew' therefore means those he determines to enter into a loving relationship with in the future.

9 Calling

The words most commonly used in the Greek to describe God's call to salvation are *kaleō* (to call) and *klēsis* (calling). They signify to invite, or to summons someone to come. The New Testament doctrine of calling can be defined as 'that gracious act of God whereby he invites sinners to accept the salvation offered in our Lord Jesus Christ'.

Theologians distinguish a twofold call:

a) The general or external call to all men.
b) The effectual or internal call to the elect.

a) The general call. The gospel is to be preached in all the world to every creature (Matthew 28:19). This means that it is to be proclaimed without any restriction to all who will hear it, because it is a universal medicine to heal the sickness of sin.

> Jesus answered and said to them, 'Those who are well have no need of a physician, but those who are sick. I have not come to call *the* righteous, but sinners, to repentance' (Luke 5:31-32).

In the parable of the Wedding Feast Christ teaches that many are invited to enter the kingdom of God, but the majority reject the invitation and only a few accept it. Why is this? Christ says:

For many are called, but few *are* chosen (Matthew 22:14).

The distinction is due to God's grace who inclines those he has chosen to receive it. The implication being that by nature and by inclination none of us if left to ourselves would accept the offer of the gospel. Paul says that salvation is solely due to the mercy of God and that he is not unjust in choosing whom he will:

> What shall we say then? *Is there* unrighteousness with God? Certainly not! For He says to Moses, '*I will have mercy on whomever I will have mercy, and I will have compassion on whomever I will have compassion.*' So then *it is* not of him who wills, nor of him who runs, but of God who shows mercy (Romans 9:14-16).

Paul preached the gospel fearlessly to all who would listen. Christ had commissioned him to do so (Acts 9:15) and he was obedient to that commission throughout his ministry. Paul was fully aware of the doctrines of foreknowledge, predestination, calling and election but this did not deter him from actively proclaiming the gospel wherever he went. For example, when he went to Athens he preached to a crowd of philosophers and others on the Areopagus. Some mocked him, some were puzzled, some disbelieved, but a few believed and were converted (Acts 17:16-34). Here is a perfect example both of the general and the effectual call of the gospel. It is proclaimed to all, some receive it but others reject it. The great English nineteenth century preacher C.H. Spurgeon said, 'We preachers are like an archer who shoots his arrow over a house. We shoot the gospel arrow but know not where it will find its mark; the All-wise God guides the arrow of conviction to its intended target in the human heart.' God has commanded the gospel to be proclaimed to all, but those who hear are completely dependent on his grace; the results are in his hands.

Why is the general call insufficient to save us? Because of our state by nature. The solemn fact is that we are not in a morally neutral state. Sin has brought us into spiritual bondage (John 8:34) and has deprived us of the ability to understand spiritual things. The Bible's analysis of our natural unregenerate condition proves this. Here is what it says:

- We are dead in trespasses and sins   – Ephesians 2:1
- Our minds are at enmity against
-               God   – Romans 8:7
- We love darkness rather than light   – John 3:19
- The things of the Spirit are
-               foolishness to us   – 1 Corinthians 2:14
- The devil blinds our minds
-               to the gospel   – 2 Corinthians 4:3
- We are alienated from the life
-               of God by sin   – Ephesians 4:18
- We are guilty before God of
-               breaking his law   – Romans 3:19
- We are slaves to sin   – John 8:34

This is the biblical diagnosis of man in sin: he is spiritually dead to God and under the power of the devil. He is a rebel against God and loves darkness rather than light. Therefore our condition as unregenerate and unrepentant sinners is a very grave one indeed. If we accept the Bible's diagnosis of our position before God we will readily understand that we are powerless and stand in urgent need of God's help and God's mercy. We need light for our darkness, life for our death, sight for our blindness, righteousness for our guilt, peace for our warfare against God, forgiveness for our rebellion, healing for our sickness and liberty for our bondage: our condition could hardly be worse!

b) The effectual call. When God calls us he gives us the ability to respond, to hear and to obey. The effectual call brings with it the power that we stand in need of. When Lazarus had died and been buried in the tomb, according to the custom of the day, his body was tightly bound with grave clothes. Even if he had been alive he would have been unable to move hand or foot:

> He [Jesus] cried with a loud voice, 'Lazarus, come forth!' And he who had died came out bound hand and foot with grave clothes, and his face was wrapped with a cloth. Jesus said to them, 'Loose him, and let him go' (John 11:43-44).

Lazarus received the call of Jesus to come out of his grave! Humanly speaking he could not do so because his hands and feet were bound. It was possible only because there was miracle-working power in the word of Jesus. It is just the same with us in our unconverted state; we need God's power to call us from the grave of sin. This God gives us in the effectual life-giving call of the gospel.

Although God is a Spirit and therefore infinite he is also a Person. His relationship with his creatures is therefore a personal one. In the Garden he said to Adam, 'Where are you?' (Genesis 3:9) At the burning bush he called, 'Moses, Moses!' (Exodus 3:4) In the tabernacle he called, 'Samuel!' to the child who would one day become the great prophet of Israel (1 Samuel 3:4). To Israel God said, 'I have called you by your name' (Isaiah 43:1). Jesus says concerning his sheep, 'he calls his own sheep by name' (John 10:3). God's effectual life-changing call addresses us by name! This brings us into a living relationship with the infinite-personal God. How can God call us to himself? Because he already knows us by name!

Because we are spiritually dead and at enmity with God we are totally dependent upon him to breathe new life into our souls. Only when he calls us by name, just as Jesus called Lazarus, are we able to respond and turn to him. Having thus been given the capacity to hear and understand God's word, the call of God is made effectual by the gift of life and of faith.

There are numerous examples in the New Testament of God's effectual call. For example:

> God *is* faithful, by whom you were called into the fellowship of His Son, Jesus Christ our Lord (1 Corinthians 1:9).

> But when it pleased God, who separated me from my mother's womb and called *me* through His grace to reveal His Son in me ... (Galatians 1:15-16).

> Who has saved us and called *us* with a holy calling, not according to our works, but according to His own purpose and grace which was given us in Christ Jesus before time began (2 Timothy 1:9).

> But you *are* a chosen generation, a royal priesthood, a holy nation, His own special people, that you may proclaim the praises of Him who called you out of darkness into His marvellous light (1 Peter 2:9).

But it may be asked, what are we called for, what purpose has God in mind in calling us? God is building his church, called a holy temple (Ephesians 2:21), which is a new humanity being recreated in the image of his Son. God wants us, and has destined us, to be like His Son, this is the purpose of his calling. Christ is our pattern; the firstborn among many brethren:

> And we know that all things work together for good to those who love God, to those who are the called according to *His* purpose. For whom He foreknew, He also predestined *to be* conformed to the image of His Son, that He might be the firstborn among many brethren (Romans 8:28-29).

10 Five difficulties

There can be no doubt that the doctrine of predestination is deeply disturbing and even offensive to many Christian people. By implication, it seems to deny the very fundamentals of the good news preached by the Lord Jesus to lost souls. The following are some of the fears that are commonly expressed:

i) Predestination denies man's free will and reduces man to being little more than a robot.

ii) How can God be just if he arbitrarily chooses some to salvation and rejects others?

iii) If God has already chosen those who will be saved what is the point of preaching the gospel or engaging in missionary work?

iv) Predestination appears to contradict all those verses in the Bible that say, 'Whosoever will may come.'

v) Predestination is dangerous to morality, encouraging men to believe that no matter how they live they will have a place in Heaven.

It is perfectly true that the doctrine of predestination does confront us with some really difficult questions, but the word is used several times in the New Testament, which is inspired by the Holy Spirit, so we must try to understand what it means. For example look at the following verse;

> For whom He foreknew, He also predestined *to be* conformed to the image of His Son, that He might be the firstborn among many brethren. Moreover whom He predestined, these He also called; whom He called, these

He also justified; and whom He justified, these He also glorified (Romans 8:29-30).

In these amazing verses Paul unveils the whole panorama of our salvation from eternity past to eternity future, from before time began to when time will be no more.

We will now try to answer the fears expressed by many Christian people in connection with this doctrine.

a) Predestination denies man's free will. We have sought to show in the section, 'The insufficiency of the general call', that in a spiritual sense we are all dead, blind and in bondage to sin and to Satan. We are by nature enemies of God and spiritual things are foolishness to us. If this is true, then we do not have either the will or the desire to acknowledge these things, or accept Christ as Lord and Saviour. There is a bias in our wills toward sin and to be independent of God. In other areas of life we are free to do what we want and go where we want. However in matters of salvation the Bible says that our wills are in bondage to sin and to Satan. This means we are totally dependent on the mercy of God

b) How can God be just in choosing some to salvation and not others? In Romans 9:6-33, Paul deals with this problem of the apparent injustice of God in choosing Jacob rather than Esau:

> What shall we say then? *Is there* unrighteousness with God? Certainly not! For He says to Moses, '*I will have mercy on whomever I will have mercy, and I will have compassion on whomever I will have compassion.*' So then *it is* not of him who wills, nor of him who runs, but of God who shows mercy (verses 14-16).

Paul concludes that because God is the holy, wonderful, all-wise God that he is, it is impossible for him to do anything unjust. In other words, the glorious character of God forbids us to think he can be either unkind or unjust. Since all men are God's creatures, He is sovereignly right to choose whom He will. Since we are all dead in trespasses and sin it is purely of God's mercy that any are saved!

c) What therefore is the use of preaching the gospel? We do so because God has commanded us to, and because he has promised to save men and women by these means. We follow the example of the apostle Paul who, although he believed in predestination, nonetheless was an indefatigable missionary all his life. We preach the gospel to all men, but God saves whom he will. Many are called (invited) by the gospel but few are chosen.

d) Predestination seems to contradict other verses in the Bible. It is perfectly true that there are many verses, such as 1 Timothy 2:4, John 3:16 and Revelation 22:17, which invite all who want salvation to come to Christ and believe. This is fully in accord with Christ's mandate to preach the gospel (Matthew 28:19) in all the world to every creature. As already described, it is God who is at work bringing souls to Himself, and He does so by inviting all to come to Him. Sadly it is also true, that without His grace we cannot come to Christ, because in and of ourselves we will never want to. For this reason Jesus said, 'Many are called but few are chosen' (Matthew 22:14). Predestination is therefore not inconsistent with those verses that invite all men to believe the Gospel and come to Christ. God invites all, but has to regenerate the elect before they will want to repent and believe the gospel:

> For as the Father raises the dead and gives life to *them*, even so the Son gives life to whom He will (John 5:21).

e) Predestination is dangerous to morality, encouraging men to believe that no matter how they live they will have

a place in heaven. This objection assumes that confidence in God's promise of a place in heaven will lead some Christians to the conclusion that therefore they may sin as much as they please. That an unconverted person might draw this conclusion we agree, but not one who has been born of God. When a man becomes a new creation in Christ Jesus '... old things have passed away; behold all things have become new' (2 Corinthians 5:17). This does not by any means make him sinless or immune to temptation, but it does give him a new heart with new affections, new desires, a love for God, for righteousness and for Christian brethren. He now hates what formerly he loved and loves what formerly he hated. When he does fall into sin he does not continue in it, but rather feels a sense of grief and self-loathing. He says with David, 'Against You, You only, have I sinned, and done this evil in Your sight ...' (Psalm 51:4). This objection incorrectly assumes that the only motive for living a holy life is the fear of losing one's salvation. The new heart, that God gives us through the new birth, gives us new motives for holy living and loving God.

Questions

1   Explain the difference between election and predestination

2   Explain the meaning of the word 'foreknowledge'

3   What is the difference between the 'general' and the 'effectual' call?

4   Why is it not unjust of God to choose some to salvation and not others?

CHAPTER EIGHTEEN

BAPTISM

1 The meaning of the word

2 The baptism of John

3 Christian baptism

    a) Link between repentance, faith and the Holy Spirit
    b) A sign of union with Christ by faith
    c) A sign of cleansing from sin
    d) A sign and seal of God's grace

4 What therefore is the purpose of baptism?

    Four answers

5 What about infant baptism?

    a) Jesus and the children
    b) Does the covenant of grace include children of Christian parents?

6 Infant baptism in the early church

    a) Development in preparation for baptism
    b) Development in administration of baptism
    c) Development in understanding of baptism
    d) Tertullian

What is baptism? Is it a sacrament essential to salvation or only a symbol of cleansing?

1 The meaning of the word

***Bapto, baptizo* means to:**
- dip in or under
- dye
- immerse
- sink
- drown
- bathe
- wash

These words and their derivatives are used 109 times in the New Testament, but in the vast majority of cases the reference is to Christian baptism. The significance of the rite is to dip, to immerse a person, symbolising the washing away of sins and their union with Christ in his death, burial and resurrection.

2 The baptism of John

The Gospel of Mark begins with John the Baptist preaching a baptism of repentance for the remission of sins:

> John came baptizing in the wilderness and preaching a baptism of repentance for the remission of sins. And all the land of Judea, and those from Jerusalem, went out to him and were all baptized by him in the Jordan River, confessing their sins (Mark 1:4-5).

John's ministry was seen by Mark as 'the beginning of the gospel of Jesus Christ'. His role was that of a messenger, or forerunner, sent by God to prepare the way for the coming of God's kingdom:

> In those days John the Baptist came preaching in the wilderness of Judea, and saying, 'Repent, for the kingdom of heaven is at hand!' (Matthew 3:1-2).

He told his fellow Jews this was to be a turning point in their history, a climactic event in God's dealings with Israel. They must cleanse themselves in preparation for the imminent arrival of one whose sandal strap John was not worthy to unloose. The prophets had foretold his coming; he would baptize them with the Holy Spirit and with fire and would rigorously expel all sin and hypocrisy from his presence (Luke 3:16-17).

Those who came to John for his baptism of repentance were conscious of failure and guilt. They confessed their sins and committed themselves to a life of holiness. But John rebuked those who came to him for baptism whose motives were not sincere. He warned them not to pride themselves on their being the physical descendants of Abraham, but to make a full repentance of their sins, by confessing and forsaking them and turning whole-heartedly to God.

We can therefore discern two main elements in John's baptism:

i) To preach repentance through baptism, for the forgiveness of sins (Luke 3:3).

ii) To prepare people to receive Christ who would bring in the kingdom of God and baptize them with the Holy Spirit and with fire (Luke 3:16).

John's baptism was only preparatory, to make ready a people through repentance and faith who would receive the coming King and his kingdom.

If this is so, why then did Jesus himself come to John to be baptized? What sins did he have to confess and what repentance did he have to make?

> And John *tried to* prevent Him, saying, 'I have need to be baptized by You, and are You coming to me?' But Jesus answered and said to him, 'Permit *it to be so* now, for thus it is fitting for us to fulfil all righteousness.' Then he allowed Him (Matthew 3:14-15).

The answer is that Jesus took upon himself human nature and the form of a servant in order to be the human sin-bearer, the Lamb of God, that takes away the sin of the world. He had to be fully identified with fallen men in order to save them through dying on the cross:

> Inasmuch then as the children have partaken of flesh and blood, He Himself likewise shared in the same, that through death He might destroy him who had the power of death, that is, the devil... Therefore, in all things He had to be made like *His* brethren, that He might be a merciful and faithful High Priest in things *pertaining* to God, to make propitiation for the sins of the people (Hebrews 2:14,17).

By being baptized by John Jesus took a further step of submission and humiliation in the process that began at Bethlehem and ended at Calvary.

When Jesus submitted himself to baptism, God the Father showed his approval by speaking from heaven, 'This is My beloved Son, in whom I am well pleased' (Matthew 3:17).

3 Christian baptism

The first example of Christian baptism is found in Acts Chapter Two. Three thousand people who heard Peter's sermon on the day of Pentecost believed and were baptized:

> Then Peter said to them, 'Repent, and let every one
> of you be baptized in the name of Jesus Christ for the
> remission of sins; and you shall receive the gift of the Holy
> Spirit' (Acts 2:38).

Christian baptism was administered to those who repented
and believed the gospel. In what respects therefore was it
any different from the baptism of John?

**a) Christian baptism links repentance and faith with the gift
of the Holy Spirit.** The order of events for Christian baptism
in the New Testament is as follows:

- Repentance toward God and faith in Jesus Christ.
- Reception of the Holy Spirit.
- Baptism.

This is seen in the text quoted above (Acts 2:38). On the Day
of Pentecost Peter promised the gift of the Spirit to all who
believe. It is seen also in the conversion of the Apostle Paul:

> And Ananias went his way and entered the house; and
> laying his hands on him he said, 'Brother Saul, the Lord
> Jesus who appeared to you on the road as you came,
> has sent me that you may receive your sight and be filled
> with the Holy Spirit.' Immediately there fell from his eyes
> *something* like scales, and he received his sight at once;
> and he arose and was baptized (Acts 9:17-18).

See also Acts 10:45-48; 19:5-6; 1 Corinthians 12:13; Titus 3:5-7.
   [See Chapter Nine, 'Regeneration', section (4), 'Is
baptism a cause?' In this section we show that faith and
repentance almost always precede baptism in the New
Testament.]
   The exception to this general rule (where the gift of the
Holy Spirit is received at baptism) is the case of the Samari-
tans in Acts 8:4-17. Why was this? The answer is highly

significant: this was the Church's first step outside Judaism. When Christ sent his disciples to preach to the lost sheep of the house of Israel he had *forbidden* them to preach to the Samaritans (Matthew 10:5-6). Even though he had preached the gospel to a Samaritan woman (John 4:4-42) and stayed two days in a Samaritan village, the apostles were still very reluctant to have any contacts with Gentiles (see Acts 10 and 11). But God had other plans for the gospel of his Son! He therefore withheld the gift of his Holy Spirit from the believing Samaritans until the apostles Peter and John could lay hands upon them as a sign of their reception into the church. They then received the Holy Spirit (Acts 8:14-17). In the case of the household of Cornelius the gift of the Spirit was the sign that these Gentile believers should be baptized (Acts 10:44-48). In this way God taught them that from now on he was including Samaritans and Gentiles in his kingdom. The same is true of the followers of John the Baptist whom Paul met in Ephesus (Acts 19:1-7).

b) Christian baptism is a sign that we have been united with Christ by faith. Baptism is an outward and visible sign that an inward and spiritual grace has taken place in our souls. This spiritual grace comes to us when we believe: faith always precedes baptism. Many verses underline the fact that we are baptized *into* Christ and *into* the Trinity. The word *into* is significant because it suggests union with Christ and with the Trinity. For example:

> For as many of you as were baptized into Christ have put on Christ (Galatians 3:27).

> Do you not know that as many of us as were baptized into Christ Jesus were baptized into His death? Therefore we were buried with Him through baptism into death, that just as Christ was raised from the dead by the glory of the Father, even so we also should walk in newness of life. For if we have been united together in the likeness

> of His death, certainly we shall also be *in the likeness of His* resurrection, knowing this, that our old man was crucified with *Him*, that the body of sin might be done away with, that we should no longer be slaves of sin (Romans 6:3-6).

> For by one Spirit we were all baptized into one body (1 Corinthians 12:13; see also Matthew 28:19; 1 Corinthians 1:13; 10:2; Colossians 2:11-12).

When the Bible says we are baptized into Christ it means nothing less than that we have been spiritually united to him. Baptism therefore speaks to us in the first place of our union with Christ. This is its primary meaning. As Christ died and rose again, so too the believer in virtue of his being united to Christ, dies to sin and rises again to newness of life in him.

c) Christian baptism is a sign of cleansing from sin. One of the meanings of the word *baptizō* is 'washing'. In New Testament times when persons went down into a river or lake it was usually in order to wash themselves. The waters of baptism symbolize the fact that we have been cleansed by the blood of Christ. Our old sins and manner of life are washed away when we emerge from the water to begin a new life in Christ.

> And now why are you waiting? Arise and be baptized, and wash away your sins, calling on the name of the Lord (Acts 22:16).

> Not by works of righteousness which we have done, but according to His mercy He saved us, by the washing of regeneration and renewing of the Holy Spirit (Titus 3:5; see also 1 Corinthians 6:11; 1 Peter 3:21).

d) Christian baptism is both a 'sign' and a 'seal' of God's grace. When God called Abraham out of paganism to be his servant, he promised to do three things for him: to give him a land, to make of him and of his descendants a great nation, and to bless the whole world through him (Genesis 12:1-3). He also graciously made a covenant with Abraham in which he solemnly promised to do all these things (Genesis 15:7-21; 17:10-14). There was really no need for God to make a covenant with Abraham, because his own word of promise was sufficient. Nevertheless because of his gracious nature, and his compassion for man in his weakness, he very kindly made an agreement (covenant) binding him to do all that he had promised. This was to encourage Abraham's faith whenever it might waver, and he be tempted to doubt the reality of God's promise to do these things for him. God then commanded Abraham to circumcise himself and all his male descendants as a sign of the covenant that he had made with him. Paul explains the significance of this:

> And he received the sign of circumcision, a seal of the righteousness of the faith which *he had while still* uncircumcised, that he might be the father of all those who believe, though they are uncircumcised, that righteousness might be imputed to them also (Romans 4:11).

Circumcision was the outward sign confirming (sealing) the genuineness of the inward work of faith that had taken place in his heart fourteen years before. For his descendants circumcision was the mark of entry into the old covenant. The outward sign only gave one the right to the privileges of the old covenant. It did not guarantee faith or holiness of life. An inward circumcision of the heart was therefore also necessary (Romans 2:28-29). Baptism on the other hand is administered as an outward rite but only as a consequence of a faith and repentance encounter with God. We receive the sign of baptism as a seal of the genuineness of our faith in the death and resurrection of Christ for us. Baptism is therefore the sign and seal that God has done something in our conscious experience bringing us to repentance and faith in Christ. The sign and the seal are the outward and inward aspects of Christian baptism.

4   What therefore is the purpose of baptism?

• Baptism is a sign and a seal that we have received forgiveness of sins and justification by faith.

• Baptism is a sign and a seal that we have been born again, united to Christ, and have received the Holy Spirit.

• Baptism is a public confession of our faith in Jesus Christ as Lord and Saviour.

• Baptism is a consecration of ourselves, not only to believe in Christ, but also to follow him day by day.

5   What about infant baptism?

The following arguments are advanced in favour of baptizing infants:

a) Jesus invited the children to come to him. Jesus welcomed the bringing of little children and infants to him (Mark 10:13-16; Luke 18:15-17) that he might pray for them and touch them. While Jesus teaches us to have the same attitude towards them as he had, there is no indication that Jesus was thinking of baptism when he received them. If he had wanted us to baptize them he could easily have said so, but he did not.

b) Does the Covenant of Grace include children of Christian parents?

i) 'You and your children' (Acts 2:39). When God made a covenant with Noah (Genesis 6:18; 9:9), with Abraham (Genesis 17:7) and with Israel (Deuteronomy 5:2-3) the children were included. Peter on the Day of Pentecost also says:

> For the promise is to you and to your children, and to all who are afar off, as many as the Lord our God will call (Acts 2:39).

In the Old Testament the rite of circumcision did not guarantee faith, purity of life or a place in heaven; it only admitted children to certain external national privileges. Children became members of the Jewish kingdom on the basis of physical descent. In the New Testament baptism was not offered, as circumcision had been to Jewish children on the basis of natural birth and a national church, but on the spiritual basis of repentance and faith – "To as many as the Lord our God will call". This implies that those who hear that call are able to understand it and respond to it. This could not apply therefore to infants who are as yet unable to understand human speech. Neither circumcision during the Old Testament nor baptism in the New Testament is of any value without faith in God.

ii) 'Children of the covenant'. Some have thought that the children of Christian parents are born with the privileges of being 'children of the covenant'. But nowhere does the New Testament say that children of Christian parents are not sinners who need to be born again. Every person still has to receive Christ for himself or herself, even though they are children born to Christian parents:

> But as many as received Him, to them He gave the right to become children of God, *even* to those who believe in His name: who were born, not of blood, nor of the will of the flesh, nor of the will of man, but of God (John 1:12-13).

That which is born of the flesh is flesh, and that which is born of the Spirit is spirit (John 3:6).

iii) 'Now are they holy'. Some Christians have supposed that the children of Christian parents are 'holy' because of the faith of their parents, 'For the unbelieving husband is sanctified by the wife, and the unbelieving wife is sanctified by the husband; otherwise your children would be unclean, but now are they holy' (1 Corinthians 7:14). Paul is writing to reassure parents of mixed marriages, where one member is an unbeliever, that their children are not regarded by God as unclean. This, however, does not mean that the unbelieving husband or wife or their children are Christians:

For how do you know, O wife, whether you will save *your* husband? Or how do you know, O husband, whether you will save your wife? (1 Corinthians 7:16).

Unbelieving husbands and wives, though they have a valid marriage, still need to be saved. Baptism is only administered in the New Testament to those who believe and are saved.

iv) Household baptisms. There are a number of examples where Paul appears to have baptized whole families at one time: Cornelius (Acts 10:24, 48); Lydia (Acts 16:15), the jailer (Acts 16:33) and Stephanas (1 Corinthians 1:16). It is suggested that some children must have been present and have been baptized. Concerning the jailer, we read that when Paul and Silas had left the prison and gone to his house:

Then they spoke the word of the Lord to him and to all who were in his house. And he took them the same hour of the night and washed *their* stripes. And immediately he and all his family were baptized (Acts 16:32-33).

If children were present they were old enough to listen to the gospel and believe it. Similarly we are told that the household of Stephanas were all devoted to the service of the church (1 Corinthians 16:15); how could this be true of young children? We are simply not told if any children were present in any of these households. An argument from silence does not therefore present any evidence in favour of baptizing infants.

v) Baptismal regeneration. Please see Chapter Nine 'Regeneration' where this is discussed.

6 Infant baptism in the early church

In the period between the death of the last of the apostles and 215 AD, there are only three descriptions of baptism in early Christian literature, all of them for adults. They are found in the following documents:

- 'The Didache' (Teaching of the Twelve Apostles). Date: 70-110 AD.
- 'First Apology', by Justin Martyr. Date: 150 AD.
- 'Apostolic Tradition', by Hippolytus. Date: 215 AD.

When we compare what they say with the New Testament teaching on baptism, three areas of development are apparent:

a) A development in the extent of preparation for baptism. 'Catechumens' was the name given to those seeking baptism. They had to serve a period of probation and training that could last up to three years before they were allowed to be baptized. Baptism therefore became a very important, solemn and holy occasion in the life of the church.

b) A development in the administration of baptism. By the time of Cyril, bishop of Jerusalem (350-386 AD), it was necessary not only to immerse the candidates three times in water, but to subject them to anointing with oil (twice), exorcism, laying-on-of-hands by a bishop, examination in the Apostles Creed and finally a declaration of forgiveness of sins. The service took place at dawn on Easter Sunday amid flaming torches and other dramatic accompaniments.

c) A development in the understanding of baptism. Because of the importance of baptism in the early church many Church Fathers made a connection between baptism and the forgiveness of sins, and also between baptism and being born again (Justin's First Apology). Much bitter debate took place as to whether post-baptismal sin could be forgiven, some saying yes, and others no. The final view was that only major sins (the seven deadly sins) could not be forgiven. By the end of 5th Century more and more infants were being baptized. The question was therefore asked, 'What sins are infants guilty of?' The answer lay in the Church's development of the doctrine of original sin, particularly by Augustine (354-420 AD). From this time onwards adult baptism declined in favour of infant baptism, because it was thought that children dying without baptism were in danger of going to hell. It was therefore important to baptize all new-born infants as soon as possible! In a short time adult baptism became a thing of the past, due to the belief that baptism secured not only forgiveness of sins but regeneration as well.

d) Tertullian (160-215).   He is regarded by some as one of the greatest of the second century Christian apologists. He wrote a treatise on baptism which contains the first historical reference to infant baptism (200 AD) but he protests against the practice saying, 'The Lord indeed says, "Forbid them not to come to Me". Let them come then when they are growing up: let them come if they are learning; if they are taught where they are coming; let them become Christians when they are able to know Christ'. His testimony is an important part of the evidence which shows that infant baptism was *not* universally accepted in the early Church. It developed in the church for the reasons given above.

From these brief remarks on the development of the doctrine of baptism in the early Church, one can see how infant baptism came to be accepted. When one studies the evidence against it, we believe we have been able to demonstrate how little support it has from the New Testament, either in precept or in practice.

Questions

1 What do we mean when we say that baptism is both a sign and a seal of God's grace?

2 Is baptism in the New Testament equivalent to circumcision in the Old Testament?

CHAPTER NINETEEN

THE CHURCH

1 Definition

2 Biblical images of the church

   a) The people of God
   b) The body of Christ
   c) The bride of Christ
   d) The building – the temple of God
   e) God's family
   f) The pillar and ground of the truth
   g) The flock of God

3 The character of the church

   a) It is apostolic
   b) It is one
   c) It is holy
   d) It is universal

4 The inner life of the church

   a) Doctrine
   b) Fellowship
   c) Breaking of Bread
   d) Prayers

5 Church discipline

What is the church? Is it an ancient institution? Is it a building? Or is it people who believe in Christ?

1 Definition

The Greek word for church is *ekklēsia*. It means those who are called out, or called together, for a particular purpose. In the New Testament it refers to those whom God has called together into an assembly. Jesus says, 'Where two or three are met together in My name, I am there in the midst of them' (Matthew 18:20). Christians are called to assemble together in his name for prayer, praise, edification, evangelism and mutual help; this is the nature of the church.

The word *ekklēsia* is used in several different ways. It can refer to:

i) A meeting of Christians in a particular assembly, e.g. Corinth

For first of all, when you come together as a church, I hear that there are divisions among you (1 Corinthians 11:18).

ii) All the Christians living in a particular place, e.g. Jerusalem

At that time a great persecution arose against the church which was at Jerusalem (Acts 8:1).

iii) A house-church

Greet the brethren who are in Laodicea, and Nymphas and the church that *is* in his house (Colossians 4:15).

iv) A number of churches

John, to the seven churches which are in Asia (Revelation 1:4).

v) The universal church

And I also say to you that you are Peter, and on this rock I will build My church, and the gates of Hades shall not prevail against it (Matthew 16:18).

The New Testament does not refer to a building as a church as we do today. In New Testament times the church simply meant a body of believers gathered together in the name of Christ in a particular place.

2 Biblical images of the church

The Bible uses a number of different word-pictures in order to describe the church. Here are the main ones: the people of God; the body of Christ; the bride; the building, i.e. temple of God; the family of God; the pillar and support of the truth; the flock of Christ.

a) The people of God. The story of the Old Testament is how God made for himself a people through whom the whole world would be blessed. It tells us how he chose one man, Abraham, and out of him made the nation of Israel:

Now the LORD had said to Abram: 'Get out of your country, from your kindred and from your father's house, to a land that I will show you. I will make you a great nation … and in you all the families of the earth shall be blessed' (Genesis 12:1-3).

Then, many years later, God sent Moses to deliver Israel from captivity in the land of Egypt, to lead them through the

wilderness, and to the border of the promised land. God
declared:

> I will take you as My people, and I will be your God.
> Then you shall know that I *am* the LORD your God who
> brings you out from under the burdens of the Egyptians
> (Exodus 6:7).

See also Exodus 19:5; Deuteronomy 14:2; Psalm 135:4.

Finally God sent Jesus to deliver mankind from the captivity of sin. He sent him to redeem, not just a random group
of individuals, but a people for himself, gathered out of all
nations, tribes, peoples and tongues:

> And she will bring forth a Son, and you shall call His
> name JESUS, for He will save His people from their sins
> (Matthew 1:21).

> Now this he did not say on his own *authority*; but being
> high priest that year he prophesied that Jesus would die
> for the nation, and not for that nation only, but also that
> He would gather together in one the children of God who
> were scattered abroad (John 11:51-52).

> Looking for the blessed hope and glorious appearing of
> our great God and Saviour Jesus Christ, who gave Himself
> for us, that He might redeem us from every lawless deed
> and purify for Himself *His* own special people, zealous for
> good works (Titus 2:13-14).

See also Acts 15:14; 1 Peter 2:9; Revelation 21:3.

Although we receive God's forgiveness and reconciliation
as individuals, it is God's will to redeem a people for himself by gathering together those of like precious faith into
his church and kingdom. We therefore find our true calling

and identity as members of the people of God. We no longer think of ourselves as isolated individuals, but as a people whom he is forming for himself out of all the nations of the world. In this way the elect of both Old and New Testament form one people, the new humanity who will inhabit the new creation that God has planned after this world has been destroyed.

b) The Body of Christ. This word-picture speaks to us of the close organic union that exists between the believer and the Lord. There can be no more intimate physical relationship than between the members or parts of the same human body (Ephesians 5:30). All its members share a common life, a common purpose, a common feeling, and common relationship within the body. Christ is called the head of the Body because he is its leader, he is in control, he is the one who feeds the body and by his wisdom regulates its life and purpose. The metaphor also speaks of our mutual dependence upon one another. The foot cannot say to the hand, 'I have no need of you', nor can the eye say to the ear, 'I have no need of you'. God has formed us into a Body in order that we might help and encourage one another (see 1 Corinthians 12:15-17). Even between the head and the body there is a mutual inter-dependence – the body cannot do without the head, nor can the head do without the body. In the life of Christ's church not only do we need him, but by his amazing grace, he also needs us to fulfil his saving purposes in the world as his church and people. We depend upon him and upon one another:

> Now you are the body of Christ, and members individually (1 Corinthians 12:27).

> For as we have many members in one body, but all the members do not have the same function, so we, *being* many, are one body in Christ, and individually members of one another (Romans 12:4-5).

But, speaking the truth in love, may grow up in all things
into Him who is the Head – Christ – from whom the whole
body, joined and knit together by what every joint supplies,
according to the effective working by which every part
does its share, causes growth of the body for the edifying
of itself in love (Ephesians 4:15-16).

c) **The Bride of Christ.** Marriage speaks to us of a unique
relationship between two human beings. Love, mutual
care and respect replace self-centredness and individual-
ism. Even in the Old Testament God spoke very tenderly of
Israel as his wife, the bride whom he loved and cherished:

For your Maker *is* your husband, the LORD of hosts is His
name (Isaiah 54:5; see also Isaiah 50:1; 62:5; Jeremiah
3:1; Hosea 2:14-20).

In the New Testament the Lord Jesus Christ also refers to
himself as the bridegroom:

So Jesus said to them, 'Can the friends of the bridegroom
fast while the bridegroom is with them? As long as they
have the bridegroom with them they cannot fast. But the
days will come when the bridegroom will be taken away
from them, and then they will fast in those days' (Mark
2:19-20).

If Christ is the bridegroom who then is the bride? The apostle
Paul tells us that the bride is the church. Christ not only loved
her, he died for her. And in the age to come he will present
her to himself, perfect and sinless. Christ, as our heavenly
bridegroom, loves and cares for his Church with a pure and
everlasting love:

Husbands, love your wives, just as Christ also loved the
church and gave Himself for it, that He might sanctify and
cleanse it with the washing of water by the word, that He

might present it to Himself a glorious church, not having spot or wrinkle or any such thing, but that it should be holy and without blemish. So husbands ought to love their own wives as their own bodies; he who loves his wife loves himself. For no one ever hated his own flesh, but nourishes and cherishes it, even as the Lord *does* the church (Ephesians 5:25-29).

Then one of the seven angels who had the seven bowls filled with the seven last plagues came to me and talked with me, saying, 'Come, I will show you the bride, the Lamb's wife.' And he carried me away in the Spirit to a great and high mountain, and showed me the great city, the holy Jerusalem, descending out of heaven from God (Revelation 21:9-10; see also Revelation 19:7-9).

It is surely one of the most amazing wonders of God's grace that he loves those who are rebellious and sinful. The love of God pitied us in our darkness, in our bondage to sin and to Satan, and rescued us through the death and resurrection of Christ. He saw no beauty in us yet he loved us and gave himself for us; this is love indeed! God's love is the love of good-will, the love that always wants what is in our highest and best interests. His love is purposeful, to present us at last holy and blameless in his presence with exceeding joy!

d) The building – the temple of God. In the Old Testament God said he would come down and live in the midst of Israel. The place he chose was the innermost room of the tabernacle, called the Most Holy Place:

And let them make Me a sanctuary, that I may dwell among them. According to all that I show you, that is, the pattern of the tabernacle and the pattern of all its furnishings, just so you shall make *it* (Exodus 25:8-9).

This building was a temporary one; it could be taken down, packed on to wagons, and transported by the Jews on their way to the promised land. Later on, king Solomon built a magnificent temple of stone, to replace the tabernacle as a permanent place of worship in Jerusalem; here God said he would live among the people:

> Then Solomon said: 'The LORD said He would dwell in the dark cloud. But I have built You an exalted house, and a place for You to dwell in forever' (2 Chronicles 6:1-2).

Of course Solomon knew very well that the infinite God could not be contained in any kind of building. The important thing was that God, who inhabits eternity and is present everywhere throughout the universe, promised to be present in a special way in the temple that they had built for him.

In the New Testament Paul describes believers as being part of God's building. He also says that our bodies are living temples in which God dwells through the Holy Spirit. Not only are we collectively part of God's temple, individually we are also temples of the Holy Spirit:

> *You are* God's building (1 Corinthians 3:9).

> Do you not know that your body is the temple of the Holy Spirit *who is* in you, whom you have from God, and you are not your own? (1 Corinthians 6:19).

Paul also teaches that the church itself is like a great temple that God himself is building. This will only be completed when Jesus returns at the end of the age. Believers are likened by Peter to living stones which, one by one, God is building into the walls of his temple until the day when it reaches completion:

> Now, therefore, you are no longer strangers and foreigners, but fellow citizens with the saints and members of the

> household of God, having been built on the foundation of the apostles and prophets, Jesus Christ Himself being the chief corner*stone*, in whom the whole building, being joined together, grows into a holy temple in the Lord, in whom you also are being built together for a habitation of God in the Spirit (Ephesians 2:19-22).

> You also, as living stones, are being built up a spiritual house, a holy priesthood, to offer up spiritual sacrifices acceptable to God through Jesus Christ (1 Peter 2:5).

e) God's family. We have already seen, in the chapter on regeneration, that it is only through experiencing the new birth that we become children of God. It is only when God sends his Spirit into our hearts that we can know him as our Father and ourselves as his children by adoption:

> For you did not receive the spirit of bondage again to fear, but you received the Spirit of adoption by whom we cry out, 'Abba, Father.' The Spirit Himself bears witness with our spirit that we are children of God (Romans 8:15-16).

> Having predestined us to adoption as sons by Jesus Christ to Himself, according to the good pleasure of His will (Ephesians 1:5).

> For you are all sons of God through faith in Christ Jesus (Galatians 3:26).

> For it was fitting for Him, for whom *are* all things and by whom *are* all things, in bringing many sons to glory, to make the author of their salvation perfect through sufferings. For both He who sanctifies and those who are being sanctified *are* all of one, for which reason He is not ashamed to call them brethren (Hebrews 2:10-11).

These verses speak very clearly of God as our Father and us as his children, belonging to his family. They also imply that

we are all brethren, i.e. we belong to one another. By grace
we have been brought into a living relationship, not only with
God, but also with one another, a relationship which through
the gift of eternal life knows no end. The true church can
therefore be likened to a family, the family of the living God.

f) The pillar and ground of the truth. The only example of
this expression in the New Testament is in Paul's letter to
Timothy:

> But if I am delayed, I *write* so that you may know how you
> ought to conduct yourself in the house of God, which is ...
> the pillar and ground of the truth (1 Timothy 3:15).

In Western countries there are many people, and some theologians, who believe that because love is the distinguishing
feature of Christ's disciples (John 13:35) it is more important
than biblical truth. But Christ never taught that love was
more important than truth. Indeed he said to Pilate:

> For this cause was I born, and for this cause I have come
> into the world, that I should bear witness to the truth.
> Everyone who is of the truth hears my voice (John 18:37).

Love must never be untruthful because Christian morality is both truthful and loving. The church of Jesus Christ
must always speak the truth, God's truth. Western churches
today over-emphasize compassion and love. They seldom
tell people they are sinners who must repent if they would
know God's forgiveness. They are so 'loving' that they fail
to proclaim the truth; this is wrong. Perhaps the apostle John
speaks more about God's love than any of the New Testament
writers, yet his attitude to those who denied the deity and
work of Christ was anything but 'loving' and tolerant:

> If anyone comes to you and does not bring this doctrine,
> do not receive him into your house nor greet him; for he
> who greets him shares in his evil deeds (2 John 10-11).

Because Satan is the father of lies, he will use all manner of
heretical ideas to oppose the church and overthrow its unique
testimony to the truth. He tempts Christians to deny the faith
so that their own testimony to the truth will be compromised.
The church is the only institution in this world to which God
has committed his message of truth and of reconciliation. It
is vital therefore for Christians not only to know the truth,
believe the truth, and live the truth but also
to proclaim the truth. Only in this way will they be able to
follow him who said:

> I am the way, the truth, and the life (John 14:6).

g) The flock of God. In the Old Testament God is called the
Shepherd of Israel. He cares for his people as a shepherd
cares for and protects his sheep:

> Give ear, O Shepherd of Israel, You who lead Joseph like
> a flock; You who dwell *between* the cherubim, shine forth!
> (Psalm 80:1).

> For He is our God, and we *are* the people of His pasture,
> and the sheep of His hand (Psalm 95:7).

What is true of the people of God collectively is also true of
them individually. David realised that God was his shepherd
who cared for him and loved him:

> The LORD is my shepherd; I shall not want. He makes me
> to lie down in green pastures; He leads me beside the still
> waters (Psalm 23:1-2).

When those whom God had appointed as under-shepherds
to lead and guide his people failed to do so, he said:

> I will feed My flock, and I will make them lie down (Ezekiel 34:15).

In the New Testament Christ is called the Good Shepherd and those who follow him his sheep. The church has only one shepherd and Christ has only one flock:

> I am the good shepherd; and I know My *sheep*, and am known by My own. As the Father knows Me, even so I know the Father; and I lay down My life for the sheep. And other sheep I have which are not of this fold; them also I must bring, and they will hear My voice; and there will be one flock *and* one shepherd (John 10:14-16).

> For you were like sheep going astray, but have now returned to the Shepherd and Overseer of your souls (1 Peter 2:25).

Perhaps the main characteristic of sheep is their need of leading and protection. They are easy prey to wild animals, so they are kept together in flocks and are dependent on their shepherd. The Lord Jesus is the ideal Shepherd. Our duty is to stay close to him, not only for our sustenance and protection, but also for the guidance we need. It is very important for the believer to understand and appreciate this relationship. Jesus is the good shepherd who feeds and leads his sheep. He is the one who gathers his people together as a shepherd gathers his sheep. We need to remember too that although Jesus is the 'Chief Shepherd' (1 Peter 5:4), he has appointed men as under-shepherds or pastors to feed his sheep while he is bodily absent from them in heaven. These are called the elders or overseers of the church, and their work is to look after Christ's sheep. They are responsible for feeding and protecting the church from error. They serve Christ and his church:

He said to him again a second time, 'Simon, *son* of
Jonah, do you love Me?' He said to Him, 'Yes, Lord; You
know that I love You.' He said to him, 'Tend My sheep'
(John 21:16).

From Miletus Paul sent to Ephesus and called for the elders
of the Church. And when they had come to him he said:

Take heed to yourselves and to all the flock, among which
the Holy Spirit has made you overseers, to shepherd the
church of God which He purchased with His own blood.
For I know this, that after my departure savage wolves
will come in among you, not sparing the flock (Acts 20:
28-29).

The elders who are among you I exhort, I who am a
fellow elder and a witness of the sufferings of Christ,
and also a partaker of the glory that will be revealed:
Shepherd the flock of God which is among you, serving as overseers, not by constraint but willingly, not for
dishonest gain but eagerly; nor as being lords over those
entrusted to you, but being examples to the flock
(1 Peter 5:1-3).

3 The character of the church

It is generally agreed that there are four essential features of
God's true Church:

a)   It is **Apostolic**
b)   It is **One**
c)   It is **Holy**
d)   It is **Universal.**

a) It is apostolic. Christ chose twelve men from among the
larger number of his disciples to be with him throughout
his earthly ministry, hearing and seeing all that he did, and

being eye-witnesses of his physical resurrection (Mark 3:14; Acts 1:21-22). He also chose Paul after his resurrection to be the apostle to the Gentiles (Galatians 1:15-16). Christ commissioned these men to preach his gospel to the world. The apostles therefore occupy a unique historical position standing between Christ and all subsequent generations of men. All that we know about Christ is mediated to us through their written witness. Paul can therefore say with absolute truthfulness that the church is built upon the foundation of the apostles and prophets. Their testimony to Christ comprehends all that we know about Christ and his teaching. It must therefore be accepted as God's final word about his Son:

> Having been built on the foundation of the apostles and prophets, Jesus Christ Himself being the chief cornerstone (Ephesians 2:20).

Any church that claims to be apostolic must therefore submit completely to the biblical testimony of the apostles. Unfortunately the Roman Catholic and the Orthodox Churches, which both claim to be apostolic in their teaching and practice, assert that church tradition is of equal authority with the apostolic writings. Tradition for the Orthodox means the customs and practices of the early Church Fathers that have been handed down to the Church in an unwritten form over several centuries. 'Holy tradition', means the Bible, plus the seven Ecumenical Councils (the Creed), the later councils, the Fathers, the Liturgy, Canon Law and Icons.

For the Orthodox Churches the practice and customs of the Church during the first nine centuries (the last Ecumenical Council was the Second Council of Nicaea, 787) are received as holy tradition and are of equal authority with Holy Scripture. For example the New Testament recognizes only two sorts of leaders in each church, elders and deacons (1 Timothy 3). However St Ignatius (55-115) taught that there were three offices, not two. In addition to elders and deacons each city should have its own bishop who should rule over all the churches in his district. He made no appeal to Scripture for this idea but simply asserted, 'Let the Bishop preside in the place of God, and his clergy in place of the apostolic conclave'. St Jerome (345-419) states that the supremacy of a single bishop arose by custom rather than by the Lord's actual appointment. Yet for Roman Catholicism and for Orthodoxy the role of the monarchical bishop on the authority of Ignatius is crucial to their understanding of the church. The Orthodox Church and the Roman Catholic Church derive continuing authority not only from the Bible, but also from the theory of the apostolic succession of their bishops. They claim that their present bishops are in direct line of descent from those in apostolic times. They believe that this makes their Church the only true Body of Christ on earth, inhabited by the Holy Spirit and therefore infallible. The teaching of St Ignatius has a permanent place in both Roman Catholic and Orthodox tradition. This illustrates both the thinking and practices of churches that base their authority not on Scripture alone but on Scripture and tradition.

However, the Roman Catholic view of tradition differs considerably from that of the Orthodox Church. It maintains that through its college of bishops (cardinals), with the Pope sitting as head of that college, tradition can still be formulated, as God reveals new truths to his Church – tradition being seen as dynamic not static. For example in 1946 Pope Pius XII consulted all parts of the Roman Catholic Church to see if the bodily assumption into heaven of the Virgin Mary could be proposed as a dogma of faith. Four years later, there being overwhelming support from all sections of the Church for the idea, the Pope proclaimed it as an infallible truth in 1950.

The new *Catechism of the Catholic Church* (1992) says:

77 'In order that the full and living Gospel might always be preserved in the Church the Apostles left Bishops as their

successors. They gave them their own position of teaching authority. Indeed, the apostolic preaching, which is expressed in a special way in the inspired books, was to be preserved in a continuous line of succession until the end of time.'

78 'This living transmission, accomplished in the Holy Spirit, is called Tradition, since it is distinct from Sacred Scripture, though closely connected to it. Through Tradition, "the Church, in her doctrine, life and worship, perpetuates and transmits to every generation all that she herself is, all that she believes. . ."'

79 'The Father's self-communication made through His Word in the Holy Spirit, remains present and active in the Church: "God who spoke in the past, continues to converse with the spouse of His beloved Son"'...

82 'As a result the Church, to whom the transmission and interpretation of Revelation is entrusted, "does not derive her certainty about all revealed truths from the Holy Scriptures alone. Both Scripture and Tradition must be accepted and honoured with equal sentiment of devotion and reverence"'.

The Roman Catholic Church claims that its 'Magisterium' (the Pope together with the college of bishops) can infallibly determine the meaning of both Scripture and tradition and in a sense is superior to both!

891 'The Roman Pontiff, head of the college of Bishops, enjoys this infallibility in virtue of his office, when as supreme pastor and teacher of all the faithful ... he proclaims by a definitive act a doctrine pertaining to faith and morals. The infallibility promised to the Church is also present in the body of Bishops when, together with Peter's successor, they exercise the supreme Magisterium ... This infallibility extends as far as the deposit of divine Revelation itself.'

At the Reformation the Protestant Church vigorously protested that the customs and practices of the post-apostolic age of the Church had gradually distorted and perverted the truths of the New Testament, just as the traditions of the scribes and Pharisees had distorted the truths of the Old Testament. Where, for example, in the New Testament do you find the worship of Mary as the sinless Mother of God to whom prayer is made? Or the doctrine of the mass and transubstantiation? Or the bowing-down and praying to icons and images in contradiction to the second commandment? Or praying to the saints?

All these doctrines are justified by Orthodoxy and by Roman Catholicism in the name of holy tradition. But the Lord Jesus severely rebuked the Scribes and Pharisees for elevating their tradition above the word of God with these words:

> But He answered and said to them, 'Why do you also transgress the commandment of God because of your tradition? For God commanded, saying, "*Honour your father and your mother*"; and, "*He who curses father or mother, let him be put to death.*" But you say, "Whoever says to *his* father or mother, 'Whatever profit you might have received from me has been dedicated *to the temple – is released from* honouring his father or mother." Thus you have made the commandment of God of no effect by your tradition' (Matthew 15:3-6).

Protestant Churches claim to be apostolic because they base all their teaching on the words of the apostles and believe that when they died all revelation ceased. Church tradition must be tested by Holy Scripture, not the other way round. This accords with the teaching of Jude when he says:

> Beloved, while I was very diligent to write to you concerning our common salvation, I found it necessary to write to you exhorting you to contend earnestly for the faith which was once for all delivered to the saints (Jude 3).

By the time Jude wrote his epistle the gospel revelation had been completed and nothing more needed to be added to it. The Scriptures are therefore the only foundation on which a Church can base its claim to be truly apostolic.

b) It is one. When Our Lord returned to heaven he left behind him a small group of his followers in the city of Jerusalem, who were united together in one church. Through the successful preaching of the gospel throughout the Roman World groups of Christians were gathered together in many different countries and cultures. The churches in Judea were composed mainly of Jewish believers. Their style of worship, where the reading and explanation of the scriptures were central, was modelled on the Jewish synagogue from which they had come. James in his letter actually uses the word 'synagogue' to describe a Christian meeting (James 2:2). On the other hand the church in Corinth had a high proportion of Gentiles and their style of worship appears to have been far less formal than that in Judea (see 1 Corinthians 14:23-33). Variation in styles of worship did not threaten the basic unity of the churches neither did the different spiritual gifts which were exercised in the Church in those days; there was diversity in unity. What did threaten the unity of the churches was the activity of heretical teachers who infiltrated themselves into the assemblies of believers. John opposed the spread of Gnosticism (religious ideas based on Greek philosophy, astrology and mystery religions) while Paul opposed Jewish legalism (salvation by observing laws and regulations). Both of these teachings threatened to divide the early church into different factions by perverting the truths of the gospel.

Christ taught that once a person is born again by the Holy Spirit he becomes a child of God and is joined to the Lord in one spirit (1 Corinthians 6:17). This means that he is united to God in such a way that his whole being becomes God-centred, leading to a complete change in his behaviour, values and views. Not only is he united to God in one spirit, but he also becomes united to all those who have shared in the same life-changing experience. Christian unity is therefore the result of this experience in which the newborn soul is united with God and with all those who truly believe in Christ as Saviour and Lord. The unity that exists between the Father and the Son exists also between Christ and believers, but Christ prayed that the unity between believers be clearly understood and practised:

> That they all may be one, as You, Father, *are* in Me, and I in You; that they also may be one in Us, that the world may believe that You sent Me. And the glory which You gave Me I have given them, that they may be one just as We are one: I in them, and You in Me; that they may be made perfect in one, and that the world may know that You sent Me, and have loved them as You have loved Me (John 17:21-23).

Christ is praying that God would unite all those who truly believe so that their witness to the world would be effective. Believers are unitedly to testify that the Father sent the Son to be the Saviour of the world (1 John 4:14); this is the message that brings salvation. Believers are called upon to preserve and to show forth an outward and visible unity, one that already exists inwardly and spiritually. Paul says:

> Endeavouring to keep the unity of the Spirit in the bond of peace. *There is* one body and one Spirit, just as you were called in one hope of your calling; one Lord, one faith, one baptism; one God and Father of all, who *is* above all, and through all, and in you all (Ephesians 4:3-6).

Why then is Christendom so divided? Why are there so many denominations, many claiming to be the one true church? Divisions have often occurred needlessly over non-essential points of doctrine, i.e. over things that are not essential to salvation. There is no excuse in many cases for so many denominations.

On the other hand divisions have often occurred because of error and heresy. For example in the sixteenth century the Roman Catholic Church had become so corrupt and heretical that the gospel of grace had been radically transformed into a system of salvation by human efforts. Similarly in the twentieth century some Protestant denominations had become so theologically liberal that they denied almost everything in the Bible. In both instances there was no hope of reforming the corrupt parent bodies and new ones therefore had to be formed. The true unity in the Holy Spirit of all born again believers is a fact irrespective of outward denominational disunity. The New Testament call for unity is a summons to keep and to maintain the fundamental oneness of life that the Holy Spirit has already given.

The sixteenth century Reformers distinguished between the invisible church (all God's elect who are truly one in Christ) and the visible church (a mixed company of regenerate and unregenerate persons). Both the Roman Catholic and the Orthodox Churches claim to be the one true and visible manifestation of the Church on earth, yet both lack the true marks of Biblical apostolicity discussed in the previous paragraph. Christians today must labour to show and to preserve unity with all those who believe the basic doctrines of salvation, i.e. the Trinity, the gospel of God's grace through faith, the deity of Christ, the inspiration and infallibility of the Bible and the substitutionary sacrifice of Christ on the cross for our sins. These are matters that are essential to salvation and thus of primary and lasting importance. Those who believe and preach them have a unity in the basic doctrines of salvation. This should lead them into a visible union, even though they might differ on issues of secondary importance, i.e. church government, the mode of baptism, etc. God has given a basic and fundamental unity to all his children; their duty is to demonstrate and preserve it in a visible and public manner.

c) It is holy. Since a church is a gathering together of those who claim to believe in Christ and to follow Christ, it follows that such people must demonstrate in their lives that they are obedient to His commandments:

> He who says, 'I know Him,' and does not keep His commandments, is a liar, and the truth is not in him. But whoever keeps His word, truly the love of God is perfected in him. By this we know that we are in Him. He who says he abides in Him ought himself also to walk just as He walked (1 John 2:4-6).

> In this the children of God and the children of the devil are manifest: Whoever does not practise righteousness is not of God, nor *is* he who does not love his brother (1 John 3:10).

> But you are a chosen generation, a royal priesthood, a holy nation, His own special people, that you may proclaim the praises of Him who called you out of darkness into His marvellous light (1 Peter 2:9).

The question may be asked, is a true church perfectly holy? Are all its members sinless? The answer, of course, is, No. The letter that John wrote, and which is quoted above, begins by saying:

> If we say that we have no sin, we deceive ourselves, and the truth is not in us. If we confess our sins, He is faithful and just to forgive us *our* sins and to cleanse us from all unrighteousness (1:8-9).

The true believer practises righteousness, he follows Christ, he keeps his word, and he abides in him. But this does not mean he never sins and never makes a mistake. It means he does not continue in the ways of sin as though it were the normal thing to do. He hates sin, but he is not immune to the temptations of the devil and sometimes he falls. Since a church is a gathering of individual Christians, it follows that the quality of spiritual life in a given church will be no higher or lower than that of its members. When Christ spoke to the seven churches of Asia after his ascension he told each of them, 'I know your works'. He knew every detail of their service to him and also every detail of their failures. He commends their virtues and sternly reproves their sins. Only two of the churches are faithful, all the others are warned to repent of their sins or else they will be punished. For example he says to the church at Ephesus:

> Remember therefore from where you have fallen; repent and do the first works, or else I will come to you quickly and remove your lampstand from its place – unless you repent (Revelation 2:5).

Christ tells this church that if it does not repent he will remove the light of his presence and, so far as he is concerned, they will cease to be his church, even though they may continue to meet and hold services. Without holiness of life and purity of doctrine Christ refuses to acknowledge any gathering of people as a true church of his. Any church therefore that claims to be an apostolic church of Christ must be able to demonstrate, among other things, that its members are holy people who show by their words and deeds that they belong to Christ and follow Christ. The apostle Peter strongly emphasizes this in writing to newly founded churches in his day:

> As obedient children, not conforming yourselves to the former lusts, *as* in your ignorance; but as He who called you *is* holy, you also be holy in all *your* conduct, because it is written, '*Be holy, for I am holy*' (1 Peter 1:14-16).

d) It is universal. By word and by deed Christ showed that the gospel he came to preach was for all men and women regardless of their nationality, social position, colour or moral condition. Unlike Judaism the Christian faith is not racially exclusive. Christ's parting words to his disciples were:

> All authority has been given Me in heaven and on earth. Go therefore and make disciples of all the nations, baptising them in the name of the Father and of the Son and of the Holy Spirit (Matthew 28:18-19).

One of the marks of a truly apostolic church is that it refuses to identify itself with any particular nationality or class. It is a missionary church, opening its doors and its heart to all men everywhere. It refuses to become associated with the rich and powerful, because Christ by example and by word preached the gospel to the poor and was himself a poor man as were his apostles. Too often church leaders seem to like the rich and powerful. In so doing they give the impression that the church is a rich man's club concerned only with those who can endow it with favours and gifts (see James 2:2-3).

4 The inner life of the church

The day of Pentecost (see Acts 2) has been called the birthday of the church. After his resurrection Jesus told his disciples to wait in Jerusalem until they had been baptised with the power of the Holy Spirit. Only when this had happened would they be able to witness effectively for him throughout the world.

As soon as this miraculous event had taken place Peter preached the first sermon of the newborn church and three thousand souls repented and were baptised. What did the Apostles do with this great crowd of new believers?

> Then those who gladly received his word were baptized; and that day about three thousand souls were added *to them*. And they continued steadfastly in the apostles' doctrine and fellowship, in the breaking of bread, and in prayers (Acts 2:41-42).

There were four activities that the apostles emphasized and these four activities formed the basis of the life of the church. They were:

a) Doctrine
b) Fellowship
c) Breaking of Bread
d) Prayers

a) Doctrine. This is placed first in order of importance by the apostles and was their main work:

> And daily in the temple, and in every house, they did not cease teaching and preaching Jesus *as* the Christ (Acts 5:42).

Teaching: To give instruction, to explain Christian truth and its implications.
Preaching: To proclaim publicly, as a herald, the truth about Christ.

The apostles used both methods to communicate the truths about Jesus Christ. They did this in a more private way in people's houses as well as publicly in the open-air.

As the number of Christians in Jerusalem began to grow, so also did the need to administer and organise the meetings and to meet the various material needs of so many people. In the end this became so great that the apostles found that it was interfering with their ministry. The time they should have been devoting to preaching and teaching was having to be spent on administrative matters:

> Then the twelve summoned the multitude of the disciples and said, 'It is not desirable that we should leave the word of God and serve tables. Therefore, brethren, seek out from among you seven men of *good* reputation, full of the Holy Spirit and wisdom, whom we may appoint over this

business; but we will give ourselves continually to prayer
and the ministry of the word (Acts 6:2-4).

Why did the apostles place such a high priority on teaching
the word of God? Because, as Jesus himself had shown, the
truths of the gospel must be well understood if disciples are
to be able to witness and live effectively for him. It is essential
therefore to have competent teachers in the church who can
give proper instruction. There are three main reasons for this:

i)   Teaching strengthens our faith and helps us to grow
     spiritually.
ii) Teaching equips us to serve others.
iii) Teaching equips us to defend the church against heresy.

i) Teaching strengthens our faith and helps us to grow.

And He Himself gave some *to be* apostles, some prophets, some evangelists, and some pastors and teachers,
for the equipping of the saints for the work of ministry, for
the edifying of the body of Christ, till we all come to the
unity of the faith and the knowledge of the Son of God, to
a perfect man, to the measure of the stature of the fulness
of Christ (Ephesians 4:11-13).

What happens if there is no teaching? What will be the
inevitable result? The next verse tells us:

That we should no longer be children, tossed to and fro and
carried about with every wind of doctrine, by the trickery
of men, in the cunning craftiness by which they lie in wait
to deceive (verse 14).

(See also 1 Corinthians 3:1-3; Hebrews 5:10-14 and 1 Timothy
4:13-16).

ii) Teaching equips us to serve others

You therefore, my son, be strong in the grace that is in Christ Jesus. And the things that you have heard from me among many witnesses, commit these to faithful men who will be able to teach others also (2 Timothy 2:1-2).

See also 1 Corinthians 3:1-3; Hebrews 5:10-14 and Colossians 3:16.

iii) Teaching equips us to defend the church against heresy

As you have therefore received Christ Jesus the Lord, so walk in Him, rooted and built up in Him and established in the faith, as you have been taught, abounding in it with thanksgiving. Beware lest anyone cheat you through philosophy and empty deceit, according to the tradition of men, according to the basic principles of the world, and not according to Christ (Colossians 2:6-8)

See also Ephesians 4:11-15; Acts 20:27-31; Jude 3-4.

Who is to do the teaching? Paul appointed elders in every church to be rulers and teachers (Acts 14:23; Titus 1:5), responsible for feeding and protecting the people of God (Acts 20:28). Not all elders are gifted to teach publicly (but see 1 Timothy 3:2); this is a special gift that is not given to all (Romans 12:7), but at least one of them must be able to do so and should give himself completely to this task:

Let the elders who rule well be counted worthy of double honour, especially those who labour in the word and doctrine (1 Timothy 5:17).

Let him who is taught the word share in all good things with him who teaches (Galatians 6:6).

If the apostles (Acts 6:4), and men like Titus and Timothy (1 Timothy 4:13-16), saw the need for giving themselves fully to teaching the Word surely we should also see a similar need in our own day. Why is this vital part of the church's ministry ignored? Is it not the cause of many of the tragedies we are experiencing at the present time? Teachers must be competent to explain the meaning, not only of all the books of the Bible, but also the main truths of the Christian faith. Teachers are God's gift to his church; we should give them the help they need to exercise their ministry.

b) Fellowship. The word in the Greek (*koinōnia*) with its derivatives, is a very strong word and means to share something with another person. It is always used of personal relationships and is translated in different ways throughout the New Testament. For example:

i) Paul says that the cup we drink at the Lord's Supper is 'a *sharing* in the blood of Christ'. The cup symbolizes our sharing in the fruits of the sacrifice of Christ on the cross. We are sharing in the salvation he obtained for us at Calvary (1 Corinthians 10:16).

ii) Peter and Andrew, James and John, were partners in a fishing business before Jesus called them to follow Him. The word *'partners'* comes from the same Greek word (Luke 5:10).

iii) When some of the early Christians suffered persecution, lost their homes and personal property, and were put in prison, there were those who supported them and as a result suffered the same fate. They became *'companions'* of the prisoners and shared their sufferings (Hebrews 10:33). This word too comes from *koinōnia*.

iv) Poor believers in Greece organised a collection of money for their Jewish brethren in Jerusalem who were in great need. By giving them their money they were entering into sharing with them by sharing their sufferings (2 Corinthians 9:13).

When Christ suffered and died for us, he did so in order that we could share in the blessings and the fruits of his death. It is by giving us *himself* that he has fellowship with us. Only when we share the sufferings of others by giving them food, clothing and a place in our homes are we are having fellowship with them. When we see a brother or sister in great financial need and we give them some money then we are having fellowship with them. If they are sick or in prison and we visit them to relieve their suffering then we are having fellowship with them. When the early Christians sold their property and worldly goods so that no one should be in material need, that was true fellowship! Fellowship means sharing our *lives* with others.

True fellowship is the outcome of Christian love. Christ said, 'By this all will know that you are My disciples, if you have love for one another' (John 13:35). Clearly men have to see something tangible if they are to know what Christian love really is. What can they see? When Christians give their time, their concern, their sympathy, their homes, and their money to one another in a sacrificial way, this is a visible demonstration of Christian love. This is what fellowship means: a sharing of ourselves with others.

c) Breaking of bread. Christ is our life, our hope and our foundation (Colossians 3:4; 1 Timothy 1:1; 1 Corinthians 3:11). Our lives are built upon him and especially upon his atoning death on the cross for us. When he instituted the Lord's Supper (Luke 22:17-20), he told his disciples to eat bread and drink wine in order to remember that he was about to offer his body and blood upon the cross for them. This is the central point of our faith, 'that Christ died for our sins according to the Scriptures.' (1 Corinthians 15:3). In the

Lord's Supper we remember that we owe everything to him. Christ said, 'Do this in remembrance of Me' (Luke 22:19). At the Lord's Supper we should therefore:

- Thank him for his love, because he died for us.
- Renew our faith in his atoning death.
- Confess our sins, asking for fresh forgiveness and cleansing.
- Praise him, our great High Priest whose blood atones for our sins.
- Ask for strength to live to please him in the future.
- Join together with his people according to his command.

The Last Supper was instituted at the end of the Jewish Passover (Luke 22:15), a feast that commemorated God's deliverance of Israel from the awful slavery of Egypt. Each family was saved from God's judgement by killing a lamb and putting its blood on the doorposts of their houses. Seeing the blood, the angel of death passed over all Jewish homes. The sacrifice of Jesus, the Lamb of God, was pre-figured in the Jewish Passover. His sacrificial death delivers, not just Jews, but all who believe in him, from the slavery of sin and the dominion of Satan; 'Christ, our Passover, was sacrificed for us' (1 Corinthians 5:7).

At the Last Supper Jesus said, 'This cup is the new covenant in My blood, which is shed for you' (Luke 22:20). What is this new covenant? It was prophesied in Jeremiah 31:31-34 and is described in detail in Hebrews 8:7-13. In this wonderful new covenant, given to us through the blood of Jesus, God promises to do five things:

i) To put his laws into our minds and write them on our hearts.
ii) To be our God and we to be his people.
iii) That we shall all know him.
iv) To be merciful to our unrighteousness.
v) To remember our sins and iniquities no more.

The early church remembered the Lord in the breaking of bread on the first day of each week (Acts 20:7). The Lord's Supper is a proclamation by the church of the Lord's death until he comes again (1 Corinthians 11:26).

d) Prayers. The early Church learnt to depend upon God for its very survival through united prayer (Acts 4:24-31). When their leader, Peter, was put in prison he was miraculously delivered in answer to the united prayers of the church (Acts 12:5-11). Prayer is a mighty weapon and the Church learnt to use it against all its enemies. Prayer expresses the fact that we are completely dependent upon God for all our needs. Jesus often prayed to his Father and taught his followers to do the same. He told us to do so at all times (Luke 18:1), privately (Matthew 6:6), and with others (Matthew 18:19-20). He emphasized that faith in God's ability to answer prayer is essential if we want to receive answers from him (Matthew 21:21-22). Prayer must always be made in the name of Christ (John 14:13), and our requests must be in accordance with God's revealed will (1 John 5:14).

There are different types of prayer:

- Thanksgiving
- Praise
- Adoration
- Confession of sin
- Supplication for others
- Petition for ourselves

The Lord's Prayer (Matthew 6:7-15) is regarded as a model prayer in that it shows us the correct order for our prayers. It begins and ends with God and his kingdom, our own requests are in the middle and there is the ever-present consciousness of the need to ask for his forgiveness.

i) We have noted four main attributes or characteristics of the true church. The church is: Apostolic; One; Holy and Universal.

ii) We have noted the four main activities of the Church. They are: Preaching and Teaching; Fellowship; Breaking of Bread and Prayers.

To this we should add praise. Singing God's praise is an important part of our worship and can be expressed either in psalms, hymns or spiritual songs (Ephesians 5:19).

But what about the all-important subject of evangelism? Should not this be added to the four main marks of the church? Yes, indeed it should! Thus in the book of Acts we see God leading his infant (Jewish) church to open the door of faith to the Gentiles (Acts 10:28-40). Not only that but we see that the New Testament church was born in a great evangelistic meeting on the Day of Pentecost (Acts 2:1-41). The gospel, with signs following, was quickly spread among the Jews by the disciples, in spite of a hostile reaction and persecution (Acts 11:19; 21:20).

God also sent Philip to preach the gospel to an Ethiopian (Acts 8:27-38) so that the gospel might go to Ethiopia, and God ordained Paul to be the Apostle of the Gentiles (2 Timothy 1:11) so that the gospel would spread throughout the Roman world. Thus the parting words of Christ to his disciples began to be fulfilled, and are the Church's mandate until the end of time (Matthew 28:19-20).

The Protestant Reformers maintained there are three marks of a true church:

i)   Preaching the Word
ii) Dispensing the sacraments
iii) The exercise of discipline

We have already spoken about the first two. The third is also very important. Where there is no proper leadership and discipline, sin and folly will, if uncontrolled, destroy any church. We see that when the church in Corinth was in danger of being destroyed by unruly internal divisions, pride and immorality, Paul had to exercise strong and severe discipline in order to restore harmony and save it from destroying itself. The administration of discipline is therefore an essential mark of the church.

5 Church discipline

God's attitude to sin, whether at the personal or at the national level, is always the same – light cannot co-exist with darkness, nor can God ever be friends with Mammon:

> What agreement has the temple of God with idols? For you are the temple of the living God. As God has said: *'I will dwell in them and walk among them. I will be their God, and they shall be My people.'* Therefore *'Come out from among them and be separate, says the Lord. Do not touch what is unclean, and I will receive you. I will be a Father to you, and you shall be My sons and daughters, says the LORD Almighty* (2 Corinthians 6:16-18).

See also Ezekiel 43:5-7.

However, all believers experience a continual conflict with sin, with the world and with their enemy the Devil:

> The flesh lusts against the Spirit, and the Spirit against the flesh; and these are contrary to one another, so that you do not do the things that you wish (Galatians 5:17).

See also Romans 7:18-25.

In every believer and in every living church this conflict
continues without intermission day and night, for Satan
never sleeps! Therefore the leaders of the churches have to
be watchful both of themselves and of the sheep committed to their care. Indeed it is the responsibility of individual
Christians to be watchful not only of their own conduct but
also their relationship with fellow believers in their church
fellowship.

When disagreements, arguments and disputes break out
between individuals, what should be done? Jesus gives very
clear guidance how to resolve personal disputes so that sin
is properly dealt with:

> Moreover if your brother sins against you, go and tell
> him his fault between you and him alone. If he hears
> you, you have gained your brother. But if he will not hear
> *you*, take with you one or two more, that '*by the mouth of
> two or three witnesses every word may be established*'
> [see Deuteronomy 17:6; 19:15]. And if he refuses to hear
> them, tell *it* to the church. But if he refuses even to hear
> the church, let him be to you like a heathen and a tax
> collector (Matthew 18:15-17).

The main object of this disciplinary process is reconciling
believers and restoring fellowship (see also Galatians 6:1).
Putting people out of the church (excommunication) is
meant to be the last resort when all else has failed to achieve
reconciliation.

The church is called to be a holy community in which God
lives by his Spirit:

> Now, therefore, you are no longer strangers and foreign-
> ers, but fellow citizens with the saints and members of the
> household of God, having been built on the foundation of
> the apostles and prophets, Jesus Christ being the chief
> corner*stone*, in whom the whole building, being joined
> together, grows into a holy temple in the Lord, in whom

you also are being built together for a habitation of God in the Spirit (Ephesians 2:19-22).

It is therefore the responsibility of the leaders of the local church to ensure that God's community is cleansed from unrepentant members who persist in open sin. The New Testament mentions several examples so that we may be in no doubt about the kinds of sin that need their attention:

- Those who cause divisions and oppose biblical teaching (Romans 16:17; Titus 3:10).
- Those who commit adultery and other sexual sins (1 Corinthians 5:1-5; 6:9).
- Those who are covetous, idolaters, revilers, drunkards or swindlers (1 Corinthians 5:11).
- Those who reject plain Bible teaching (2 Thessalonians 3:14-15).
- Those who blaspheme (1 Timothy 1:9).
- Those who promote and teach heresy (2 John 10-11).

How should discipline be exercised? And by whom? Discipline must be first exercised privately and personally to see if repentance can be achieved (see Matthew 18:15-17). If the person(s) will not repent and is defiant and disobedient Jesus says, 'Tell it to the church' (v.17). The leaders, having investigated the case and interviewed the individual concerned must, after conferring together, summon the whole church and inform them of the facts of the case. Having obtained the consent of the church, the leaders proceed to announce the excommunication of the individual from church fellowship:

In the name of our Lord Jesus Christ, when you are gathered together, along with my spirit, with the power of our Lord Jesus Christ, deliver such a one to Satan for the destruction of the flesh, that his spirit may be saved in the day of the Lord Jesus (1 Corinthians 5:4-5).

Those thus excommunicated are not to be regarded as our enemies; rather, if we have the opportunity, we must admonish them in the hope of their recovery (2 Thessalonians 3:15). But until there is repentance we can have no social contact with them (1 Corinthians 5:11; 2 Thessalonians 3:6; 2 John 10) so that they may recognise the gravity of the sin(s) that has placed them outside the church into the world in which Satan reigns. Should the excommunicated person publicly and honestly repent, he or she must be welcomed back into the fellowship of the church (2 Corinthians 2:6-8).

What are the main purposes of church discipline? The Westminster Confession (30:3) mentions the following:

- To reclaim and recover those who have erred from God's Word.
- To warn and deter others from falling into similar offences.
- To purge out the evil leaven lest it affect the whole church.
- To preserve the honour of Christ and the profession of his gospel.
- To prevent the wrath of God from falling on the church.

Questions

1 Describe what the New Testament means by a Church.

2 What metaphors are used in the New Testament to describe the church?

3 What are the four main characteristics of the church?

4 What are the four main activities of the church?

5 On what grounds do the Roman Catholic and the Orthodox Churches say that they are the only truly Apostolic Churches?

6 Why is church discipline important?

CHAPTER TWENTY

THE SECOND COMING OF CHRIST

1 Be prepared

    a) Christ said he would come again
    b) The angels said he would come again
    c) The apostles said he would come again

2 Events that must precede his coming

Five events

3 The time of the Second Coming

4 The nature of the Second Coming

    a) A personal and physical return
    b) A visible return
    c) A sudden return
    d) A triumphant return

5 The purpose of the Second Coming

    a) To complete the work of redemption
    b) To deliver the Church
    c) To resurrect the dead – the evil and the good
    d) To judge the living and the dead

6 The millennium

    a) Premillennial view
    b) Postmillennial view
    c) Amillennial view

1 Be prepared

In Matthew 25 Christ's disciples ask him three questions:

i) When will Jerusalem and the Temple be destroyed?
ii) When will his Second Coming occur?
iii)When will be the end of the world? (Matthew 24:3)

Christ answers these three questions in some detail in this
chapter and also in Mark 13 and Luke 21. He then warns them
to be prepared for his coming, and not to be like Noah's generation, who disbelieved the patriarch's warnings and were
unprepared for the great flood that was coming:

> But of that day and hour no one knows, no, not even the
> angels of heaven, but My Father only. But as the days
> of Noah *were*, so also will the coming of the Son of Man
> be ... Therefore you also be ready, for the Son of Man is
> coming at an hour when you do not expect *Him* (Matthew
> 24:36,37,44).

> Watch therefore, for you know neither the day nor the
> hour in which the Son of Man is coming (Matthew 25:13).

In chapter twenty-five Jesus tells two parables, the parable of
'the wise and foolish virgins' and the parable of the 'talents'.
He did this to emphasise the need not only to be ready for his
coming, but also to be faithfully serving him in the meantime.
Those who do so will receive his commendation:

> His lord said to him, 'Well *done*, good and faithful servant;
> you were faithful over a few things, I will make you ruler
> over many things. Enter into the joy of your lord' (Matthew
> 25:21).

a) Christ said he would come again.

Then the sign of the Son of Man will appear in heaven, and then all the tribes of the earth will mourn, and they will see the Son of Man coming on the clouds of heaven with power and great glory (Matthew 24:30).

And if I go and prepare a place for you, I will come again and receive you to Myself; that where I am, *there* you may be also. (John 14:3)

b) The angels said he would come again.

And while they looked steadfastly towards heaven as He went up, behold, two men stood by them in white apparel, who also said, 'Men of Galilee, why do you stand gazing up into heaven? This *same* Jesus, who was taken up from you into heaven, will so come in like manner as you saw Him go into heaven' (Acts 1:10-11).

c) The apostles said he would come again.

For this we say to you by the word of the Lord, that we who are alive and remain until the coming of the Lord will by no means precede those who are asleep. For the Lord Himself will descend from heaven with a shout, with the voice of an archangel, and with the trumpet of God. And the dead in Christ will rise first (1 Thessalonians 4:15-16).

And that He may send Jesus Christ, who was preached to you before, whom heaven must receive until the times of restoration of all things, which God has spoken by the mouth of all His holy prophets since the world began (Acts 3:20-21).

When will he come? Only God the Father knows the exact time (Matthew 24:36), but when he does come it will be like a thief in the night (1 Thessalonians 5:2). It will be totally unexpected (Matthew 24:44), and it will be very sudden (Revelation 22:7). The Bible says that before his Second Coming certain events must have taken place. These are as follows:

2 Events that must precede his coming

i) The preaching of the gospel to every nation. Christ said that his gospel must be preached universally. This means it will be recognized and understood in every nation of the world:

> And this gospel of the kingdom will be preached in all the world as a witness to all the nations, and then the end will come (Matthew 24:14).

> Go therefore and make disciples of all the nations, baptizing them in the name of the Father and of the Son and of the Holy Spirit (Matthew 28:19).

Isaiah had prophesied that the Messiah's mission was not only to the Jews but also to the Gentiles:

> Behold! My Servant whom I uphold, My Elect One *in whom* My soul delights! I have put My Spirit upon Him; He will bring forth justice to the Gentiles ... I, the LORD, have called You in righteousness, and will hold Your hand; I will keep You and give You as a covenant to the people, as a light to the Gentiles (Isaiah 42:1,6).

Simon Peter was the person God chose to be the first to preach the gospel to the Gentiles, when Cornelius the Roman centurion and his household became the first Gentile converts (Acts 10:1-48):

> Simon has declared how God at the first visited the Gentiles to take out of them a people for His name (Acts 15:14).

Christ also prophesied that although he had been sent to the lost sheep of the house of Israel he had also come as the Good Shepherd of the Gentiles as well:

> And other sheep I have which are not of this fold; them also I must bring, and they will hear My voice; and there will be one flock *and* one shepherd (John 10:16).

See also Isaiah 11:10; Matthew 8:11; Luke 2:29-32; Romans 9:24-26; Ephesians 2:11-13.

Paul says that the future conversion of Israel will not take place until the full number of the Gentiles are saved:

> For I do not desire, brethren, that you should be ignorant of this mystery, lest you should be wise in your own opinion, that hardening in part has happened to Israel until the fullness of the Gentiles has come in (Romans 11:25).

ii) The conversion of the Jews. God sent Christ to the lost sheep of the house of Israel (Matthew 15:24) but its leaders rejected him, so the kingdom of God was taken from them (Matthew 21:43) and given to the Gentiles. This does not mean that God has totally rejected the Jews and will never have any dealings with them again in the future. In Romans chapters nine, ten and eleven Paul explains that God's rejection of them at the time of Christ is not final but only temporary. He mentions seven things:

- Israel is still a separate and distinct nation. (9:4)
- Their covenant promises and blessings are still valid. (9:4-5)
- God has definitely not finally rejected Israel. (11:1-5)
- The fall of Israel is only temporary. (11:11)
- God has plans to accept them again in great blessing. (11:12-15)
- Israel is God's olive tree. The branches that he broke off he will graft in again. (11:20-23)

- When the full number of Gentiles is saved God will remove Israel's hardness of heart and save them too. (11:25-26)

> Now if their fall *is* riches for the world, and their failure riches for the Gentiles, how much more their fullness! ... For if their being cast away is the reconciling of the world, what *will* their acceptance *be* but life from the dead? (Romans 11:12, 15).

> For I do not desire, brethren, that you should be ignorant of this mystery, lest you should be wise in your own opinion, that hardening in part has happened to Israel until the fulness of the Gentiles has come in. And so all Israel will be saved, as it is written: '*The Deliverer will come out of Zion, and He will turn away ungodliness from Jacob; for this is My covenant with them, when I take away their sins*' (Romans 11:25-27).

These three chapters in Romans show that God has plans to save his ancient people before Christ comes again. Some Christians believe that the restoration of the Jewish state in 1948, and the return of Jerusalem to Israel's sovereignty in 1967, are signs that God is beginning to fulfil his promise. They say that the following texts refer to a gathering of Jews, not just from Babylon, but from all over the world; Isaiah 11:11 & 12; Ezekiel 36:24-28; Amos 9:14-15 and Zechariah 8:1-8. They see these events as the first fruits of greater blessings still to come. However, other Christians are not so sure. They point out that those Jews who have returned to Israel have not, with few exceptions, accepted Jesus as Messiah, nor come back with new hearts (Deuteronomy 30:1-10).

iii) The apostasy and great tribulation. In Matthew 24:4-14 Jesus tells his disciples of specific 'signs of the times' that will herald the end of the age. One of them is the great apostasy. In verses 15-22 he warns them about the terrible events surrounding the fall of Jerusalem. In verses 23-28 he alerts to the appearance of false Christs and false prophets. From verses 29-31 he speaks of the final events. It appears that just before his coming, days of great tribulation will occur:

> Immediately after the tribulation of those days the sun will be darkened, and the moon will not give its light; the stars will fall from heaven, and the powers of the heavens will be shaken (Matthew 24:29).

During this time there will also be a great falling-away from the faith:

> And shall God not avenge His own elect who cry out day and night to Him, though He bears long with them? I tell you that He will avenge them speedily. Nevertheless when the Son of Man comes will He really find faith on the earth? (Luke 18:7-8).

> Now, brethren, concerning the coming of our Lord Jesus Christ and our gathering together to Him, we ask you, not to be soon shaken in mind or troubled, either by spirit or by word or by letter, as if from us, as though the day of Christ had come. Let no one deceive you by any means; for *that Day will not come* unless the falling away comes first, and the man of sin is revealed, the son of perdition (2 Thessalonians 2:1-3).

iv) The revealing of the Man of Sin, the Antichrist. Ever since the Garden of Eden Satan has been working against God, seeking to frustrate his purposes and to defeat his people. He has many fallen angels and evil spirits who work with him and appear in many different forms. One of these is the antichrist, who pretends to be something like Christ, but in reality works to overturn and destroy all that Christ has done. Even in the days of the apostle John many antichrists were appearing:

> Little children, it is the last hour; and as you have heard that Antichrist is coming, even now many antichrists have

come, by which we know it is the last hour ... Who is a liar
but he who denies that Jesus is the Christ? He is antichrist
who denies the Father and the Son (1 John 2:18, 22).

And every spirit that does not confess that Jesus Christ has
come in the flesh is not of God. And this is the *spirit* of the
Antichrist which ... is now already in the world (1 John 4:3).

Paul tells us that one deadly form the Antichrist will assume
is that of a person, the Man of Sin:

Let no one deceive you by any means; for *that Day will
not come* unless the falling away comes first, and the
man of sin is revealed, the son of perdition, who opposes
and exalts himself above all that is called God or that is
worshipped, so that he sits as God in the temple of God,
showing himself that he is God (2 Thessalonians 2:3-4).

In Revelation 13 John sees a vision of two terrible beasts of
prey emerging, one out of the earth and one out of the sea.
They serve the great red dragon who has seven heads and
ten horns – the Devil mentioned in the previous chapter. The
beast who emerges out of the sea has great power and even
greater arrogance against God:

Then he opened his mouth in blasphemy against God,
to blaspheme His name, His tabernacle, and those who
dwell in heaven. And it was granted to him to make war
with the saints and to overcome them. And authority was
given him over every tribe, tongue, and nation. And all who
dwell on the earth will worship him, whose names have
not been written in the Book of Life of the Lamb slain from
the foundation of the world (Revelation 13:6-8).

In this devilish beast we can see certain characteristics that
will also be true of the Man of Sin – blasphemy against God,
opposition to God's people and the acceptance of worship
as though he was God! He is definitely a person, and will

be the very incarnation of the spirit of Antichrist that is already at work in the world.

v) Signs in heaven and earth. In Matthew 24 Jesus tells his disciples that certain events will characterise the times between his first and second comings. This period is referred to in the New Testament as 'the last times' (Hebrews 1:1-2; 2 Timothy 3:1-5). Jesus tells them that they will see various things, which he calls 'the beginning of sorrows' (v.8):

- Nation fighting against nation
- Kingdom fighting against kingdom
- Famines
- Pestilences
- Earthquakes
- Persecutions
- False Christs and false prophets
- Worldwide lawlessness
- Apostasy

Towards the end of the age these things will give place to celestial disorders and signs:

- The sun, moon and stars will show signs
- International distress and anxiety will be widespread
- The heavenly powers will be shaken
- The sun and moon will be darkened
- The stars will fall
- The sign of the Son of Man will appear in heaven

A conjunction of all these things will bring home to all who live on the earth that its end is near:

> Then they will see the Son of Man coming in a cloud with power and great glory. Now when these things begin to happen, look up and lift up your heads, because your redemption draws near (Luke 21:27-28).

3 The time of the Second Coming

Throughout history there have been those who have confidently predicted the exact date of the Second Coming. Thousands of people have believed them only to be disappointed when the day came and nothing happened! Christians should never make this mistake because it is written:

> But of that day and hour no one knows, no, not even the angels of heaven, but My Father only (Matthew 24:36).

If our Lord Jesus Christ did not know the exact date of his return how much less should any human being try to predict when that day will be. The Bible tells us to do two things:

i) To be prepared for it.
ii) To observe the signs which will precede it.

4 The nature of the Second Coming

a) A personal and physical return. We are told to expect Jesus to return to this world in the same way in which he left after his resurrection, but this time he will return publicly and gloriously:

> Men of Galilee, why do you stand gazing up into heaven? This *same* Jesus, who was taken up from you into heaven, will so come in like manner as you saw Him go into heaven (Acts 1:11).

Although Jesus now has a glorified body he will still be recognizable to those who saw him on earth:

> Behold, He is coming with clouds, and every eye will see Him, and they *also* who pierced Him. And all the tribes of the earth will mourn because of Him. Even so, Amen (Revelation 1:7)

See also Philippians 3:20; Colossians 3:4; 1 Thessalonians 2:19; 3:13, 4:15-17.

b) A visible return. Some Christians believe that there will be two Second Comings, one will be secret and one will be public, the first when Jesus comes *for* his church and the second when he comes *with* his church at the end of the age. But Jesus never said there would be two comings, but only one, and that it would be visible to the whole world.

> Jesus said to him, '*It is as* you said. Nevertheless, I say to you, hereafter you will see the Son of Man sitting at the right hand of the Power, and coming on the clouds of heaven' (Matthew 26:64).

> Looking for the blessed hope and glorious appearing of our great God and Saviour Jesus Christ (Titus 2:13).

See also 2 Thessalonians1: 3-10; Hebrews 9:28.

c) A sudden return. Although the coming of the Lord will be preceded by certain signs and events, the vast majority of mankind will be totally unprepared for it. Just as it was before the flood when, in spite of many warnings, people went on with their lives as before and so judgement took them completely by surprise, so for the majority of mankind the Second Coming will be sudden and unexpected:

> For you yourselves know perfectly that the day of the Lord so comes as a thief in the night. For when they say, 'Peace and safety!' then sudden destruction comes upon them, as labour pains upon a pregnant woman. And they shall not escape (1 Thessalonians 5:2-3).

> He who testifies to these things says, 'Surely I am coming quickly.' Amen. Even so, come Lord Jesus! (Revelation 22:20).

> Watch therefore, for you know neither the day nor the hour in which the Son of Man is coming (Matthew 25:13).

d) A triumphant return. When Christ first came to this world he came as a helpless baby born to a poor family. When he died his only material possessions were a cloak and a pair of sandals. When he returns it will be as King of Kings and Lord of Lords. The body of his humiliation has already been transformed into a glorified body. His appearing will be dramatic and glorious:

- The clouds of heaven will be his chariot.
- His army will be thousands of angels.
- Arch-angels will be his heralds.
- The saints will be his retinue.
- Trumpets and a great shout will announce his arrival. (Matthew 24:30-31; 26:64; 1 Thessalonians 4:16).

5 The purpose of the Second Coming

a) To complete the work of redemption. Christ came to seek and to save the lost and to gather together into his church both Jew and Gentile in one body. He began this great work but after his resurrection it was given to the Holy Spirit, working through the church, to apply Christ's salvation to men and women all over the world until the day that Jesus returns:

> Now this he did not say on his own *authority*; but being high priest that year he prophesied that Jesus would die for the nation, and not for that nation only, but also that He would gather together in one the children of God who were scattered abroad (John 11:51-52).

> Simon has declared how God at the first visited the Gentiles to take out of them a people for His name (Acts 15:14).

The church of Christ is likened to a holy temple under construction. God is the builder and every believer a stone whom he shapes, sizes and builds into the walls of his mighty temple:

> Having been built on the foundation of the apostles and prophets, Jesus Christ Himself being the chief corner-*stone*, in whom the whole building, being joined together, grows into a holy temple in the Lord (Ephesians 2:20-21).

Once the number of the elect has been completed this will signify that God's holy temple is finished and Christ's work of redemption fulfilled. The temple is now ready to be a habitation of God through the Spirit.

b) To deliver the church. It appears that at the time of the Second Coming the world will be in a state of turmoil, wickedness will be everywhere rampant, and the church under persecution. Christ's appearance will therefore coincide with a period of great trial and anguish for those believers still left on the earth:

> Men's hearts failing them from fear and the expectation of those things which are coming on the earth, for the powers of heaven will be shaken. Then they will see the Son of Man coming in a cloud with power and great glory. Now when these things begin to happen, look up and lift up your heads, because your redemption draws near (Luke 21:26-28).

> I was watching; and the same horn was making war against the saints, and prevailing against them, until the Ancient of Days came, and a judgement was made *in favour* of the saints of the Most High, and the time came for the saints to possess the kingdom (Daniel 7:21-22).

See also 1 Corinthians 15:24-25; Revelation 6:10-11.

c) To resurrect the dead – the evil and the good. At his appearing the dead will be raised from their graves or wherever they have died. This is called the general resurrection. Christ will bring with him from heaven those saints who died in the Lord, and their spirits will be reunited with their new, glorified bodies. The unbelieving dead will also be reunited with their bodies, a truly vast company of men and women, boys and girls, comprising all who have ever lived on the earth!

> And after my skin is destroyed, this *I know*, that in my flesh I shall see God (Job 19:26).

> Do not marvel at this; for the hour is coming in which all who are in the graves will hear His voice, and come forth – those who have done good, to the resurrection of life, and those who have done evil, to the resurrection of condemnation (John 5:28-29).

> And I saw the dead, small and great, standing before God, and books were opened. And another book was opened, which is *the Book* of Life. And the dead were judged according to their works, by the things which were written in the books. The sea gave up the dead who were in it, and Death and Hades delivered up the dead who were in them. And they were judged, each one according to his works (Revelation 20:12-13).

See also 1 Corinthians 15:51-55; 1 Thessalonians 4:14-18.

d) To judge the living and the dead. At the return of Christ all wrongs will be righted. Every soul who has ever lived will receive their just rewards. All those who escaped punishment for their crimes during this life will not escape now. Secret things, long hidden in darkness, will be exposed and brought out into the bright light of God's presence. Satan and all his wicked angels will be condemned:

> When the Son of Man comes in His glory, and all the holy angels with Him, then He will sit on the throne of His glory. All the nations will be gathered before Him, and He will separate them one from another, as a shepherd divides his sheep from the goats. And He will set the sheep on His right hand but the goats on the left ... And these will go away into everlasting punishment, but the righteous into eternal life (Matthew 25:31-33,46).

> For God will bring every work into judgement, including every secret thing, whether *it is* good or whether *it is* evil (Ecclesiastes 12:14).

> In flaming fire taking vengeance on those who do not know God, and on those who do not obey the gospel of our Lord Jesus Christ. These shall be punished with everlasting destruction from the presence of the Lord and from the glory of His power, when He comes in that Day, to be glorified in His saints and to be admired among all those who believe, because our testimony among you was believed (2 Thessalonians 1:8-10).

Christians will not come into condemnatory judgement, because Christ has already paid the penalty for their sins and has, in his grace, granted them everlasting life (John 5:24).

However, there *will* be a judgement of our service to God and a just assessment of the use we have made of our gifts, opportunities and time. Christ himself will reward those who have done well and reprove those who have not:

> For we must all appear before the judgement seat of Christ, that each one may receive the things *done* in the body, according to what he has done, whether good or bad (2 Corinthians 5:10).

> Each one's work will become manifest; for the Day will declare it, because it will be revealed by fire; and the fire will test each one's work, of what sort it is. If anyone's

work which he has built on *it* endures, he will receive a reward. If anyone's work is burned, he will suffer loss; but he himself will be saved, yet so as through fire (1 Corinthians 3:13-15).

Do not be deceived, God is not mocked; for whatever a man sows, that he will also reap. For he who sows to his flesh will of the flesh reap corruption, but he who sows to the Spirit will of the Spirit reap everlasting life (Galatians 6:7-8).

6 The millennium

This word refers to a period of one thousand years. It is mentioned in only one chapter of the Bible, Revelation 20:

He laid hold of the dragon, that serpent of old, who is the Devil and Satan, and bound him for a thousand years; and he cast him into the bottomless pit, and shut him up, and set a seal on him, so that he should deceive the nations no more till the one thousand years were finished. But after these things he must be released for a little while. And I saw thrones, and they sat on them, and judgement was committed to them. And *I saw* the souls of those who had been beheaded for their witness to Jesus and for the word of God, who had not worshipped the beast or his image, and had not received *his* mark on their foreheads or on their hands. And they lived and reigned with Christ for a thousand years (Revelation 20:2-4).

John sees this as a vision, not on the earth, but in heaven where martyr-souls reign with Christ for one thousand years. Where does this millennium, mentioned in the Book of Revelation, fit into the sequence of events described by Christ in Matthew 24 or by Paul in 2 Thessalonians 2, as there is no mention of it in these passages?

There are three main views about the millennium:

a) Premillennial. This view holds that Christ will return before the millennium. According to its advocates the order of events will be as follows:

- Before Christ's return there will be a worldwide apostasy.
- Christ comes suddenly and secretly to take his saints to heaven.
- Antichrist will rule the earth for seven years and there will be a period of great tribulation.
- Christ will then return in power and great glory. He defeats Satan at the battle of Armageddon. Christ reigns at Jerusalem for one thousand years and restores temple worship and its sacrifices. All Israel will be saved. Unbelievers who survive the great tribulation share the blessings of the millennial kingdom.
- After the millennium Satan will be released, rebel against God and be finally defeated. This will be followed by the resurrection of the wicked and the Last Judgement.

b) Postmillennial.
- This view holds that, through the preaching of the gospel, Christ's kingdom will gradually grow until the whole world shall be full of the knowledge of the glory of God as the waters cover the sea. Christianity will then prevail over the earth for one thousand years during which time Satan is bound.
- Satan will rebel and be defeated by Christ at his Second Coming.
- The dead will then be raised followed by the Last Judgement.

c) Amillennial. This view holds that the millennium mentioned in the Book of Revelation, itself a book of figurative images and language, is purely symbolic. The thousand year reign is clearly a heavenly one, not an earthly. It is a reign that believers share with Christ as he rules all things in the interests of his church. It is always a good principle of biblical interpretation that obscure and disputed parts of Scripture should be interpreted by the clear and obvious ones – not the other way round! It does not agree that the world is going to get better and better before Christ returns, as proposed by postmillennialism. It does not agree that there will be two Second Comings, nor that unbelievers will be in Christ's kingdom, nor that Jewish sacrifices in the temple will be restored, all as proposed by most forms of pre-millennialism.

The true order of events according to amillennialism is as described in Matthew 24 and 1 and 2 Thessalonians:

• After the world-wide preaching of the gospel to all nations, the conversion of the Jews, the apostasy and tribulation, the revealing of the Man of Sin, the signs and wonders in heaven and earth, Christ will come.
• Satan and the antichrist will be destroyed in the final battle.
• The dead will be raised and the saints will meet Christ in the air and receive their new bodies.
• The Last Judgement will take place; Satan and the wicked will be cast into hell and the righteous will go to be with the Lord forever.
• The earth will be destroyed by fire. God will make new heavens and a new earth in which righteousness will dwell. This new world will be inhabited by the saints for ever and ever.

Questions

1 What events must take place before the Second Coming?

2 What will Christ do at his Second Coming?

3 What are the three main views concerning the millennium?

CHAPTER TWENTY ONE

DEATH, HEAVEN, AND HELL

1 What is death?

2 Why do we die?

3 Is the soul immortal?

4 Where do we go to when we die?
The intermediate state.

   a) The unbeliever
   b) The believer
   c) The Old Testament believers are in heaven
   d) New Testament believers are in heaven

5 What are believers doing in heaven?

6 Life in the new heaven and new earth

   a) An embodied life
   b) A social life
   c) A life of service
   d) A perfect life
   f) An endless life
   g) A God-centred life

1 What is death?

Death brings to an end the existence of our physical life on this planet and separates the soul from the body. The Bible says that after physical death there is a conscious existence; the soul does not die with the body. Jesus says that there is a place called hell, as well as a place called heaven, and we must go either to one or the other:

Hell

> And I say to you, My friends, do not be afraid of those who kill the body, and after that have no more that they can do. But I will show you whom you should fear: Fear Him who, after He has killed, has power to cast into hell; yes, I say to you, fear Him! (Luke 12:4-5).

Heaven

> Then he said to Jesus, 'Lord remember me when You come into Your kingdom.' And Jesus said to him, 'Assuredly, I say to you, today you will be with Me in Paradise' (Luke 23:42-43).

2 Why do we die?

Secular philosophers and scientists look upon death as part of our natural physical existence. They believe that we share the same fate as the animals; we are born, we live and we die. All this, they say, is quite normal and reasonable; there is nothing to be afraid of since death is but the end of a physical process – everything in the universe has a beginning and ultimately an end. But the Bible sees all life as originating, not in the convergence of chance physical processes, but in the will of God, the creator of all things. Modern man is increasingly atheistic in his view of life. He does not believe in God and therefore cannot understand that there is any purpose to life. Without a belief in God the universe seems quite meaningless; for the atheist therefore there is no hope beyond the grave.

The Bible says that death came into the world when man fell into sin by disobeying God. Man was created immortal, for fellowship with God and with the rest of mankind, but forfeited everything when he sinned:

> But of the tree of the knowledge of good and evil you shall not eat, for in the day that you eat of it you shall surely die (Genesis 2:17).

> Cursed *is* the ground for your sake; in toil you shall eat *of* it all the days of your life. Both thorns and thistles it shall bring forth for you, and you shall eat the herb of the field. In the sweat of your face you shall eat bread till you return to the ground, for out of it you were taken; for dust you *are*, and to dust you shall return (Genesis 3:17-19).

> Therefore, just as through one man sin entered the world, and death by sin, and thus death spread to all men, because all sinned (Romans 5:12).

3   Is the soul immortal?

Some people, who profess to believe the Bible, say that when the unbeliever dies his soul also dies, or else is actually destroyed in hell. This teaching is known either as 'conditional immortality' or 'annihilationism'. In support of their opinion they quote the following verses:

> The wages of sin is death, but the gift of God *is* eternal life in Christ Jesus our Lord (Romans 6:23).

> ... the blessed and only Potentate, the King of kings and Lord of lords who alone has immortality, dwelling in unapproachable light, whom no man has seen or can see, to whom *be* honour and everlasting power (1 Timothy 6:15-16).

> The dead do not praise the LORD, nor any who go down into silence (Psalm 115:17).

Annihilationists believe that eternal life is something that a man can only receive by faith from God, who alone is immortal and without whom there can be no eternal existence. The sinner although physically alive is spiritually dead, and therefore when his body dies so does his soul. It is destroyed by God's righteous judgement and ceases to exist altogether. However, as we shall see in the next section, the souls of both unbelievers and believers continue their conscious existence either in hell or in heaven.

Some people believe that though the soul is immortal it 'sleeps' at the moment of death and awakes only at the resurrection day; the righteous to eternal life and the wicked to eternal punishment. But this view ignores all those verses in the Bible that speak of a conscious existence after death, both of the evil and the good.

4 Where do we go when we die? The intermediate state

The Bible says that the separation of body and soul is not a permanent but a temporary condition. Believers are destined to inherit a kingdom called 'a new heaven and a new earth' in which righteousness will dwell (Revelation 21:1; see also 2 Peter 3:13). At the Second Coming Christ will bring with him the souls of believers who were in heaven, and they will receive new bodies. Those believers who are alive when he returns will also receive new bodies. The kingdom will not only be physical but also spiritual.

a) **The unbeliever.** When the unbeliever dies his soul goes
to hell where he suffers for his sin, rebellion and rejection
of Christ as Saviour and Lord. His body decays but will
be resurrected on the day of judgement. It will then be
reunited with his soul, awaiting the final sentence of judgement on the whole of humanity by the risen Christ.

> So it was that the beggar died, and was carried by the
> angels to Abraham's bosom. The rich man also died and
> was buried. And being in torments in Hades, he lifted up
> his eyes and saw Abraham afar off, and Lazarus in his
> bosom (Luke 16:22-23).

> And do not fear those who kill the body but cannot kill the
> soul. But rather fear Him who is able to destroy both soul
> and body in hell (Matthew 10:28).

> And I saw the dead, small and great, standing before God,
> and books were opened. And another book was opened
> which is *the Book* of Life. And the dead were judged ac-
> cording to their works, by the things which were written
> in the books. The sea gave up the dead who were in it,
> and Death and Hades delivered up the dead who were
> in them. And they were judged each one according to his
> works. Then Death and Hades were cast into the lake of
> fire. This is the second death (Revelation 20:12-14).

> To take part in this ministry and apostleship from which
> Judas by transgression fell, that he might go to this own
> place (Acts 1:25). [Judas is called 'the son of perdition'
> (John 17:12)].

> All the nations will be gathered before Him, and He will
> separate them one from another, as a shepherd divides
> his sheep from the goats ... And these will go away into
> everlasting punishment, but the righteous into eternal life
> (Matthew 25:32,46).

b) The believer. The Bible clearly teaches that when the believer dies his body decays, but his soul does not sleep but goes immediately into the presence of God in heaven. This condition will last until the Second Coming of Christ and is referred to as 'the intermediate state', because only when Jesus returns will body and soul be reunited. The believer will then receive a glorified body, and will inhabit the new heaven and new earth which God will make to replace the present world that is awaiting judgement and complete destruction.

c) Old Testament believers are in heaven.

For You will not leave my soul in Sheol, nor will You allow Your Holy One to see corruption. You will show me the path of life; in Your presence *is* fulness of joy; at Your right hand *are* pleasures forevermore (Psalm 16:10-11).

You will guide me with Your counsel, and afterward receive me *to* glory. Whom have I in heaven *but You*? And *there is* none upon earth *that* I desire besides You (Psalm 73:24-25).

Now even Moses showed in the *burning* bush *passage* that the dead are raised, when he called the Lord, '*the God of Abraham, the God of Isaac, and the God of Jacob.*' For He is not the God of the dead but of the living, for all live to Him (Luke 20:37-38).

... and He was transfigured before them. His clothes became shining, exceedingly white, like snow, such as no launderer on earth can whiten them. And Elijah appeared to them with Moses, and they were talking with Jesus (Mark 9:2-4).

d) New Testament believers are in heaven.

For to me, to live *is* Christ, and to die *is* gain ... For I am hard pressed between the two, having a desire to depart and to be with Christ, *which is* far better (Philippians 1:21, 23).

We are confident, yes, well pleased rather to be absent from the body and to be present with the Lord (2 Corinthians 5:8).

For if we believe that Jesus died and rose again, even so God will bring with Him those who sleep in Jesus (1 Thessalonians 4:14).

But you have come to Mount Zion and to the city of the living God, the heavenly Jerusalem, to an innumerable company of angels, to the general assembly and church of the firstborn *who are* registered in heaven, to God the Judge of all, to the spirits of just men made perfect (Hebrews 12:22-23).

When He opened the fifth seal, I saw under the altar the souls of those who had been slain for the word of God and the testimony which they held. And they cried with a loud voice, saying, 'How long, O Lord, holy and true, until You judge and avenge our blood on those who dwell on the earth?' (Revelation 6:9-10).

5 What are believers doing in heaven?

They are present with the Lord	–	2 Corinthians 5:8
They see his face	–	Revelation 22:4
They rest from their labours	–	Revelation 14:13
They enter into the joy of their Lord	–	Matthew 25:21
They are made perfect	–	Hebrew 12:23
They are comforted	–	Luke 16:25

They receive their eternal inheritance	–	1 Peter 1:4
They are glorified	–	Romans 8:30
They sing the praise of God and the Lamb	–	Revelation 7:10
They are satisfied	–	Revelation 7:17
They serve God in his temple	–	Revelation 7:15

6 Life in the new heaven and new earth

a) An embodied life. At the resurrection we will receive new spiritual bodies (i.e. bodies for the Spirit) which will be immortal (1 Corinthians 15:44, 53) and made like Christ's glorious body (Philippians 3:21). We shall see him as he is and be like him (1 John 3:2). All created things are looking forward to this moment, as they too will have a place and a part in the glorious liberty of the children of God (Romans 8:19-22). We will have a conscious bodily life in a new and redeemed physical environment. We will be given new powers yielding a far higher and more glorious existence than anything we have known before.

b) A social life. The Bible pictures the heavenly life, not as a solitary existence but as a corporate experience, which we will share with all those who have been redeemed. It is a kingdom (Hebrews 12:28), a city (Revelation 21:2), a temple (Revelation 7:15), a wedding feast (Revelation 19:9). The heavenly life will be the fulfilment of all God's good purposes for his children. Even the most happy and blessed human relationships which we have enjoyed on earth will be sublimated and exalted to a yet higher and more glorious level of experience.

c) A life of service. In the new heavens and new earth God's servants will serve him (Revelation 22:3). We will be living a life that is active and responsible. The degree of responsibility that will be entrusted to us will depend upon how faithfully we have served the Lord in this life; see the parable of the minas (Luke 19:11-26; see also Matthew 24:45-47 and Luke 16:9-14.) In the future age the saints will judge the world and angels (1 Corinthians 6:2-3).

d) A perfect life. There will be no sin, no sorrow, no sickness and no temptation. The limitations of flesh and blood will be gone forever. Our relationship with God will be sacred yet intimate. All our desires and aspirations will be in total harmony with the divine will. Our delight will be, not only to see him, but also to serve him. He will make us drink from living streams of heavenly water, proceeding from the throne of God and of the Lamb (Revelation 7:15-17).

e) An endless life. Eternal life is something that every believer receives when they are born-again of the Holy Spirit (John 3:16). The life then given knows no end because it comes from God who is himself immortal. It is begun on earth but it is consummated in the new heaven and new earth. This life is so glorious and joyful that it is compared to a kingly life: 'And they shall reign forever and ever.' (Revelation 22:5). We will be with him forever throughout the countless ages of eternity.

f) A God-centred life. The central and most significant experience of heaven is that we will always be in the very presence of God and of the Lamb: 'Thus we shall always be with the Lord' (1 Thessalonians 4:17). To be in the presence of his bright glory and spotless holiness will be the crowning experience of the resurrected believer. This experience will never fade, but grow and grow. Throughout eternity we will find out more and more of God's unutterable majesty, holiness, love, beauty, wisdom and grace towards us. To him be glory forever and forever. Amen.

Questions

1   What happens to the unbeliever at death?

2   What happens to the believer at death?

3   Describe the final state of the believer in the new creation.

Bible Teaching Plan
Year One

Week	subjects for Sundays	subject for midweek	chapter
1	God has spoken	The canon of Scripture	2
2	The origin and inspiration of Scripture	Relationship between Old and New Testaments	2
3	The only rule of faith and conduct	Understanding and interpreting God's Word	2
4	The Lord's use of Scripture	The use of Scripture in worship	2
5	Can God be known? the Bible	Methods of studying	2
6	The nature of God; his spirituality	How should we worship God?	3
7	The nature of God; his infinity and eternity	The names of God – Old Testament	3
8	His immutability	The names of God – New Testament	3
9	His knowledge and wisdom	Foreknowledge/ foreordination	3
10	His will	Guidance	3
11	His power	Can God do everything?	3
12	His holiness	Can man resist God's will?	3

Week	subjects for Sundays	subject for midweek	chapter
13	His justice	God's moral government: why does God allow war, illness etc?	3
14	His goodness	God's love: general benevolence or dynamic power?	3
15	His truth	The Bible frequently ascribes change to God	3
16	His sovereignty	The kingdom of God	3 & 9
17	The Trinity: a Christian Doctrine	Heretical views	3
18	The Trinity: mutual relationships and activities of the persons	The doctrine of the Nicene Creed	3
19	The Fatherhood of God	False views: universal fatherhood and brotherhood	3
20	The Son of God: his divinity	Christ's pre-existence, OT aspect	3 & 5
21	The Son of God: his manhood	False views of Christ	3 & 5
22	The Holy Spirit: his personality	False views of the Spirit	3 & 8
23	The Holy Spirit: his work in redemption	The Holy Spirit in the Old Testament	3 & 8
24	The Holy Spirit: his work in sanctification	Pentecost: its implications	3 & 8
25	The Holy Spirit: his work in the world – common grace	The gifts of the Spirit	3 & 8

Week	subjects for Sundays	subject for midweek	chapter
26	The Holy Spirit: his work in the church	Grieving and quenching the Spirit	3 & 8
27	God's decrees	All events included	2
28	God's decrees in action: Creation	Modern objections	2
29	God's decrees in action: Providence	Providence in my life	2
30	God's decrees in action: Miracles	Do miracles happen today?	2
31	God's decrees in action: election and reprobation	Is God unfair?	9
32	Man – his original state	The soul	4
33	Man – his fall	The consequences today	4
34	Sin – original and actual	False theories of sin	4
35	Total depravity	The bearing of total depravity on evangelism	4
36	The covenant of works	The relation of law to the Christian	13
37	The covenant of grace	The plan of salvation	17
38	The mediator of the covenant	Christ: human and divine	6
39	His mediation as prophet – his teaching	Comparison of OT prophets and prophecy	6
40	His mediation as priest – his perfect life	Can Christ's teaching be lived today?	6

Week	subjects for Sundays	subject for midweek	chapter
41	His mediation as priest – his atoning death	Objections to the evangelical view of substitutionary atonement	6
42	His mediation as priest – his resurrection	For whom did Christ die?	6
43	His mediation as priest – his intercession	Aaronic and Melchizedek priesthood as types	6
44	His mediation as king – his dominion and kingdom	Characteristics and duties of citizens	6
45	Lord of the Church	His body, his bride	19
46	His triumphant return	'When shall these things be – what shall be the sign?'	21

Bible Teaching Plan

Year Two

Week	subjects for Sundays	subject for midweek	chapter
1	The Christian's death and resurrection	The present state of the dead	21
2	Heaven, Paradise, Sheol, Hades	Old Testament concepts	18
3	Hell	The error of purgatory	18
4	The good news – its content	Is there a second chance?	11 & 13
5	The call of God – general and effectual	The gospel in the Old Testament	9
6	Regeneration	Preaching in the New Testament: preparation and delivery of sermons	11
7	Repentance	The marks of true repentance	13
8	Faith: saving and dead	The relationship of faith and prayer	13
9	Faith and works	Good works	10 & 13
10	Assurance	When is assurance not presumption?	16
11	Justification	Comparison and contrast of Roman Catholic and Protestant views	10

Week	subjects for Sundays	subject for midweek	chapter
27	The Christian's enemies: Satan – his person and work	Objections to a personal devil	
28	The Christian's enemies: Satan – his defeat	Temptation – our Lord's experience	
29	The Christian's enemies: the world	Recognising temptation	
30	The Christian's enemies: the flesh	Spiritual discipline	
31	Means of grace: the Word	Bible study methods	2
32	Means of grace: prayer	Prayer problems	19
33	Means of grace: fellowship	Relations with Christians of other denominations	19
34	Means of grace: breaking of bread	Necessary preparation for the Lord's Supper	19
35	Means of grace: baptism	Why don't we baptise infants?	20
36	The Christian in the world	Social commitments	
37	The Christian in his job	'Full time service'	
38	The Christian in his home	The problems of a non-Christian home	
39	The Christian citizen	The NT Church's contacts with the State	
40	The Christian in his church	The requirements for church officers	19

Week	subjects for Sundays	subject for midweek	chapter
41	The Christian under trial	Must I expect persecution?	
42	The Christian pilgrim	'This world is not my home'	
43	The Christian and his possessions	Tithing	
44	The Christian and his time	Priorities	
45	The Christian hope: the Lord's return	How should it affect me now?	21
46	The Christian hope: new heavens and a new earth	Safeguards against apostasy	21